# EMERGING ADULTS' RELIGIOUSNESS AND SPIRITUALITY

# Emerging Adults' Religiousness and Spirituality

Meaning-Making in an Age of Transition

Edited by

## Carolyn McNamara Barry
## Mona M. Abo-Zena

**OXFORD**
UNIVERSITY PRESS

## OXFORD
### UNIVERSITY PRESS

Oxford University Press is a department of the University of Oxford.
It furthers the University's objective of excellence in research, scholarship,
and education by publishing worldwide.

Oxford   New York
Auckland   Cape Town   Dar es Salaam   Hong Kong   Karachi
Kuala Lumpur   Madrid   Melbourne   Mexico City   Nairobi
New Delhi   Shanghai   Taipei   Toronto

With offices in
Argentina   Austria   Brazil   Chile   Czech Republic   France   Greece
Guatemala   Hungary   Italy   Japan   Poland   Portugal   Singapore
South Korea   Switzerland   Thailand   Turkey   Ukraine   Vietnam

Oxford is a registered trademark of Oxford University Press
in the UK and certain other countries.

Published in the United States of America by
Oxford University Press
198 Madison Avenue, New York, NY 10016

© Oxford University Press 2014

Library of Congress Cataloging-in-Publication Data
Emerging adults' religiousness and spirituality: meaning-making in an age of
transition / edited by Carolyn McNamara Barry, Mona M. Abo-Zena. — 1 [edition].
    pages cm.—(Emerging adulthood series)
Includes bibliographical references and index.
ISBN 978–0–19–995918–1
1. Teenagers—Religious life—United States.   2. Young adults—Religious
life—United States.   3. Spiritual formation.   4. Meaning (Philosophy)
I. Barry, Carolyn McNamara, editor of compilation.
BL625.47.E44 2014
200.84´20973—dc23
2014000152

# CONTENTS

# Series Foreword  ▲

The *Emerging Adulthood Series* examines the period of life starting at age 18 and continuing into and through the third decade of life, now commonly referred to as emerging adulthood. The specific focus of the series is on flourishing (i.e., factors that lead to positive, adaptive development during emerging adulthood and the successful transition into adult roles) and floundering (i.e., factors that lead to maladaptive behaviors and negative development during emerging adulthood as well as delay and difficulty in transitioning into adult roles) in the diverse paths young people take into and through the third decade of life.

There is a need to examine the successes and struggles in a variety of domains experienced by young people as they take complex and multiple paths in leaving adolescence and moving into and through their twenties. Too often the diversity of individual experiences is forgotten in our academic attempts to categorize a time period. For example, in proposing his theory of emerging adulthood, Arnett (2000, 2004) identified features of the development of young people, including *feeling in-between* (emerging adults do not see themselves as either adolescents or adults), *identity exploration* (especially in the areas of work, love, and worldviews), *focus on the self* (not self-centered, but simply lacking obligations to others), *instability* (evidenced by changes of direction in residential status, relationships, work, and education), and *possibilities* (optimism in the potential to steer their lives in any number of desired directions). Although this is a nice summary of characteristics of the time period, the scholarly examination of emerging adulthood has not always attempted to capture and explain the within-group variation that exists among emerging adults, often making the broad generalization that they are a relatively homogenous group. For example, emerging adults have been categorically referred to as "narcissistic," "refusing to grow up," and "failed adults." While there certainly are emerging adults who fit the profile of selfish, struggling, and directionless, there are others who are using this period of time for good. Indeed, there is great diversity of individual experiences in emerging adulthood. Hence, there is a need to examine better various beliefs/attitudes, attributes, behaviors, and relationships during this period of time that appear to reflect positive adjustment, or a sense of flourishing, or conversely those that lead to floundering.

For example, recent research (Nelson & Padilla-Walker, 2013) shows that young people who appear to be successfully navigating emerging adulthood tend to engage in identity exploration, develop internalization of positive values, participate in positive media use, engage in prosocial behaviors, report healthy relationships with parents, and engage in romantic relationships that are characterized by higher levels of companionship, worth, affection, and emotional support. For others who appear to be floundering, emerging adulthood appears to include anxiety and depression, poor self-perceptions, greater participation in risk behaviors, and poorer relationship quality with parents, best friends, and romantic partners. Thus, while various profiles of flourishing and floundering are starting to be identified, the current work in the field has simply provided cursory overviews of findings. This series provides a platform for an in-depth, comprehensive examination into some of these key factors that seem to be influencing, positively or negatively, young people as they enter into and progress through the third decade of life and the multiple ways in which they may flourish or flounder. Furthermore, the series attempts to examine how these factors may function differently within various populations (i.e., cultures and religious and ethnic subcultures, students vs. non-students, men vs. women). Finally, the series provides for a multidisciplinary (e.g., fields ranging from developmental psychology, neurobiology, education, sociology, criminology) and multimethod (i.e., information garnered from both quantitative and qualitative methodologies) examination of issues related to flourishing and floundering in emerging adulthood.

It is important to make one final note about this series. In choosing to employ the term "emerging adulthood," it is not meant to imply that the series will include books that are limited in their scope to viewing the third decade of life only through the lens of emerging adulthood theory (Arnett, 2000). Indeed, the notion of "emerging adulthood" as a universal developmental period has been met with controversy and skepticism because of the complex and numerous paths young people take out of adolescence and into adulthood. It is that exact diversity in the experiences of young people in a variety of contexts and circumstances (e.g., cultural, financial, familial) that calls for a book series such as this one. It is unfortunate that disagreement about emerging adulthood theory has led to a fragmentation of scholars and scholarship devoted to better understanding the third decade of life. Hence, although the term "emerging adulthood" is employed for parsimony and for its growing familiarity as a term for the age period, this series is devoted to examining broadly the complexity of pathways into and through the third decade of life from a variety of perspectives and disciplines. In doing so, it is my hope that the series will help scholars, practitioners, students, and others better understand, and thereby potentially foster, the lives of young people in the various paths they may take to adulthood.

In *Emerging Adults' Religiousness and Spirituality*, Drs. Carolyn M. Barry and Mona M. Abo-Zena have assembled a strong contingent of authors to provide an extensive examination into the religious and spiritual development of emerging adults. This topic was selected to be the focus of the first book in the series because it reflects the intent of this series to address topics in emerging adulthood that are often misunderstood and are in need of greater attention. Indeed, when thinking of religious and spiritual development in emerging adulthood, many are quick to dismiss its relevance because it is becoming increasingly well known that outward religious participation declines significantly for the majority of young people in the third decade of life (e.g., Smith, 2009). However, there is a much richer story to be told regarding the individual variation that exists in the role that religion and spirituality plays in young people's identity development, strivings for meaning-making, relationships, and behaviors.

This book succeeds in both examining challenging questions and raising important issues related to individual variation in the religious and spiritual lives of emerging adults and the ways in which this variation may be tied to flourishing and floundering in the third decade of life. For example, chapters unpack both the potential benefits of religion and spirituality versus the potential dark side of religious extremism. Other chapters examine how parents still matter to young people in this particular domain and what other socializing agents (e.g., media, peers, universities) and contexts (e.g., culture, religious communities) might play more of a role. Other chapters delve into complicated issues regarding religion and the law, gender, sexuality, and sexual minorities as well as what it means to be nonreligious and the variation that exists within that segment of emerging adults. These are complex issues that have often been overlooked due to the sweeping generalization that is too often made that religion and spirituality are not important domains of development in emerging adulthood. The editors and authors of this volume have shed light on these multifaceted issues and have demonstrated the importance of examining the religious and spiritual development of emerging adults in order to understand better the variation in flourishing and floundering in the third decade of life.

**Larry J. Nelson**
Series Editor

# FOREWORD ◢

Social science research on the lives of emerging adults in the United States and in many other countries has become a major growth industry in the last decade. Jeffrey Arnett's coining of the idea of emerging adulthood in 2004 and his explaining how and why it has become such an important part of the American life course has generated a ground-swell of interesting and important research on many aspects of emerging adulthood as a cultural fact and an experience. During the same time period, research on the religious and spiritual lives of teenagers and emerging adults, and on the dynamic processes involved in the intergenerational faith transmission from parents to children, also burgeoned. This was partly due to the influence of my own National Study of Youth and Religion, but also to a broad, rising, self-generated interest in these topics among scholars across a range of disciplines and fields. As a result, today we currently enjoy a number of valuable studies of the religious and spiritual lives of young people that draw upon a variety of data sources and methodological designs and offer multiple perspectives on this complex topic. Our knowledge, understanding, and explanations of the facts and dynamics at work in this area have thus expanded greatly. Now is just a great time to be studying young people in their teenage years and twenties.

To this happily developing body of scholarly knowledge, the book you hold in your hand, *Emerging Adults' Religiousness and*

*Spirituality: Meaning-Making in an Age of Transition*, makes a very important and unique contribution. Here we have collected in one volume many serious, in-depth, and informative chapters engaging, synthesizing, and developing empirical and theoretical understandings of the role and meaning of religion and spirituality (as well as nonreligion and atheism) in the lives of emerging adults. For the growing number of interested readers, both academic and nonacademic, this book will provide an excellent one-stop learning resource on the issues the book addresses. I am extremely pleased to see that Carolyn McNamara Barry and Mona Abo-Zena took the initiative and did the extensive work to organize the volume, pull the chapters together, and see it through to publication. It is much needed and timely.

A simple review of the table of contents reveals some of the major strengths of this work: The focuses of the different chapters are carefully chosen to address all major concerns in play, the authors are highly qualified to write their particular contribution, the approach taken is not narrow but multidisciplinary, and the entire project is nicely framed by solid foundational chapters. I am very impressed by the breadth, balance, and competence reflected in the pieces that together comprise this book. The mix of the larger developmental approach, the substantive topic areas of inquiry, and the fair readiness to see both the positive and negative sides of religious (and nonreligious) experience here are admirable. I am confident that *Emerging Adults' Religiousness and Spirituality* will come quickly to serve as an authoritative reference point for future students and scholars interested in learning about and further developing study in these areas.

*Emerging Adults' Religiousness and Spirituality* deserves to become widely available in many kinds of libraries and on many bookshelves, including those of colleges and research universities, seminaries and divinity schools, local public libraries, research hospitals, religious organizations, and all social science scholars who study emerging adults, whether or not religion and spirituality are their primary interests. Readers from all of those institutional backgrounds will benefit by studying and referencing the important chapters found in what follows. I myself look forward to studying this book more closely and returning to it repeatedly in the future as my own studies of emerging adults unfold.

**Christian Smith, PhD**
*University of Notre Dame*

# Acknowledgments ▲

Since the fall of 2011 when Carolyn was first approached about writing a book on emerging adults' religiousness and spirituality, this book has been a tremendous gift for us. We are grateful to our Oxford University Press Editors, Sarah Harrington and Andrea Zekus, and Series Editor, Larry Nelson, for providing their unyielding support throughout the project's duration. Carolyn is indebted to her Department Chair, Dr. Beth Kotchick, and Dean, Rev. James Miracky, S. J., for their allowance of using course releases and a portion of her sabbatical time to complete this book. Mona would like to thank TERC and the postdoctoral fellowship that supported her during the preparation of this volume, as well as Fran Jacobs, Ellen Pinderhughes, Martha Pott, and George Scarlett from Tufts University for nurturing her scholarly focus on meaning-making. We also wish to thank Jeff Barnett, David Dollahite, and Kathryn Wentzel for their input at formative stages of this project. We appreciate the generous and conscientious feedback and guidance from Chris Boyatzis, Richard Lerner, and Kate Loewenthal. We are deeply appreciative of the support and collegiality of Christian Smith, who has pioneered the scholarship on religious and spiritual lives of emerging adults, for his generous foreword and welcoming of an interdisciplinary approach to understand this understudied topic and population better. This book would not be possible without the expertise of each of our chapter authors: Sameera Ahmed, Piotr Bobkowski, Jennifer

Christofferson, Paul Deal, Graciela Espinosa-Hernandez, Luke Galen, Meghan Gillen, Perry Glanzer, Jonathan Hill, Pamela Ebstyne King, Roger Levesque, Gina Magyar-Russell, Jacqueline Mattis, Larry Nelson, Geoffrey Ream, Todd Ream, Eric Rodriguez, Tara Stoppa, Tucker Brown, and William Whitney. We deeply appreciate their willingness to be part of this journey with us. Our rich exchanges about religiousness and spirituality have enhanced our understanding of this topic in such profound ways; we are delighted to share this collective product with them, and to continue our conversations about meaning-making during the third decade and beyond with them and others in the years to come.

As we reflected on our emerging-adult years and what has transpired since then, we also want to thank our religious community leaders and families. Carolyn is particularly grateful for the amazing religious mentors that she had as an emerging adult (Sr. Margaret Dincher, Mary Ann Psomas-Jacklowski, and Rick Hess), close friends from varying faith traditions (Anne Richardson Hansen, Stacey Horn, Nisha Pandya, and Larry Nelson), and her parents (Jim and Connie McNamara), all of whom provided a safe space for her to explore her own faith more deeply. She feels especially blessed to have her husband, Dan, as her partner for life, and for sharing their faith with their children, Kevin and Ryan, who seek honest and rich answers to their profound questions about God and the purpose of life. They have strengthened her faith and enriched her life in immeasurable ways. As Mona reflects on her own meaning-making, she thanks her parents (Mahmoud Abo-Zena and Fifi Elshaarawey) for their guidance and patience throughout her lifelong journey. She thanks her husband, Mohamed Hassan, for his unending support in their journey together and commitment to support Abdelrahman, Mariam, Noor, and Abdallah in their own meaning-making process, and she is inspired by their wonder and search for the sacred. Finally, we thank all those who have contributed to our individual and collective meaning-making process, including friends and classmates, teachers and students, the religious and nonreligious, and the old and young. Ultimately, we ground ourselves in our own respective tradition, and thank God. As we continue to reflect on the process of writing and compiling this book, we appreciate the many life experiences from our own childhood memories, including religious celebrations and other experiences that have led us to wonder and search for the sacred to late-night discussions about faith during college with peers; some of these experiences have continued with those same peers as we have included others along our respective journeys as we seek the deeper meaning to life's mysteries about sickness and health, prosperity and tribulation, and the vastness of the world around us.

Serendipity (or some higher power or destiny) brought us together at the Conference of Emerging Adulthood in Providence, Rhode Island, in a paper symposium on emerging adults' religiousness. Together we have copiloted this atmospheric journey, and we have enjoyed the vistas along the way. The countless hours that we have spent primarily over the phone and e-mail were filled with fascinating dialogue ranging from scholarly ideas to reflecting on our own emerging-adult meaning-making process and others with whom we have encountered in our lives to sharing each other's faith traditions, religious socialization practices, and current family lives more broadly. We feel most blessed for this collaboration turned friendship. We only wish others, particularly emerging adults, could engage in such a deep and ongoing ecumenical dialogue in a safe space that we have had the distinct opportunity to do.

And to demonstrate the importance of understanding meaning in context, we share perspectives from our respective traditions that speak to the value of ecumenism that we treasure so deeply:

*How can we live in harmony? First we need to know we are all madly in love with the same God.*

— St. Thomas Aquinas

*Verily, in the creation of the heavens and the earth, and in the alternation of night and day, there are indeed signs for people of understanding.*

—Qur'an 4:190

# About the Editors ▲

**Carolyn McNamara Barry** earned her BS in psychology from Ursinus College in May 1996, with minors in secondary education, sociology, and Spanish. She graduated summa cum laude with departmental honors in psychology. While in college, she was inducted into Phi Sigma Iota, Psi Chi, and Phi Beta Kappa. Thereafter she pursued her PhD in human development at the University of Maryland, College Park, where she was inducted into Kappa Delta Pi. Immediately after completing her PhD in 2001, she served as an assistant professor in psychology, and in 2008 was granted tenure and promotion to rank of associate professor at Loyola University Maryland (formerly known as Loyola College in Maryland). In 2011, she earned the Faculty Award for Excellence in Service-Learning and Engaged Scholarship, from Loyola University Maryland. Dr. Barry serves on the editorial boards for the *International Journal for Behavioral Development* and the *Journal of Youth and Adolescence*. She holds professional memberships in the Society for Research in Child Development, Society for Research in Adolescence, Society for the Study of Emerging Adulthood, American Psychological Association (Divisions 2 and 36), and the Association for Psychological Science. She currently is serving on the executive board for the Society for the Psychology of Religion and Spirituality (Division 36, APA) in the capacity as member-at-large. She also received the Girl Scout Gold Award in 1992.

**Mona M. Abo-Zena** earned her BA in sociology from the University of Chicago; her EdM in administration, planning, and social policy from Harvard University; and her PhD in applied child development from Tufts University. She completed a postdoctoral research fellowship at TERC, and is currently a visiting assistant professor in education and human development at Brown University. Mona's work focuses on the role of religion and religious/spiritual development (broadly defined) as a way of knowing and being. She has published in the areas of religion, identity development, research methodology, and education; her work has contributed to receiving a Gold EXCEL Award for journal feature article, the National Association for Multicultural Education's Philip C. Chinn Multicultural Book Award, and to an encyclopedia that received an Outstanding Reference Award. She is currently coediting a volume on the development of immigrant-origin children and adolescents for New York University Press (Carola Suárez-Orozco, Mona M. Abo-Zena, and Amy Kerivan Marks, Eds.). She has been recognized with awards by Tufts University for Outstanding Undergraduate Teaching and for Public Service, and as an Emerging Leader by Phi Delta Kappa for her work and advocacy in education. She holds memberships in the American Psychological Association (Division 36), Association for Psychological Science, National Association for the Education of Young Children, Phi Delta Kappa, Society for Research on Adolescence, Society for Research on Child Development, Society for Research on Identity Formation, and the Society for the Study of Human Development. Mona's work is informed by over 15 years of teaching, administrative, and board experience in public and Islamic schools.

# Contributors

**Mona M. Abo-Zena**
Brown University
Providence, RI

**Sameera Ahmed**
Family & Youth Institute
Canton, MI

**Carolyn McNamara Barry**
Loyola University Maryland
Baltimore, MD

**Piotre S. Bobkowski**
University of Kansas
Lawrence, KS

**Iain Tucker Brown**
Northern New Mexico College
Española, NM

**Jennifer L. Christofferson**
Johns Hopkins University
Baltimore, MD

**Paul J. Deal**
Loyola University Maryland
Baltimore, MD

**Graciela Espinosa-Hernandez**
University of North Carolina
Wilmington
Wilmington, NC

**Luke W. Galen**
Grand Valley State University
Allendale, MI

**Meghan M. Gillen**
Penn State University, Abington
Abington, PA

**Perry L. Glanzer**
Baylor University
Waco, TX

**Jonathan Hill**
Calvin College
Grand Rapids, MI

**Pamela Ebstyne King**
Fuller Theological Seminary
Pasadena, CA

**Roger J. R. Levesque**
Indiana University
Bloomington, IN

**Gina Magyar-Russell**
Loyola University Maryland
Baltimore, MD

**Jacqueline S. Mattis**
New York University
New York, NY

**Larry J. Nelson**
Brigham Young University
Provo, UT

**Geoffrey L. Ream**
Adelphi University
Garden City, NY

**Todd C. Ream**
Taylor University
Upland, IN

**Eric M. Rodriguez**
City University of New York,
Brooklyn
Brooklyn, NY

**Tara M. Stoppa**
Eastern University
St. David's, PA

**William B. Whitney**
Fuller Theological Seminary
Pasadena, CA

# Part I ▲
## INTRODUCTION

# 1 ▲

# Seeing the Forest and the Trees: How Emerging Adults Navigate Meaning-Making

CAROLYN McNAMARA BARRY AND MONA M. ABO-ZENA

*Sarah got into her dream college, where students seemed so friendly and the campus was big, but not overwhelming. However, after a semester she found her classmates to be fake, cliquish, and only into partying. Thankfully, she connected with her resident assistant, Molly, who invited her to go to a Campus Ministry small group designed to promote spirituality through authentic relationships. At first, she was reluctant to attend, fearing that a particular religious doctrine would be forced upon her, but Molly persisted in reassuring her that it would not be like that. Through these weekly chat sessions, she met like-minded others who also wanted to share their challenges of being a first-year student and to discuss the big questions of life that regularly emerged in their liberal arts core classes. By the end of her first year, Sarah felt at home at her college.*

Although most children in the United States are raised in a faith tradition, their outward religious expression declines significantly by the time they are in their twenties, even though many claim religion and spirituality to be important (Smith, 2005, 2009). Reasons for this sharp change in religious behavior may be attributed in part to adolescents' forging of their identity, including their religious and spiritual beliefs (Erikson, 1968). This religious and spiritual identity developmental process takes on even greater prominence during the third decade (Arnett, 2004). This change also can be explained by emerging adults' increasing immersion in contexts beyond their family, at work and school. In such settings, they are more likely to encounter others who have religious and spiritual beliefs that differ from their own. Moreover, they live in a media-saturated world, and media in its multitude of types conveys a wide variety of values and beliefs (Roberts, Foehr, Rideout, & Brodie, 2003). Thus, this third decade is a time that is ripe for religious and spiritual development, which is the central topic of this book. In this introductory chapter we first provide a justification for why emerging adults are a robust group for the study of religiousness and spirituality, followed by a discussion of the utility of a developmental as well as contextual lens for this exploration. Lastly, we provide an overview of the different parts of the book, including a description of each chapter. In sum, we strive to provide both the breadth (forest) and depth (trees) on how emerging adults make meaning out of their lives.

## ▲ Why Emerging Adults?

According to Arnett (2006), few young people enter their twenties with clear ideas about their values, beliefs, and worldviews, but few leave without having reached some resolution to them. This capacity for exploration about religiousness and spirituality occurs due in part to their neurological maturation (Paus, 2009), increasing cognitive-affective flexibility (Labouvie-Vief, 2006), and increased emotional-regulation capacities (Steinberg, 2008) amid increasingly diverse social contexts (Settersten & Ray, 2010). Not surprisingly then, emerging adults encounter experiences that mark turning points (e.g., applying for jobs, attending a university, breaking up with a romantic partner, traveling internationally), and in turn they strive to make sense out of them, a process known as meaning-making (McLean & Breen, 2009; McLean & Pratt, 2006). Emerging adults' meaning-making has been associated with positive adjustment (McAdams, Reynolds, Lewis, Patten, & Bowman, 2001), which might yield opportunities for flourishing. Yet for those who do not engage in meaning-making or who do so in the absence of sufficient emotional and structural supports, they tend to be lost in transition, and such floundering may result in perilous developmental outcomes (i.e., immorality, consumerism, substance abuse, unsatisfying sexual experiences, and civic and political disengagement), according to Smith (2011). Although sociologists (e.g., Smith, 2009) have conducted large-scale studies on emerging adults' religiousness and spirituality, psychologists have given less attention to this topic among those in the third decade relative to other decades. Consequently, in this volume we seek to contribute to the developmental psychological literature, particularly given that scholars in the fields of psychology and human development recognize that the process of meaning-making is a central, yet overlooked aspect of human behavior (Holden & Vittrup, 2009; Tarakeshwar, Stanton, & Pargament, 2003). Specifically, we seek to describe how the developmental process of meaning-making encompasses the religious and spiritual experiences of emerging adults in the United States.

In fact, much debate has ensued as to whether this decade constitutes a separate life stage, which some refer to as youth (Keniston, 1971), or more recently, emerging adulthood (Arnett, 2004), while others (e.g., Bynner, 2005) consider this time a delayed adolescence and launch into adulthood. In fact, even Stanley Hall (1904) envisioned adolescence as ending around age 25. Arnett (2004) has long maintained that this stage only applies to those with particular cultural and demographic conditions, including those in pursuit of higher education and with delayed entry into marriage and parenthood, and he proposed five features of the stage (i.e., identity exploration, instability, self-focus, feeling in-between, possibility). For the purpose of this volume, we do not take sides on this ongoing stage debate (for fuller description of a series of debates on this issue, see Arnett, Kloep, Hendry, & Tanner, 2011). Rather, we simply maintain that the third decade of life is an unclearly defined time in the United States, given that many young people delay their entry into adult roles. For some, they invest in educational and/or job training, as well as relationship experiences that lead to successful adoption of adult roles by age 30 (flourishing), whereas others drift into and out of different relationships, jobs, and schooling that do not adequately prepare them for the adoption of adult roles (floundering). Thus, throughout the book, authors may refer to those in this decade as emerging adults, early adults, or young adults.

## ▲ Toward Defining the Scope of Religiousness and Spirituality

As summarized by Pargament, Mahoney, Exline, Jones, and Shafranske (2013), psychologists predominantly have focused on investigating those who are religious dwellers (those who reside within a religious community), and only more recently included spirituality (i.e., "individualized, experientially based pursuit of positive values," p. 11), thereby allowing for a broader range of experiences. Indeed, religiousness and spirituality are multifaceted (Moberg, 2002). In an effort to parse these terms, psychologists (many of whom are less religious than the population in the United States at large; McMinn, Hathaway, Woods, & Snow, 2009) have tended to polarize the terms, such that spirituality has been viewed favorably, while religion has been viewed unfavorably (Pargament et al., 2013). Thus, we adopt Pargament's (1999) definition of spirituality as searching for the sacred, while religiousness involves this search within an institution established to promote spirituality (Pargament et al., 2013).

## ▲ How Development Matters

### Developmental Insights on Emerging Adults

As developmental psychologists focus on a specific age group, the broader lifespan perspective that considers how each developmental phase is interrelated may sometimes be lost. While this volume focuses on those during the emerging-adult years, it also uses a developmental lens, highlighting how salient aspects of early and middle childhood and adolescence may inform attitudes and actions during this third decade, which in turn informs experiences anticipated later in adulthood. This developmental approach further considers continuities and discontinuities in development, especially because discontinuities may contribute to personal challenges in the process of meaning-making, and in some cases instances of person-context mismatch during this third decade.

### Integrated Across Developmental Domains and Processes

The literature on the psychology of religion and spirituality includes developmental domains such as physical, cognitive, social, and emotional development. A holistic developmental perspective, though, considers how growth and change within a particular domain is integrated across development. This volume not only delineates the developmental underpinnings of meaning-making but explores how this process results through the mutual informing of developmental domains (e.g., how cognitive approaches including beliefs and doubts interact with socialization by peers, families, and religious communities, and are expressed by the individual).

## ▲ How Context Matters

### Contextually Grounded

Theoretical assumptions about the mutually constitutive developmental processes between individual and context guide developmental systems perspectives (Lerner & Overton, 2008). Consequently, this volume embeds discussions of religiousness and spirituality in emerging adults in the many levels of context in which they live, including the goodness of fit between individuals and their context. Although the volume focuses on emerging adults in the United States, other contexts are incorporated as illustrations of person-context fit where applicable. This volume highlights the range of experiences and perspectives of emerging adults in the United States grounded in social context (e.g., university and non-university students), social position (e.g., race, socioeconomic status, gender, sexual orientation), and religious or spiritual identification (e.g., nonreligious, nontheistic, religious majority, religious minority, denomination, level of practice and belief). Building upon theorists who focus on ecological and cultural nature of development (Bronfenbrenner, 1979; Rogoff, 2003), context may be as broad as how the media portrays the social values and laws framing religion and spirituality within a society, to the particular patterns and variations in a geographic region, to the environment of a particular belief-influenced institution within a particular town, to the contextual features of a particular family, residence hall, or bedroom and how meaning is operationalized in daily life.

## ▲ Summary

Due to the heightened self and identity exploration during the third decade (Erikson, 1968), coupled with other cognitive, physical, and socioemotional developmental advances, emerging adults are the ideal age group for the study of religiousness and spirituality. In this volume, we adopt a developmental as well as contextual lens for this exploration in order to situate emerging adults within the broader lifespan and in their nested contexts. In the remainder of the introduction, we outline the remaining parts of this volume, including summaries of each of the chapters.

## ▲ Overview

### Part II: Foundational Perspectives

Much theoretical work has been done on religious and spiritual theories; however, limited work exists that is tailored to emerging adults. This section begins by exploring theories and conceptual frameworks of religious and spiritual development. Then, how and to what extent religious and spiritual contexts may be associated with flourishing versus floundering are discussed.

#### Religious and Spiritual Development During Emerging Adulthood

Given the central task of the third decade is the solidification of one's identity (Arnett, 2004), Barry and Abo-Zena (Chapter 2) discuss how emerging adults carve out their religious and spiritual components of themselves during this decade. Specifically, the authors review research on how developmental advances in the physical, cognitive, social, and emotional domains support emerging adults' religious and spiritual development. Then, the authors delineate trends in religious and spiritual beliefs and practices across the third decade. Finally, the authors conclude with research on how religious and spiritual development intersects with the physical, cognitive, social, and emotional domains.

#### Potential Benefits and Detriments of Religiousness and Spirituality to Emerging Adults

While the literature generally links religiousness and spirituality to a range of potential benefits (Lefkowitz, Gillen, Shearer, & Boone, 2004; Regnerus, 2003), like any phenomena, there are also possible detriments. In Chapter 3, Magyar-Russell, Deal, and Brown first provide a cultural and historical setting under which emerging adults forge their religious and spiritual values and beliefs. Thereafter, they review the individual and collective benefits of religiousness and spirituality, such as well-being, purpose, and health outcomes. They next document the detriments of religiousness and spirituality, including cases of extreme religious views. The authors then note how religiousness and spirituality likely influence these varied outcomes. Lastly, they conclude with a discussion of emerging adults' missed opportunities for meaning-making.

## Part III: Contexts and Socializing Agents in Emerging Adults' Religious and Spiritual Lives

Socialization encompasses the diverse processes by which human beings safely coexist and maintain diverse communities and cultures (Grusec & Hastings, 2007). This section is grounded in a sociocultural perspective that assumes that social context and development are essential aspects of one another (Berk & Winsler, 1995), and that influences are bidirectional. Individuals are embedded in a variety of nested contexts that directly and indirectly influence development; contexts are also influenced by the individuals inhabiting them (i.e., media; Bronfenbrenner, 1979). The fluid contexts are inherently social and cultural by nature, and they are not necessarily separated physically or theoretically (Rogoff, 2003). This section explores socialization agents most relevant to the religious and spiritual lives of emerging adults.

### Parents

Given that parents are the primary socializing agents of religiousness and spirituality, it is logical to begin with this agent (Smith, 2003). In Chapter 4, Nelson notes the plentiful challenges that parents face in their emerging-adult children's religious and spiritual development. Nelson organizes the chapter by first discussing how parents have socialized their children concerning religiousness and spirituality in the first two decades, and then discussing the more limited research on the socialization of emerging-adult children. Then, he reviews the literature on parenting and the parent–child relationship on children's, adolescents', and emerging adults' religious and spiritual development. Finally, he discusses the future work that is needed, which includes both scholarship on the direct and indirect effects of parents on emerging adults' religious and spiritual development as well as the role of the parent–child relationship, child characteristics, and contextual factors that are likely to shape this socialization process.

## Peers

As emerging adults become more invested in the social worlds beyond their families (Carbery & Buhrmester, 1998), they are increasingly likely to interact with those who have differing values and beliefs from their own, including those about religion and spirituality. In Chapter 5, Barry and Christofferson first discuss the nature and types of peer relationships as well as the process by which peers socialize each other. Then, they summarize empirical work on the relation between religiousness and spirituality for each of the four types of peer relationships: siblings, friends, romantic partners, and other peer relationships. The authors conclude by noting existing research limitations, future research directions, and implications of the findings.

## Media

Given that emerging adults currently live in a media-saturated world (Roberts et al., 2003), in Chapter 6 Bobkowski reviews the role of this socializing agent on emerging adults' religiousness and spirituality. According to Arnett (1995) and Brown (2006), media serves as a form of self-socialization given substantial variability as to what type, content, and frequency of media one consumes at any given instance. Media varies substantially in its content and the values and beliefs that are represented in that content. Thus, Bobkowski first provides an overview of the Media Practice Model (e.g., Shafer, Bobkowski, & Brown, 2012). Then each moment of the model is discussed in the subsequent sections. Therefore, he discusses how individuals select media that is religious or nonreligious in nature followed by how emerging adults process the varying content of the media. Lastly, he summarizes research on how emerging adults incorporate media messages into their religious mosaics.

## The Law's Promise of Religious Freedom

Around the world, the role of religion varies. The United States is a particular context that is founded on freedom of religion and where religion is considered to be a private affair not to be established by the government. Nonetheless, there are signals within the United States that condone a theistic perspective, and where many assume a Christian foundation to an increasingly religiously pluralistic nation (Eck, 2002). Emerging adults from the United States are considered to be more observant and religiously committed than are those in other industrialized nations (Inglehart, Basañez, Dàez-Medrano, Halman, & Luijicx, 2004). In Chapter 7, Levesque examines Constitutional law as well as Supreme Court cases involving religion, thereby showing how the court's view of the relation between law and religion has changed over time. Then, he identifies the lessons learned from legal cases, and how they apply to emerging adults. He concludes that the United States in a sense has adopted a "religion" by grounding its faith in the Constitution.

## Religious Communities

Congregations are a central feature of religious life generally and a physical site for personal and collective transformation (Ammerman, 1997), but the field of congregational studies has paid minimal attention to the ways that congregational life relates to the religious and spiritual development of its younger members (Regnerus, Smith, & Smith, 2004). For a subgroup of emerging adults, such communities are central and provide an invaluable source of comfort and grounding amid the instability of this developmental period (Roehlkepartain & Patel, 2006). Yet many other emerging adults avoid organized and informal religious communities. In Chapter 8, Whitney and King explore the ways in which formal and informal religious communities provide a range of ecological contexts for the religious and spiritual development of young people. First, they document trends in emerging adults' participation in religious congregations and communities and provide key definitions for terms relating to religious and spiritual development. Second, these scholars explore the lives of emerging adults who regularly participate in formal religious congregations and/or informal communities. Lastly, Whitney and King unpack how the ecological systems context of a religious community can shape emerging adults' identity formation, which promotes meaning-making opportunities.

## Universities

The university context can shape emerging adults' religious and spiritual lives through a variety of mechanisms (Calhoun, Aronczyk, Maryl, & VanAntwerpen, 2007). In Chapter 9, Glanzer, Hill, and Ream note that four changes in higher education are likely to contribute to emerging adults' religious and spiritual development: the increasing secularization in higher education; cocurricular offerings of religion on secular campuses; the diminishment of religion in secular institutions' curriculum; and the distinctive role of faith-based colleges and universities. Lastly, they discuss how higher education is likely to influence its students' religious and spiritual beliefs.

### Part IV: Variations

Human development is understood and enhanced by studying development in context. This section considers the variation in emerging adults' religious and spiritual development as deriving from systemic relationships between diverse individuals and their complex and dynamic cultural and ecological contexts. The authors of these five chapters incorporate a person-based and systems-based analysis of the similarities and regularities of differences within and between individuals and their cultural and community contexts.

### Gender

In Chapter 10, Mattis documents the long-standing findings that women report higher levels of religiousness and spirituality than do men (Desmond, Morgan, & Kikuchi, 2010). However, the universality of this finding has some important caveats and varies upon closer examination of personal piety, organizational participation, and among religious minorities (for a review, see Sullins, 2006). For instance, exceptions to this finding include cases where privilege is often afforded to men in religious contexts and how that bears on the religious and spiritual development experiences of men and women (Smith, 1991). Thus, Mattis provides a careful examination that incorporates theory and research to unpack the gender–religiousness connection and the conditions that surround them. Recognizing that much of this research focuses on college students and has a Christian bias, Mattis argues for a need to broaden the range of contexts in which we study this link among emerging adults. She concludes with a call to incorporate gender and feminist theory in an interdisciplinary research approach to the study of religion and spirituality.

### Heterosexual Sexuality

Issues related to sexuality are central to the lived experiences of emerging adults, given their desire to achieve intimacy, and emerging adults must navigate the range of socializing messages they receive about how, when, and with whom to achieve intimacy. In Chapter 11, Stoppa, Espinosa-Hernandez, and Gillen utilize a contextual and developmental lens to review the extant research on the heterosexual relationships among emerging adults in the United States amid acknowledging the range of contextual influences, including religious communities, close relationships, and media. Next, they review research on religiousness (including religious affiliation) and spirituality on emerging adults' sexual beliefs and behaviors as well as other sex-related issues, including abortion, pornography, and romantic relationships. Then, they discuss developmental processes designed to promote adaptive integration between religious, spiritual, and sexual identity and behaviors. They conclude by identifying key limitations of this research topic (e.g., over- versus underreporting of sexual activities depending upon religious affiliation) and appropriate future research directions.

### Sexual Minorities

Given that most mainstream religions in the United States do not openly endorse having a same-sex or bisexual orientation (Russell, 2002), the religious and spiritual lives of emerging adults who are gay men, lesbian women, or bisexual men or women are likely to differ from their heterosexual counterparts, which warrants a separate chapter for consideration. In Chapter 12, Ream and Rodriguez commence with a bird's-eye view of the issue by articulating societal forces at play in the religious-ideological struggles as they affect emerging adults in the United States today, including what historical effects that the current cohort experienced as adolescents. Next, they address individual-level developmental tasks for sexual minorities, namely the process of coming out to self and others, joining a sexual-minority community, and resolving issues of cognitive dissonance between religious/spiritual and sexual-minority identity for those who belong to religious communities who do not endorse and/or support this identity. Ream and Rodriguez thereafter delineate opportunities for self, religious, and/or spiritual development that result from belonging to the current cohort. They conclude by providing directions for practice and research in the future.

### Culture, Context, and Social Position

Increasingly, emerging adults in the United States are navigating the meaning-making process within a religiously and culturally pluralistic society. In Chapter 13, Abo-Zena and Ahmed explore how religion and spirituality overlap with culture, which consists of the complex personal and social contexts in which an individual interacts and develops over time. Further, they attempt to clarify how cultural variations may inform the meaning-making process of individuals' religious and spiritual developmental processes and experiences. They present a general conceptualization of the interaction of religion, culture, and context, while highlighting the sources and possible reasons for variation that include how layers of culture are embedded in social and personal contexts. In addition, the authors highlight implications of the interaction between religion and culture for research and applied interventions.

### Nonreligious and Atheist Emerging Adults

In order to represent the range of religious and spiritual beliefs and experiences, it is essential to include those who are not devoted, particularly since this group of young people is growing in our nation today (Kosmin, Keysar, Cragun, & Navarro-Rivera, 2009) and this cohort is less religious than previous cohorts (Pew Research Center, 2010). Therefore, in Chapter 14, Galen focuses on the substantial number of emerging adults who identify as either completely nonreligious, unaffiliated, or who have at least some period of religious doubting. He summarizes the basic demographic and cognitive characteristics of the nonreligious. Then, he reviews the research on the educational, personality, familial, and social influences on emerging adults who self-identify as nonreligious. In so doing, he provides an analysis of the tremendous within-group variation in the processes and outcomes associated with the unaffiliated.

### Part V: Conclusion

We conclude with highlighting the overall state of the field exploring religion and spirituality. In discussing key findings, we also highlight what we do not know about the religiousness and spirituality of emerging adults as part of their self-development during this time period. Given that emerging adults' religiousness or spirituality is generally fluid, context-dependent, and integrated with other aspects of identity, we carefully examine how specific sources of variation weave together to create a holistic view of the person. Moreover, we discuss how such variations may be managed within individual and broader contexts. Lastly, we discuss the implications of these findings for emerging adults themselves, their parents, and the subsequent implications for those who work with emerging adults (e.g., religious leaders, university faculty and staff, social service agency personnel, and military officers).

## ▲ References

Ammerman, N. T. (with Farnsley, A. E.). (1997). *Congregation and community*. New Brunswick, NJ: Rutgers University Press.

Arnett, J. J. (1995). Broad and narrow socialization: The family in the context of a cultural theory. *Journal of Marriage and Family, 57*, 617–628. doi: 10.2307/353917

Arnett, J. J. (2004). *Emerging adulthood: The winding road from late teens through the twenties*. New York, NY: Oxford University Press.

Arnett, J. J. (2006). A longer road to adulthood. In J. J. Arnett & J. L. Tanner (Eds.), *Emerging adults in America: Coming of age in the 21st century* (pp. 3–25). Washington, DC: American Psychological Association.

Arnett, J. J., Kloep, M., Hendry, L. B., & Tanner, J. L. (2011). *Debating emerging adulthood: Stage or process*. New York, NY: Oxford University Press.

Berk, L., & Winsler, A. (1995) *Scaffolding children's learning: Vygotsky and early education*. Washington, DC: National Association for the Education of Young Children.

Bronfenbrenner, U. (1979). *The ecology of human development: Experiments by nature and design*. Cambridge, MA: Harvard University Press.

Brown, J. D. (2006). Emerging adults in a media-saturated world. In J. J. Arnett & J. L. Tanner (Eds.), *Emerging adults in America: Coming of age in the 21st century* (pp. 279–299). Washington, DC: APA. doi: 10.1037/11381-012

Bynner, J. (2005). Rethinking the youth phase of the life course: The case of emerging adulthood? *Journal of Youth Studies, 8*, 367–384.

Calhoun, C., Aronczyk, M., Mayrl, D., & Van Antwerpen, J. (2007). *The religious engagements of American undergraduates*. Social Science Research Council. Brooklyn, NY. Retrieved from: http://religion.ssrc.org/reguide/printable.html

Carbery, J., & Buhrmester, D. (1998). Friendship and need fulfillment during three phases of young adulthood. *Journal of Social and Personal Relationships, 13*, 393–409. doi:10.1177/0265407598153005

David, J. A., Smith, T. W., & Marsden, P. V. (2007). *General Social Surveys, 1972–2006: Cumulative Codebook (National Data Program for the Social Sciences Series, no. 18)* Chicago, IL: National Opinion Research Center.

Desmond, S. A., Morgan, K. H., & Kikuchi, G. (2010). Religious development: How (and why) does religiosity change from adolescence to young adulthood? *Sociological Perspectives, 53*, 247–270. doi: 10.1525/sop.2010.53.2.247.

Eck, D. L. (2002). A new religious America: How a "Christian country" has become the world's most religiously diverse nation. San Francisco, CA: Harper.

Erikson, E. H. (1968). *Identity: Youth and crisis.* New York, NY: Norton.

Grusec, J. E., & Hastings, P. D. (Eds.). (2007). *Handbook of socialization: Theory and research.* New York, NY: Guilford.

Hall, G. S. (1904). *Adolescence: Its psychology and its relation to physiology, anthropology, sociology, sex, crime, religion, and education* (Vol. 1). Englewood Cliffs, NJ: Prentice-Hall.

Holden, G. W., & Vittrup, B. (2009). Religion. In M. H. Bornstein (Ed.), *Handbook of cultural developmental science* (pp. 279–295). New York, NY: Routledge.

Inglehart, R., Basañez, M., Da.ez-Medrano, J., Halman, L., & Luijicx, R. (2004). *Human beliefs and values: A cross-cultural sourcebook based upon the 1999-2002 values surveys.* Mexico City, Mexico: Siglo Veintiuno Editores.

Keniston, K. (1971). *Youth and dissent: The rise of a new opposition.* New York, NY: Harcourt Brace Jovanovich.

Koenig, L. B., McGue, M., & Iacono, W. G. (2008). Stability and change in religiousness during emerging adulthood. *Developmental Psychology, 44,* 532–543.

Kosmin, B. A., Keysar, A., Cragun, R. T., & Navarro-Rivera, J. (2009). *American nones: The profile of the no religion population.* Hartford, CT: Institute for the Study of Secularism in Society and Culture.

Labouvie-Vief, G. (2006). Emerging structures of adult thought. In J. J. Arnett & J. L. Tanner (Eds.), *Emerging adults in America: Coming of age in the 21st century* (pp. 59–84). Washington, DC: American Psychological Association.

Lefkowitz, E. S., Gillen, M. M., Shearer, C. L., & Boone, T. L. (2004). Religiosity, sexual behaviors, and sexual attitudes during emerging adulthood. *The Journal of Sex Research, 41*(2), 150–159. doi: 10.1080/00224490409552223

Lerner, R. M., & Overton, W. F. (2008). Exemplifying the integrations of the relational developmental system: Synthesizing theory, research, and application to promote positive development and social justice. *Journal of Adolescent Research, 23*(3), 245–255. doi: 10.1177/0743558408314385

Mattis, J. (2005). Religion in African American family life. In V. C. McLoyd, N. E. Hill, & K. A. Dodge (Eds.), *African American family life: Ecological and cultural diversity* (pp. 189–210). New York, NY: Guilford.

McAdams, D. P., Reynolds, J., Lewis, M., Patten, A. H., & Bowman, P. J. (2001). When bad things turn good and good things turn bad: Sequences of redemption and contamination in life narrative and their relation to psychosocial adaptation in midlife adults and in students. *Personality and Social Psychology Bulletin, 27,* 474–485. doi:10.1177/0146167201274008

McLean, K., & Breen, A. V. (2009). Processes and content of narrative identity development in adolescence: Gender and well-being. *Developmental Psychology, 45,* 702–710. doi:10.1037/a0015207

McLean, K. C., & Pratt, M. W. (2006). Life's little (and big) lessons: Identity statuses and meaning-making in the turning point narratives of emerging adults. *Developmental Psychology, 42,* 714–722. doi:10.1037/0012-1649.42.4.714

McMinn, M. R., Hathaway, W. L., Woods, S. W., & Snow, K. N. (2009). What American Psychologist Association leaders have to say about psychology of religion and spirituality. *Psychology of Religion and Spirituality, 1,* 3–13. doi: 10.1037/a0014991

Moberg, D. O. (2002). Assessing and measuring spirituality: Confronting dilemmas of universal and particular evaluative criteria. *Journal of Adult Development, 9*, 47–60. doi: 10.1023/A:1013877201375

Pargament, K. I. (1999). The psychology of religion and spirituality? Yes and no. *The International Journal for the Psychology of Religion, 9*, 3–16. doi: 10.1207/s15327582ijpr0901_2

Pargament, K. I., Mahoney, A., Exline, J. J., Jones, J. W., & Shafranske, E. P. (2013). Envisioning an integrative paradigm for the psychology of religion and spirituality. In K. I. Pargament (Ed.), *APA handbook of psychology, religion, and spirituality: Vol. 1. Context, theory, and research* (pp. 3–19). doi: 10.1037/14045-001

Paus, T. (2009). Brain development. In R. Lerner & L. Steinberg (Eds.), *Handbook of adolescent psychology* (3rd ed., Vol. 1, pp. 95–115). New York, NY: Wiley.

Pew Research Center (2012).*"Nones" on the rise: One-in-five adults have no religious affiliation.* http://www.pewforum.org/uploadedFiles/Topics /Religious_ Affiliation/ Unaffiliated/NonesOnTheRise-full.pdf

Regnerus, M. D. (2003). Religion and positive adolescent outcomes: A review of research and theory. *Review of Religious Research, 44*(4), 394–413.

Regnerus, M. D., Smith, C., & Smith, B. (2004). Social context in the development of adolescent religiosity. *Applied Developmental Science, 8*(1), 27–38. doi: 10.1207/S1532480XADS0801_4

Roberts, D. F., Foehr, U. G., Rideout, V. J., & Brodie, M. (2003). *Kids and media in America.* New York, NY: Cambridge University Press.

Roehlkepartain, E. C., & Patel, E. (2006). Congregations: Unexamined crucibles for spiritual development. In E. C. Roehlkepartain, P. E. King, L. Wagener, & P. L. Benson (Eds.), *The handbook of spiritual development in childhood and adolescence* (pp. 324–336). Thousand Oaks, CA: Sage.

Rogoff, B. (2003). *The cultural nature of human development.* New York, NY: Oxford University Press.

Russell, S. T. (2002). Queen in America: Citizenship for sexual minority youth. *Applied Developmental Science, 6*(4), 258–263. doi: 10.1207/S1532480XADS0604_13

Shafer, A., Bobkowski, P. S., & Brown, J. D. (2012). Sexual media practice: How adolescents select, engage with, and are affected by sexual media. In K. Gill (Ed.), *The Oxford handbook of media psychology* (pp. 223–251). New York, NY: Oxford University Press.

Settersten, R., & Ray, B. E. (2010). *Not quite adults: Why 20-somethings are choosing a slower path to adulthood, and why it's good for everyone.* New York, NY: Bantam Books.

Smith, C. (2003). *The secular revolution: Power, interests, and conflict in the secularization of American public life.* Berkeley, CA: University of California Press.

Smith, C. (with Christofferson, K., Davidson, H., & Herzog, P. S.) (2011). *Lost in transition: The dark side of emerging adulthood.* New York, NY: Oxford University Press.

Smith C. (with Denton, M. L.) (2005). *Soul searching: The religious and spiritual lives of American teenagers.* New York, NY: Oxford University Press.

Smith, C. (with Snell, P.). (2009). *Souls in transition: The religious and spiritual lives of emerging adults.* New York, NY: Oxford University Press.

Smith, C. (with Christoffersen, K., Davidson, H., & Snell Herzog, P.). (2011). *Lost in transition: The dark side of emerging adulthood.* New York, NY: Oxford University Press.

Smith, H. (1991). *The world's religions: Our great wisdom tradition.* New York, NY: HarperOne.

Steinberg, L. (2008). A social neuroscience perspective on adolescent risk-taking. *Developmental Review, 28,* 78–106. doi: 10.1016/j.dr.2007.08.002

Sullins, D. P. (2006). Gender and religion: Deconstructing universality, constructing complexity. *American Journal of Sociology, 112,* 838–880. doi: 10.1086/507852

Tarakeshwar, N., Stanton, J., & Pargament, K. I. (2003). Religion: An overlooked dimension in cross-cultural psychology. *Journal of Cross-Cultural Psychology, 34*(4), 377–394. doi: 10.1177/0022022103253184.

# Part II ▲
## FOUNDATIONAL PERSPECTIVES

# 2 ▲

# Emerging Adults' Religious and Spiritual Development

CAROLYN MCNAMARA BARRY AND MONA M. ABO-ZENA

> *After reflecting on several Muslim suicide bombers'*
> *trajectories, Eboo Patel saw parallel life experiences*
> *of feeling excluded from mainstream society because*
> *of racist bullying, which was inadequately assuaged*
> *with his mother's encouragement to pray more. To*
> *him, religious leaders were busy building mosques, but*
> *not building the assets of young people. Distancing*
> *himself in college from his Muslim faith, Patel became*
> *immersed in social justice work with the Catholic*
> *Worker Movements, which espoused that God is*
> *the source of love, equality, and connection. Years of*
> *service later while visiting his grandmother in India, he*
> *became distraught by its caste system. He questioned*
> *the appearance of a young woman in their home who*
> *neither seemed a servant nor a friend. Patel learned*
> *that the woman had been abused and was being housed*
> *by the grandmother until she located a viable housing*
> *alternative. Astonished by his grandmother's actions*
> *that may have jeopardized the family's safety, he was*
> *amazed to learn that she had provided a safe haven*
> *for nearly 100 women over the last 45 years. The*
> *grandmother explained that she is Muslim, and merely*
> *doing what Muslims do. Thereafter, Eboo recommitted*
> *to his own Muslim faith* (Patel, 2007).

Emerging adults seek to create a set of values, beliefs, and worldviews that are uniquely their own (Arnett, 2004). Many emerging adults value religiousness and spirituality and explore such beliefs as they strive to develop their identities further. As illustrated in the epigraph to this chapter, it was only through interactions with others of differing faiths, heightened self-exploration, and then significant personal life events that Eboo Patel returned to his faith of origin, but then at a more internalized and committed state. Some emerging adults (e.g., Catholics) are more likely to change their religious affiliation than are others (Smith, 2009). Nevertheless, the importance of religious beliefs remains stable in the United States throughout the emerging-adults years, even while religious participation declines across the twenties, especially during the first few years (Koenig, McGue, & Iacono, 2008). However, much of the existing literature on emerging adults combines them with adolescents or adults, thereby not (1) situating them developmentally nor (2) reflecting the variation in culture, context, and religious content. For example, Yonker, Schnabelrauch, and DeHaan (2012) predicted that age would moderate the relation between spirituality/religiousness and risk behavior; however, their meta-analytic review of the literature (i.e., 75 studies published between 1990 and 2010) found an insufficient number of studies that examined these differences among adolescents and emerging adults.

Given the state of the literature, in this chapter, we review research on emerging adults' religious and spiritual development, which we define as a process of meaning-making designed to facilitate the search for the sacred that may or may not involve connections to religious institutions (Pargament, Mahoney, Exline, Jones, & Shafranske, 2013). We acknowledge that religious and spiritual development may have parallel or orthogonal trajectories across individuals during their emerging-adult years. All developmental domains and contextual factors associated with a given individual have the potential to influence religious and spiritual development, and in turn promote flourishing versus floundering. First, we discuss developmental advances that shape emerging adults' religious and spiritual development. Second, we document the trends in this development over the emerging-adult years. Third, we review theories of religious and spiritual development as they apply to emerging adults. Finally, we review literature on how religious and spiritual development intersects with the physical, cognitive, emotional, and social domains.

## ▲ Developmental Underpinnings

The advances in all developmental domains undergird religious and spiritual development in the third decade of life. Along with increased life experiences, emerging adults undergo physiological, cognitive, and emotional changes, which converge to influence how they may engage in religious and spiritual contexts. Such changes intersect with significant social context changes; thus, emerging adults spend less time at home, and more time with peers who may influence their meaning-making.

Concerning physical development, adolescents have undergone tremendous pubertal changes in addition to brain maturation, involving synaptic pruning, myelinization of the prefrontal cortex, and limbic system changes, even though their prefrontal cortex is not fully mature until approximately age 25 (Paus, 2009). Thus, emerging adults increasingly are able to engage in higher levels of metacognition, planning, and abstract thinking, all of which support a more complex understanding of religious and spiritual issues. For instance, they can more deeply contemplate the existence of God, and cognitively grasp many of the theologically, spiritually, philosophically, and epistemologically complex readings and ideas that are espoused by organized religious doctrine, scholarly theological and philosophical writings, and by spiritual leaders. Additionally, their thinking is principled and characterized by cognitive-affective flexibility (Labouvie-Vief, 2006). Relatedly, scholars have shown connections between adults' spirituality and the brain at the neurochemical level (e.g., serotonin systems; Borg, Soderstrom, & Farde, 2003) as well as within the temporal lobe (Beauregard, 2012).

Socialization agents and conditions influence young people's faith, particularly through their cognitions, which in turn promote the internalization of their values and beliefs (Levenson, Aldwin, & D'Mello, 2005). Although parents are often the primary early religious and spiritual socialization agents, emerging adults forge their own values and beliefs (which may differ from their parents'), while they renegotiate their relationship with their parents. Specifically, emerging adults no longer merely act in ways that carry out parental wishes, but rather make their own decisions while seeking input from a wide array of individuals, which may include parents, which Tanner and Arnett (2011) refer to as recentering (see Chapter 4). Young adults explore beliefs further through other socialization agents, such as peers (friends, romantic partners, classmates, and coworkers; see Chapter 5) who may hold more religiously diverse views than their own. Given the intensity of and time spent in these peer relationships, they may serve as important religious and spiritual socialization agents as emerging adults tackle conversations about the meaning of life. Peer interaction can occur in a range of contexts, such as higher education and religious communities, and can be accessed through technology (see Chapters 6, 8, and 9).

Amid these peer relationships other salient developmental issues emerge (e.g., sexuality) that intersect with religious and spiritual development. For instance, 84% of 18- to 23-year-old young emerging adults have sex with a peer (Regnerus & Uecker, 2011; see Chapters 11 and 12). These scholars further argue that while previous cohorts of young adults have engaged in sex, factors related to social media have shifted the social context from one where such discussions and behaviors were taboo, to one where discussions and behaviors are expected or even encouraged. The prevalence of sexual activity raises a range of physical issues that may differ by gender and within and across religious traditions on such issues as contraception, protection from sexually transmitted infections, pregnancy, and body image. The manner and extent to which sexual issues arise depend upon sexual orientation, marital status, and how sexuality and sexual activities are understood within particular theology and faith communities. Particularly for mainstream Protestant and Catholic emerging adults attending secular universities in the United States, Freitas (2008) finds that their quest for a life partner often can result in divorcing their moral compass from their sexual behavior, which ironically leaves them less satisfied with their love lives. Alternately, the integration of sexuality with spirituality in the sanctification of sex in loving, nonmarital relationships (i.e., the belief that God is present in sexual relations between two loving partners) was found to be associated with greater sexual satisfaction in a primarily Roman Catholic and Protestant subsample of 65 college students (Murray-Swank, Pargament, & Mahoney, 2005).

During this third decade often characterized with less direct mentorship and more autonomy, emerging adults are exposed to greater diversity in religious and spiritual perspectives, and are more capable of engaging with them and with others about matters of faith given their physical, cognitive, and socioemotional advances. We next discuss the nature of religiousness and spirituality across this third decade of life.

## ▲ Prevalence of Religiousness and Spirituality Across Emerging-Adult Years

### Beliefs

The third decade of life consists of much variation in emerging adults' religiousness and spirituality. According to Smith (2011), two-thirds of emerging adults are moral relativists, agnostics, or skeptics, with the remaining third being strongly opposed to moral relativism. Nevertheless, seven out of ten emerging adults in a national survey responded that religion is important or very important in their lives (Harvard IOP, 2008). Further, more students reported a strengthening of religious convictions and beliefs by the end of college than did those who reported a weakening in religious beliefs (Lefkowitz, 2005).

While some, particularly many religious minority and conservative persons, adhere strictly to their faith of origin, the predominant set of beliefs for Catholic and Protestant emerging adults in the United States (Smith, 2009) can be characterized as a more diffuse version of "moralistic therapeutic deism" (MTD, Smith, 2005, p. 163) than they reported as adolescents. In other words, they view God as creator, advocate of goodness and justice, yet marginal in their daily lives. Further, they believe that heaven welcomes all good people, and self-fulfillment is the goal in one's life. In fact, most Millennials in the United States identify as *spiritual, but not religious* (Jones, Cox, & Banchoff, 2012). Moreover, religious beliefs vary by gender, economic status, ethnicity (David, Smith, & Marsden, 2007), religious affiliation (Smith, 2009), and immigrant status (Suárez-Orozco, Singh, Abo-Zena, Du, & Roeser, 2011), and these patterns are increasingly complex when multiple demographics are considered within a given person. For example, a middle-income Latina-American, Roman Catholic woman who is a recent immigrant is likely to report stronger religious beliefs and practices than is a similar profile woman who was born in the United States and/or who is of a higher income. Nevertheless, on average, both of these women are likely to report stronger beliefs than a European-American, mainline Protestant, middle-income man.

## Practices

While beliefs remain important, religious and spiritual practices decline until the age of 30 upon entry into marriage and parenthood (Smith, 2009; Stolzenberg, Blair-Loy, & Waite, 1995). In contrast, Smith (2009) found increases among a subgroup of nonreligious adolescents who became religious as emerging adults. Compared to adolescents, he further documented an increase in syncretistic spiritual practices, particularly from Buddhism and Hinduism, among emerging adults of all religious affiliations, but especially among Jewish and Mormon emerging adults. Thus, the pattern of religious and spiritual beliefs and practices across the emerging-adult years is quite complex. Having delineated the developmental issues that support religiousness and spirituality as well as the trends across these years, we next review existing theories of how emerging adults' religious and spiritual beliefs grow and change.

## ▲ Theories of Religious and Spiritual Development

Theories of religious and spiritual development generally have highlighted the cognitive processes needed to engage with meaning-making. Although emerging adults' cognitive functioning supports advances in religious and spiritual understandings, the theoretical literature on religious and spiritual development has not given explicit attention to emerging adults, and primarily considers them as part of a larger group of 18- to 39-year-olds (for a full review of theories on religious and spiritual development, see Oser, Scarlett, & Bucher, 2006). Instead, this section outlines key features of theories of religious and spiritual development as applied to emerging adults.

### Stage Models

Stage models of seminal theories like that of Piaget have been applied to the study of religious thinking (see Oser et al., 2006). The most well-known stage theory, the structural theory of faith development (Fowler & Dell, 2006), assumes an invariant and culturally universal sequence of meaning-making across the lifespan. Even prior to the modern-day delay of entry into adult roles until the twenties, which Arnett (2004) calls emerging adulthood, Fowler contended that the lack of critical thought and articulation capacity of adolescents is replaced by a qualitatively different *individuative-reflective faith* among those in early adulthood, wherein they come to distinguish their beliefs from others and then internalize them over the third decade before forming a *conjunctive faith* at age 30, which involves an overt commitment to one's faith. Although the exact number and features of stages vary across theories, they generally include an invariant sequence of increasingly complex thinking. Moreover, the mechanism by which individuals progress through these stages is a deep mother structure, which becomes integrated into one's larger set of worldviews and results in a mature faith (Oser et al., 2006). Although the projected ages for each stage are not delineated, empirical findings (Fowler & Dell, 2006) support the notion that abstract thought is a necessary precondition for more advanced religious and spiritual thinking. In sum, the stage models have advanced the field by describing the structure that guides transitions in emerging adults' religious thinking. While stage models provide a framework from which to explore these primarily cognitive changes surrounding religiousness for particular age groups, they are inherently limited by discontinuous views of development.

## Non-Stage Models

In contrast to stage theories' assumption of a universal telos or endpoint, which inherently is biased toward or against particular religions (Oser et al., 2006), scholars have investigated religious and spiritual development in other ways. Among those who focus on cognition, cognitive-cultural theories (Johnson & Boyatzis, 2005) contend that individuals have an intuitive ontology as well as a counterintuitive system that reflects cultural, religious, heritable, and other socialization factors. For instance, religious development has been seen as a form of transformation that moves from a self-sufficient, closed system to a more open system by first recognizing and accepting one's personal limits (Brown & Miller, 2005); emerging adults' increased cognitive capacity known as pragmatic thought can be seen as a mechanism that promotes such religious development (Labouvie-Vief, 2006).

According to the trait approach, people are conceptualized as having extrinsic, intrinsic, and/or quest religious orientations (Batson, Schoenrade, & Ventis, 1993). Consistent with adult findings, college students with intrinsic orientation reported greater levels of psychospiritual health than did the other orientations (Genia, 1996), yet they have been shown to report levels of all three religious orientations (Kneipp, Kelly, & Dubois, 2011). Relatedly, Piedmont, Ciarrochi, Dy-Liacco, and Williams (2009) have documented that spiritual transcendence is a sixth personality trait or factor across wide samples of adults (including emerging adults), which together with religious sentiments explains a range of psychosocial adjustment indicators.

Utilizing a person-centered approach, Kwilecki (1999) asserts that religious and spiritual development grows quantitatively across adulthood (not childhood), involves imagination rather than reason, and is best understood when considering a person's life circumstances. Therefore, emerging adults would be at a less mature level of their religious and spiritual development, which is further understood by considering the instability of their circumstances and limited experiences of their life circumstances. Tisdell (2003) contends that spiritual development is a spiral process akin to models of adult learning, such that after separating and evaluating one's formative set of beliefs (which is a hallmark developmental task for emerging adults), one later returns to acknowledge their role in one's life, and possibly rejects their continued function. Further, work by Kass, Friedman, Zuttermeister, and Benson (1991) emphasizes the value of having core spiritual experiences, which involves having a spiritual event and a subsequent cognitive evaluation that identifies a person's belief in a higher power as well as having a personal relationship with that higher power. Indeed, Astin, Astin, and Lindholm (2011) have shown that some college students through their curricular choices, interactions with faculty, and personal practices are likely to report spiritual experiences from which they derive personal meaning and contribute to their evolving spirituality. Similarly, Benson and Roehlkepartain (2008) put forth a consensus-based framework for spiritual development for youth (including emerging adults). Such development involves the intersection of three processes (awareness or awakening, interconnecting and belonging, and a way of living), which are situated within a framework involving other developmental domains as well as beliefs and practices from one's social contexts, culture, metanarratives, and other significant life events.

Scholars note that young people's beliefs about existential issues (which may be framed through their religiousness and spirituality) are essential to the formation of a stable identity (Markstrom, 1999), a key developmental task for emerging adults. Building upon the classic Eriksonian work (1968), some scholars (Marcia, 1966) investigate religiousness and spirituality as part of identity during the second and third decades of life. Most young people are never at the same place in each domain of their identity development, and that identity status depends upon context (Solomontos-Kountouri & Hurry, 2008). Spiritual identity, in particular, has been shown to be important in constructing one's overall identity as an adult; moreover, spiritual identity may be revised over the course of adulthood, often in response to facing adversity (Kiesling, Sorell, Montgomery, & Colwell, 2006).

Many young people may question, and even doubt, their existing religiousness and spirituality. Yet among college graduates, skepticism may be a driving force of their preference for institutionalized religion (Hill, 2011). Such doubting may result in religious conversion and may be sudden and intense due to a stressful life event, or it may be a gradual conversion, often resulting from a religious significant other (Granqvist & Kirkpatrick, 2004). Although not widespread, such conversions are a central part of young people's religious and spiritual development, and therefore worthy of scholarly attention. In sum, alternatives to stage models tend to focus on a particular concept associated with religious or spiritual development and the complexity of that concept, but then lack a sequential progression across this area of development. Further, these perspectives are based on the premise that only adults (and likely after the emerging-adult years) are capable of achieving religious maturity. Clearly, the field needs to utilize both continuous and discontinuous theories of religious and spiritual development to yield a more complete picture.

## *Summary*

The religious and spiritual development literature includes both stage and non-stage theories. However, there is much need for scholars to expand upon these theories to include how emerging adults' physical, cognitive, social, and psychological development intersects with their religious and spiritual development. Nevertheless, both religious and spiritual developmental theory and research illustrates the complex processes involved in acquiring and adapting one's religious and spiritual beliefs over time. We next consider how all domains of emerging adults' development inform their religious beliefs and practices and vice versa.

## ▲ The Intersection of Religious and Spiritual Development With Developmental Domains

Providing the context of the person-centered psychological perspective, we consider how developmental perspectives may inform religious and spiritual development. Also, we consider the rich ways that religious and spiritual experiences and structures may inform these domains of development. Given the limited research that spotlights individuals in this age group, we do not have adequate empirical data to indicate how emerging adults' experiences of these common themes may compare to those during other developmental periods. Many of the religious and spiritual activities outlined next may not be specific to emerging adults; nevertheless, our review of the research is meant to bring attention as to where future research efforts on emerging adults might be directed.

## Physical

Philosophers and theologians have long contemplated the connection between body and soul (e.g., James, 1902/1985). Indeed, physical developmental changes undergird religious and spiritual development beginning at the neuronal level and progressing to the whole body's functioning. Maselko (2013) documents the neural connections to mystical experiences, certainty of religious beliefs, and prayer. The issue of physical maturity within a context of increasing social, emotional, and economic maturity, and responsibility may manifest itself in a heightened sense of urgency toward a definition of roles. Meanwhile for religious communities, age and maturity are grounded in their respective theologies (King & Roeser, 2009). Religious traditions may mark entrance to an adult community of worship by strictly physical (i.e., sexual) maturity, or a combination of physical maturity and public recognition of acquisition of knowledge and acceptance of the beliefs within a religious tradition (Smith, 1991). It is important to note that within religious traditions, this level of accountability may come at markedly younger ages such as 10–15 years. Not surprisingly then, highly religious emerging adults are more likely to abstain from premarital sex and, in turn, are more likely to marry at younger ages than are their less committed peers (Regnerus & Uecker, 2011), thereby shortening the number of emerging-adult years. For religious traditions with conservative teachings on sexuality, engaging in related activities (e.g., viewing pornography) may result in both feelings of guilt (Nelson, Padilla-Walker, & Carroll, 2010) and conflicting social pressures from the broader society and from within the religious community.

From the religious perspective, some religious practices (e.g., dietary restrictions) regulate the relation between the body and spirit, often with the goal of promoting the sanctity of the body. According to Dowling and Scarlett (2006), one common religious practice across traditions is fasting, even though the specific degree, duration, purpose, and body-spirit conceptualization vary across traditions. Religion and spirituality have been linked to body image in positive and healthy ways (i.e., a reduction in risk behaviors; Homan & Boyatzis, 2010). Yet the relations are complex, and scholars have shown religion, religiousness, and spirituality to be related to issues about the body in negative ways as well. For instance, women use religion to rationalize eating disorders as well as arbitrarily adopt aspects of religion to help recover from these disorders (Boyatzis & Quinlan, 2008).

Physical activities of multiple types mark religious behaviors, and the symbolism behind the activities infuses meaning. For instance, prayer may have physical elements, and it may be even more prevalent for religiously observant emerging adults. Whether raising one's hands, kneeling, bowing, or prostrating, the physical acts of prayer have sacred and symbolic meanings within religious contexts, as in the example in the Roman Catholic celebration of the Eucharist. Many believe that physical aspects of worship may lead to increased physical health (e.g., meditation, yoga, the prayer movements; see Benson & Kipper, 1976/2000). The participation in such rituals may be marked by other physical expression, such as shaking hands or hugging, and may be regulated or limited by physical conditions, such as when menstruation marks a woman as being ritually impure (Dowling & Scarlett, 2006). Persons of varying religions differ in their conceptualizations of injury, sickness, and disease (e.g., an expiation of sins, a blessing, a punishment), as well as their regulation of how, when, and whether one seeks medical treatment (e.g., blood transfusions), in addition to other practices to alleviate suffering (e.g., prayers, sacrifices). Physical changes and faith celebrations, such as dances, retreats, and pilgrimages, thus, can support religious and spiritual development. Greater scholarly attention is needed to see how these physical components of religion are related to emerging adults' religious and spiritual development.

## Cognitive

Emerging adults' cognitive skills are utilized in their religious and spiritual development. For example, young people who study a holy text often utilize analytical reasoning skills and proficiency in another language (e.g., Hebrew or Arabic) for textual analysis, abstract thought to envision a higher power, and memorization skills to retain a salient passage (Smith, 1991). However, others are socialized in cognitive approaches that promote less interpretation and questioning in favor of a more literal engagement with the text, which may lead to other cognitive outcomes (e.g., career and personal pursuits that are aligned with the respective tradition). Many emerging adults may have spent portions of their formative years learning about language through exposure to stories about prophets, saints, and other exemplars, which have outcomes related both to belief acquisition and understanding of abstract or metaphorical language. The particular developmental outcomes may vary according to the religious tradition and other aspects of social position, as Patel's prologue to the chapter illustrates. Cognitive changes inform the nature of perspectives on religious experiences, and such experiences may promote different religious outcomes, both cognitive and emotional.

### Emotional

As part of religious communities, emerging adults have the opportunity to experience and regulate positive (e.g., forgiveness, empathy, generosity) and negative emotions (e.g., jealousy, hatred, greed; Corrigan, 2008). Indeed, young people of varying world theologies and associated practices are likely to report having a sense of purpose and increased levels of well-being (King & Furrow, 2004). Emerging adults' emotional responses also may be unique to their religious and spiritual lives. For instance, among those emerging adults raised in a religious tradition, they may experience religious questioning or doubt, and consequently be troubled. Emerging adults in particular may be reluctant to seek counsel for this because they do not want to disappoint others (e.g., family, mentors, clergy) and may not find adequate resources to address their religious or spiritual questions or needs (Exline & Rose, 2005).

In addition, there are rich possibilities in exploring issues of the intersection of locus of control, religious teaching and life, individual development, and psychology (i.e., attribution theory). For some emerging adults, this intersection may provide personal structure in their life as well as a sense of security and comfort (amid an age of instability; Arnett, 2004); for others this intersection may contribute to a sense of being unmotivated to exert effort because things are outside of one's control (resulting potentially in a failure to launch into adulthood quickly or fully; Hood, Hill, & Spilka, 2009). Religious communities and their theology often provide a roadmap and strategies for emotional development, which have direct implications for how emerging adults engage socially, whether with others who are similar to or different from themselves.

## Social

Emerging adults have large social support networks, which consist of more fluid relationships as well as longer term family and peer relationships (Settersten & Ray, 2010). While parents (particularly mothers) often engage in spiritual disclosure with their emerging adults, which can benefit the parent–child relationship (Brelsford & Mahoney, 2008), the potential for other intimate relationships in turn promotes the opportunity for dialogue that further supports religious and spiritual exploration (see Chapters 4 and 5). Moreover, for most religious and spiritual traditions, religious communities provide particular socialization contexts (see Chapter 8). Many emerging adults may have been socialized to a range of extents within such communities. For some, this may include a baptism or ascribed inclusion in a particular religious social group. For others, this may be a more enmeshed involvement that provides social support and mentoring from nonparental adults, as well as peers (Roehlkepartain & Patel, 2006). Through exemplars, doctrines, and organizations, religious communities may promote care for or respect for others. Many religious traditions actively promote social justice and equality, as well as welfare generally (e.g., respect for elders, or care for the weak or poor). In studies of civic involvement of adolescents and emerging adults, religiousness and religious institutions consistently have been found to be significant predictors of contribution and volunteering (Gibson, 2008).

While religious communities often promote particular social ties, religion is sometimes associated with barriers to particular social connections (see Chapters 8 and 12). Religious individuals or groups that, for example, have orientations that their truth is the only pathway to salvation may have difficulty relating to others with different values (Silberman, 2005). At times, the religious teachings themselves may be interpreted explicitly as either directly badmouthing particular individuals or groups, or indirectly limiting contact with particular individuals or groups. Emerging adults who may have religious perspectives different from their families or faith communities, or seek intimate friendships or romantic relationships with people outside their religious tradition, may face additional challenges in reconciling their different social obligations. Thus, research on the intersection of religiousness and spirituality with all developmental domains illustrates some important points that have been related to emerging adults, and many more for scholars to investigate as to their relevance in their future work.

## ▲ Conclusions

Individuals in the third decade of life are developmentally poised to explore and progress in their identity development, and in some cases strengthen their religious and spiritual beliefs and practices. The research reviewed illustrates that most emerging adults in the United States consider religiousness and spirituality to be important. Despite this centrality, there is surprisingly limited theoretical and empirical scholarship that seeks to describe and predict the possible trajectories related to religious and spiritual development from adolescence into the emerging-adult years, and then from those years to the fourth decade of life (e.g., lack of engagement, fluid identity marked by exploration, commitment, and solidification of identity). Theories of religious and spiritual development have espoused the strides that come during these emerging-adult years, yet more sophisticated levels of religious and spiritual thinking can emerge later in adulthood. Indeed, religious and spiritual development does not exist in a vacuum, but intersects with all other developmental domains in any given person, and only in understanding these intersections in time as well as that person's place in the lifespan can a more authentic understanding of religious and spiritual development result. Only by situating this holistic developmental view of emerging adults amid the entire lifespan can we better understand the religious and spiritual development of any person at a single point in time.

## ▲ Acknowledgments

The authors would like to thank Chris Boyatzis for providing thoughtful recommendations on earlier drafts of this manuscript.

# ▲ References

Arnett, J. J. (2004). *Emerging adulthood: The winding road from the late teens through the twenties*. New York, NY: Oxford University Press.

Astin, A. W., Astin, H. S., & Lindholm, J. A. (2011). Cultivating the spirit: How college can enhance students' inner lives. San Francisco, CA: Jossey-Bass.

Batson, C., Schoenrade, P., & Ventis, W. (1993). *Religion and the individual*. New York, NY: Oxford University Press.

Benson, H., & Kipper, M. Z. (1976/2000). *The relaxation response*. New York, NY: HarperTorch.

Beauregard, M. (2012). Neuroimaging and spiritual practice. In L. J. Miller (Ed.), *The Oxford handbook of psychology and spirituality* (pp. 500–513). New York, NY: Oxford University Press.

Benson, P. L., & Roehlkepartain, E. C. (2008). Spiritual development: A missing priority in youth development. *New Directions for Youth Development, 118*, 13–28. doi: 10.1002/yd.253

Boyatzis, C. J., & Quinlan, K. B. (2008). Women's body image, disordered eating, and religion: A critical review of the literature. *Research in the Social Scientific Study of Religion, 19*, 183–208. doi: 10.1163/ej.9789004166462.i-299.61

Brelsford, G. M., & Mahoney, A. (2008). Spiritual disclosure between older adolescents and their mothers. *Journal of Family Psychology, 22*, 62–70.

Brown, S., & Miller, W. R. (2005). Transformational change. In W. R. Miller & H. D. Delaney (Eds.), *Judeo-Christian perspectives on psychology: Human nature, motivation, and change* (pp. 167–183). Washington, DC: American Psychological Association.

Corrigan, J. (Ed.). (2008). *The Oxford handbook of religion and emotion*. New York, NY: Oxford University Press.

David, J. A., Smith, T. W., & Marsden, P. V. (2007). *General Social Surveys, 1972–2006: Cumulative Codebook (National Data Program for the Social Sciences Series, no. 18)*. Chicago, IL: National Opinion Research Center.

Dowling, E. M., & Scarlett, W. G. (Eds.). (2006). *Encyclopedia of religious and spiritual development*. Thousand Oaks, CA: Sage.

Erikson, E. (1968). *Identity: Youth and crisis*. New York, NY: Norton.

Exline, J. J., & Rose, E. (2005). Religious and spiritual struggles. In R. F. Paloutzian & C. L. Parks (Eds.), *Handbook of the psychology of religion and spirituality* (pp. 315–330). New York, NY: Guilford Press.

Fowler, J. W., & Dell, M. L. (2006). Stages of faith from infancy through adolescence: Reflections on three decades of faith development theory. In E. C. Roehlkepartain, P. E. King, L. Wagener, & P. L. Benson (Eds.), *The handbook of spiritual development in childhood and adolescence* (pp. 34–45). Thousand Oaks, CA: Sage.

Freitas, D. (2008). *Sex and the soul: Juggling sexuality, spirituality, romance and religion on America's college campuses*. New York, NY: Oxford University Press.

Genia, V. (1996). I, E, quest, and fundamentalism as predictors of psychological and spiritual well-being. *Journal for the Scientific Study of Religion, 35*, 56–64. doi: 10.2307/1386395

Gibson, T. (2008). Religion and civic engagement among America's youth. *The Social Science Journal, 45,* 504–514. doi: org/10.1016/j.sosscij.2008.07.007

Granqvist, P., & Kirkpatrick, L. A. (2004). Religious conversion and perceived childhood attachment: A meta-analysis. *The International Journal for the Psychology of Religion, 14,* 223–250. doi: 10.1207/s15327582ijpr1404_1

Harvard IOP. (2008). *The 14th Biannual Youth Survey of Politics and Public Service.* Retrieved May 18, 2008, from http://www.iop.harvard.edu/var/czp_site/storage/fekeditor/file/spring%20poll%2008%20-%20topline.pdf.

Hill, J. P. (2011). Faith and understanding: Specifying the impact of higher education on religious belief. *Journal for the Scientific Study of Religion, 50,* 533–551.

Homan, K. J., & Boyatzis, C. J. (2010). The protective role of attachment to God against eating disorder risk factors: Concurrent and prospective evidence. *Eating Disorders, 18,* 239–258. doi: 10.1080/10640261003719534

Hood, R. W., Hill, P. C., & Spilka, B. (2009). *Psychology of religion: An empirical approach* (4th ed.). New York, NY: Guilford.

James, W. (1902/1985). *The varieties of religious experience.* Cambridge, MA: Harvard University Press.

Johnson, C. N., & Boyatzis, C. J. (2005). Cognitive-cultural foundations of spiritual development. In E. C. Roehlkepartain, P. E. King, L. M. Wagener, & P. L. Benson (Eds.), *The handbook of spiritual development in childhood and adolescence* (pp. 211–223). Thousand Oaks, CA: Sage.

Jones, R. P., Cox, D., & Banchoff, T. (2012). *Generation in transition: Religion, values, and politics among Millenials: Findings from the 2012 Millenial Values Survey.* Retrieved August 2, 2012 from http://publicreligion.org/site/wp-content/uploads/2012/04/Millennials-Survey-Report.pdf

Kass, J. D., Friedman, R., Leserman, J., Zuttermeister, P., & Benson, H. (1991). Health outcomes and a new measure of spiritual experience. *Journal for the Scientific Study of Religion, 30,* 203–211. doi: 10.2307/1387214

Kiesling, C., Sorell, G. T., Montgomery, M. J., & Colwell, R. K. (2006). Identity and spirituality: A psychosocial exploration of the sense of spiritual self. *Developmental Psychology, 42*(6), 1269–1277. doi:10.1037/0012-1649.42.6.1269

King, P. E., & Furrow, J. L. (2004). Religion as a resource for positive youth development: Religion, social capital, and moral outcomes. *Developmental Psychology, 40,* 703–713. doi: 10.1037/1941-1022.S.1.34

King, P. E., & Roeser, R.W. (2009). Religion and spirituality in adolescent development. In R. M. Lerner & L. Steinberg (Eds.), *Handbook of adolescent psychology* (3rd ed., pp. 435–478). Hoboken, NJ: Wiley.

Kneipp, L. B., Kelly, K. E., & Dubois, C. (2011). Religious orientation: The role of college environment and classification. *College Student Journal, 45,* 143–150.

Koenig, L. B., McGue, M., & Iacono, W. G. (2008). Stability and change in religiousness during emerging adulthood. *Developmental Psychology, 44,* 532–543. doi: 10.1037/0012-1649.44.2.532

Kwilecki, S. (1999). *Becoming religious.* Cranbury, NJ: Associated University Press.

Labouvie-Vief, G. (2006). Emerging structures of adult thought. In J. J. Arnett & J. L. Tanner (Eds.), *Emerging adults in America: Coming of age in the 21st century* (pp. 59–84). Washington, DC: American Psychological Association.

Lefkowitz, E. S. (2005). "Things have gotten better:" Developmental changes among emerging adults after the transition to university. *Journal of Adolescent Research, 20*, 40–63. doi: 10.1177/0743558404271236

Levenson, M. R., Aldwin, C. M., & D'Mello, M. (2005). Religious development from adolescence to middle adulthood. In R. F. Paloutzian, & C. L. Park (Eds.), *Handbook of the psychology of religion and spirituality* (pp. 144–161). New York, NY: Guilford.

Marcia, J. E. (1966). Development and validation of ego-identity status. *Journal of Personality and Social Psychology, 3*, 551–558. doi: 10.1037/h0023281

Markstrom, C. (1999). Religious involvement and adolescent psychosocial development. *Journal of Adolescence, 22*, 205–221. doi: 10.1016/j. adolescence.2004.11.007

Maselko, J. (2013). The neurophysiology of religious experience. In K. I. Pargament (Ed.), *APA handbook of psychology, religion, and spirituality: Vol. 1. Context, theory, and research* (pp. 205–220). Washington, DC: American Psychological Association. doi: 10.1037/14045-001.

Murray-Swank, N. A., Pargament, K. I., & Mahoney, A. (2005). At the crossroads of sexuality and spirituality: The sanctification of sex by college students. *The International Journal for the Psychology of Religion, 15*(3), 199–219. doi: 10.1207/s15327582ijpr1503_2

Nelson, L. J., Padilla-Walker, L. M., Carroll, J. S. (2010). "I believe it is wrong but I still do it:" A comparison of religious young men who do versus do not use pornography. *Psychology of Religion and Spirituality, 2*, 136–147. doi: 0.1037/a0019127

Oser, F. K., Scarlett, G., & Bucher, A. (2006). Religious and spiritual development throughout the lifespan. In W. Damon, R. M. Lerner (Series Eds.), & R. M. Lerner (Vol. Ed.), *Handbook of child psychology: Vol. 1. Theoretical models of human development* (6th ed. pp. 942–998). Hoboken, NJ: Wiley.

Pargament, K. I., Mahoney, A., Exline, J. J., Jones, J. W., & Shafranske, E. P. (2013). Envisioning an integrative paradigm for the psychology of religion and spirituality. In K. I. Pargament (Ed.), *APA handbook of psychology, religion, and spirituality: Vol. 1. Context, theory, and research* (pp. 3–19). Washington, DC: American Psychological Association. doi: 10.1037/14045-001.

Patel, E. (2007). *Acts of faith: The story of an American Muslim, the struggle for the soul of a generation.* Boston, MA: Beacon Press.

Paus, T. (2009). Brain development. In R. Lerner & L. Steinberg (Eds.), *Handbook of adolescent psychology* (3rd ed., Vol. 1, pp. 95–115). New York, NY: Wiley.

Piedmont, R. L., Ciarrochi, J. W., Dy-Liacco, G. S., & Wlliams, J. E. G. (2009). The empirical and conceptual value of the spiritual transcendence and religious involvement scales for personality research. *Psychology of Religion and Spirituality, 1*, 162–179. doi: 10.1037/a0015883

Regnerus, M., & Uecker, J. (2011). *Premarital sex in America: How young Americans meet, mate, and think about marrying.* New York, NY: Oxford University Press.

Roehlkepartain, E. C., & Patel, E. (2006). Congregations: Unexamined crucibles for spiritual development. In E. C. Roehlkepartain, P. E. King, L. Wagener, & P. L. Benson (Eds.), *The handbook of spiritual development in childhood and adolescence* (pp. 324–336). Thousand Oaks, CA: Sage.

Settersten, R., & Ray, B. E. (2010). *Not quite adults: Why 20-somethings are choosing a slower path to adulthood, and why it's good for everyone.* New York, NY: Bantam Books.

Silberman, I. (2005). Religious violence, terrorism, and peace: A meaning systems analysis. In R. F. Paloutzian, & C. L. Park (Eds.), *Handbook of the psychology of religion and spirituality* (pp. 529–549). New York, NY: Guilford.

Smith, C. (with Denton, M. L). (2005). *Soul searching: The religious and spiritual lives of American teenagers.* New York, NY: Oxford University Press.

Smith, C. (with Snell, P.). (2009). *Souls in transition: The religious and spiritual lives of emerging adults.* New York, NY: Oxford University Press.

Smith, C. (with Christoffersen, K., Davidson, H., & Herzog, P. S.). (2011). *Lost in transition: The dark side of emerging adulthood.* New York, NY: Oxford University Press.

Smith, H. (1991). *The world's religions: Our great wisdom tradition.* New York, NY: HarperOne.

Solomontos-Kountouri, O., & Hurry, J. (2008). Political, religious and occupational identities in context. Placing identity status paradigm in context. *Journal of Adolescence, 31,* 241–258. doi: 10.1016/j.adolescence.2007.11.006

Stolzenberg, R. M., Blair-Loy, M., & Waite, L. J. (1995). Religious participation in early adulthood: Age and family life cycle effects on church membership. *American Sociological Review, 60,* 84–103. doi: 10.2307/2096347

Suárez-Orozco, C., Singh, S., Abo-Zena, M. M., Du, D., & Roeser, R. W. (2011). The role of religion and religious organizations in the positive youth development of immigrant youth. In A. E. A. Warren, R. M. Lerner, & E. Phelps, (Eds.). *Thriving and spirituality among youth: Research perspectives and future possibilities* (pp. 255–288). Hoboken, NJ: Wiley.

Tanner, J. L., & Arnett, J. J. (2011). Presenting "emerging adulthood": What makes it developmentally distinctive? In J. J. Arnett, M. Kloep, L. B. Hendry, & J. L. Tanner (Eds.), *Debating emerging adulthood: Stage or process?* (pp. 13–30). New York, NY: Oxford University Press.

Tisdell, E. J. (2003). *Exploring spirituality and culture in adult and higher education.* San Francisco, CA: Jossey-Bass.

Yonker, J. E., Schnabelrauch, C. A., & De Haan, L. G. (2012). The relationship between spirituality and religiosity on psychological outcomes in adolescents and emerging adults: A meta-analytic review. *Journal of Adolescence, 35,* 299–314. doi: 10.1016/j.adolescence.2011.08.010

# 3 ▲

# Potential Benefits and Detriments of Religiousness and Spirituality to Emerging Adults

GINA MAGYAR-RUSSELL, PAUL J. DEAL,
AND IAIN TUCKER BROWN

> *Religion ... comprises a system of wishful illusions*
> *together with a disavowal of reality, such as we find*
> *in an isolated form nowhere else but in amentia, in a*
> *state of blissful hallucinatory confusion.*
> —Freud, 1927/1961, p. 43

> *Religion is nothing if it be not the vital act by which*
> *the entire mind seeks to save itself by clinging to*
> *the principle from which it draws its life. This act*
> *is prayer ... the very movement itself of the soul,*
> *putting itself in a personal relation of contact with the*
> *mysterious power of which it feels the presence.*
> —James, 1902/1982, p. 464

Emerging adulthood is a distinctive developmental period during the late teens through the twenties marked by identity exploration in social roles, worldviews, and relationships (Arnett, 2000). Virtually by definition then, religiousness and spirituality are to be contemplated, if not experienced, during this critical phase of human development. The quotes from eminent psychologists that open this chapter provide a glimpse into the myriad of messages that emerging adults encounter, and often ponder, as they develop their own religious and spiritual worldviews, communities, and practices.

Although a period of culturally sanctioned religious and spiritual self-discovery may seem indulgent and privileged, the decision making that takes place during this stage of life is critical for the welfare of individuals and society in the United States. Undeniably, religiousness and spirituality are psychological forces that contribute to health and well-being throughout the lifespan (Koenig, King, & Carson, 2012). Among emerging adults in particular, scholars generally agree that religiousness and spirituality can offer opportunities for constructive self-reflection that may lead to positive outcomes (Regnerus, 2003), both in the short term and over time. For instance, religiousness and spirituality can protect against engaging in "risk behaviors," such as substance use, illegal and deviant conduct, and sexual activity (Yonker, Schnabelrach, & DeHaan, 2012), that often pose immediate and long-term dangers for health and well-being. Nevertheless, we are still learning about the specific forms of religiousness and spirituality that have less beneficial, even deleterious, implications for the overall welfare of emerging adults (Exline & Rose, 2005; Koenig et al., 2012; Magyar-Russell & Pargament, 2006).

For instance, emerging adults in college report experiencing religious and spiritual struggles, which is a particular form of coping that reflects tension and strain about religious and spiritual issues within oneself, with other people, and/or with the divine (Pargament, Murray-Swank, Magyar, & Ano, 2005). Studies have shown that such struggles often have adverse implications for mental and physical health (Bryant & Astin, 2008; Exline, Yali, & Sanderson, 2000; Faigin & Pargament, 2008). In fact, the findings from several researchers suggest that an analysis of the advantages of religiousness and spirituality among emerging adults are intricately intertwined with potential disadvantages. For example, emerging adults who regularly attend religious services are more likely to be sexually abstinent; however, this same group of individuals also may be *less likely* to practice safe sex practices when they do eventually engage in sexual activities (Lefkowitz, Gillen, Shearer, & Boone, 2004; Snell, 2009).

Thus, an analysis of the benefits and detriments of religiousness and spirituality in the lives of emerging adults is complex, multifaceted, and evolving. To unravel the associations between religiousness, spirituality, and their positive and negative implications, we begin with a brief analysis of the cultural and historical setting in which emerging adults in the United States create their religious and spiritual worldviews, communities, and practices. We then review some of the identified benefits of religiousness and spirituality from empirical studies. Next we present potential detriments of religiousness and spirituality for health and well-being, including the often problematic effects of extreme views and behaviors, in the lives of emerging adults. Finally, we discuss potential "missed opportunities" for meaning-making and coming of age via religious and spiritual communities among emerging-adult cohorts.

## ▲ Creating a Religious and Spiritual Worldview

Emerging adults embody a diversity of religious and spiritual postures that resist easy categorization. Generally speaking, both mainstream culture in the United States and emerging adulthood make a sharp subjective turn away from external doctrines and toward inner experience as a primary source of significance. The inward, self-authoring focus of emerging adulthood in the United States privileges the realm of experiences as essential to identity construction. As such, becoming an authentic self depends on being true to one's experiential world of thoughts and feelings (Taylor, 2007). Notably, this process is much less common among the ethnically religious and other highly devout groups, such as Mormons (Barry & Nelson, 2005) and evangelical Protestants (Uecker, Regnerus, & Vaalar, 2007).

Though the degree of inward focus varies by family, culture, and tradition, one particularly formative phenomenon is secularism, which refers to a social atmosphere in which God or a transcendent power is no longer axiomatic, but rather one choice among competing narratives of ultimate and cosmic significance. The plurality inherent to secularism is the space where many, if not most, emerging adults in the United States create and live out their religious and spiritual worldviews. For the vast majority of emerging adults, the task to self-author their identities, worldviews, and communities leaves them less tethered to tradition and more individually focused than at any other time in development. As Cushman (1995) stated, "truth is located in the private interior of each individual" (p. 228).

If the secular is conceptualized as a marketplace of competing narratives, how do emerging adults navigate their experience of, and relation to, the sacred? What types of relationships do their particular religious traditions encourage them to have with the world, science, and even their own doubt? How much exploration and questioning is permitted and necessary to achieve a mature religious or spiritual identity and worldview? Naturally, devoted traditionalists, such as those committed to orthodox religiousness, will answer these questions differently from, for example, the often less dogmatic adherents of noncreedal religions, such as Zen Buddhism, and liberal and mainline faith communities (e.g., Protestantism and progressive Roman Catholicism). The difference lies in how porous or impermeable the boundary line is between the secular and sacred (Longest & Smith, 2011). Either way, religiousness influences the ways in which emerging adults apprehend, interact, and imbibe mainstream cultural values and norms (Barry & Nelson, 2005). This relates to behaviors of considerable import, such as choosing a college, major, and eventual career path (Longest & Smith, 2011); seeking sexual and romantic intimacy; affiliating (or disaffiliating) with a religion; and being open to experience.

## ▲ Potential Benefits of Religiousness and Spirituality

Religious and spiritual worldviews generally provide adherents with a moral order, with a sense of purpose in life and directives about what is right and wrong (Smith, 2003). Moreover, religious and spiritual worldviews offer emerging adults a distinctive set of coping strategies for dealing with life stressors (Mahoney, Pendleton, & Ihrke, 2006; Smith, 2003) and provide them with useful religious and spiritual experiences, such as group rituals, prayer, meditation, and the guidance and support of elders and moral exemplars (Smith, 2003). Religious services in particular provide emerging adults a unique intergenerational environment in which they are not age-stratified with peers (as is typical in college); rather, they are in the presence of a wide age range of individuals who can offer perspectives from different life stages. Although there appear to be few differences in outcomes between the major religious traditions among emerging adults (Smith, 2009), the following sections represent some of the more robust empirical links found between personal religiousness, spirituality, and the promotion of health and well-being in emerging adults.

### Reduction in Risk Behaviors

In a recent meta-analysis including 75 studies, Yonker, Schnabelrauch, and DeHaan (2012) found that greater levels of religiousness and spirituality were significantly and inversely linked to risk behaviors, including underage alcohol consumption, binge drinking, marijuana use, smoking, substance use, deviant behavior, and sexual activity. Likewise, the

National Study of Youth and Religion (NSYR) found that both the religiously and spirituality devoted and religious and spiritual "regulars" (5% and 14% of emerging adults, respectively) reported less engagement in risk behaviors such as drinking alcohol, smoking, fighting, and various types of sexual activity in comparison to same-aged religiously and spiritually "disengaged" peers (25.5% of emerging adults; Smith, 2009). Additionally, greater personal religiousness and spirituality was associated with lower body mass index (BMI) and greater contentment with one's body and physical appearance (Smith, 2009).

Given that young adults between the ages of 15 and 24 years acquire roughly half of all new sexually transmitted infections (U.S. Department of Health and Human Services, 2012), sexual activity and its consequences are of particular import to emerging adults. In a sample of 205 college students, aged 18 to 25 years, Lefkowitz, Gillen, Shearer, and Boone (2004) found that sexually abstinent youth reported attending religious services more frequently, adhering to their religion's teachings more closely, and that their religious beliefs had more influence in their daily lives in comparison to sexually active youth. Emerging adults who attended services more frequently also reported having fewer lifetime sexual partners compared to less religious youth (Lefkowitz et al., 2004). Similarly, Burdette, Hill, Ellison, and Glenn (2009) found that church attendance was protective against "hooking up" (a physical encounter between two people who are largely unfamiliar with one another) at college for conservative Protestant women. Taken together, these findings suggest that religiousness and spirituality may reduce the likelihood of engaging in risk behaviors by means of doctrine, group influence, or negative expectations about the experience and consequences of engaging in such activities.

### Mental Health, Well-Being, and Social Connectedness

Greater personal religiousness and spirituality generally has been associated with fewer symptoms of depression and anxiety (Smith, 2009; Yonker et al., 2012). Moreover, greater self-reported religiousness and spirituality has been linked to greater subjective well-being, greater feelings of gratitude and purpose in life, and greater sense of control over life (Smith, 2009)—all vitally important attributes for successfully negotiating the challenges faced during emerging adulthood. Finally, more religiously and spirituality devoted emerging adults generally report better quality of parental relationships; greater involvement in organized activities; less time spent on social networking Web sites; a stronger moral orientation with regard to rules, racial inequalities, and the needs of the poor and elderly; and greater perception of bonding in social relationships (Smith, 2009).

## ▲ Potential Detriments of Religiousness and Spirituality

### Health and Well-Being

Although some empirical findings document the benefits of religiousness and spirituality for emerging adults, it is also imperative to note the potential downside of religious and spiritual involvement. For instance, in the Lefkowitz et al. (2004) study described earlier, emerging adults who followed their religions more closely were less likely to believe that condoms could prevent unintended outcomes such as pregnancy or sexually transmitted diseases and were more likely to perceive barriers to condom use, such as low self-efficacy for buying and carrying condoms, and communicating with sexual partners about using condoms. Similarly, although Zaleski and Schiaffino (2000) found that higher levels of intrinsic and extrinsic religiosity were associated with lower levels of sexual activity among 231 sixteen- to twenty-year-olds, their data also revealed that religiosity was linked to less condom use among those having sex. Collectively, these findings suggest that religious identification and behavior (i.e., church attendance) may delay initiating sexual activity; however, when religious emerging adults do engage in sexual behaviors, they are less likely to do so in a manner effective to keep themselves and their partners safe from unintended consequences (see Chapter 11).

What about the potential for adverse influence of religiousness and spirituality on mental health among emerging adults? Among emerging adults in college, religious and spiritual struggles (Pargament et al., 2005b) have been linked to lower levels of self-esteem, poorer physical health (Bryant & Astin, 2008), greater risk for engaging in addictive behaviors (Faigin & Pargament, 2008), and higher levels of depression, anxiety, and even suicidality (Exline, Yali, & Sanderson, 2000) in comparison to college students who were not struggling spiritually.

Boyatzis and McConnell (2006) found that freshman and sophomore college women who have religious and spiritual quest orientation (a religious orientation marked by an appreciation for existential questions, doubt, and paradox) were more likely to report greater body dissatisfaction and greater symptoms of bulimia in comparison to upperclassman and recent college graduates. In a related study, Homan and Boyatzis (2010) found that college women with a secure attachment to God had reduced levels of risk factors for disturbed eating, whereas college women with an anxious insecure attachment to God were at greater risk for body dissatisfaction. These authors postulate that higher quest orientation, emphasizing questioning and doubting, and an anxious insecure attachment to God may exacerbate emerging adults' vulnerability to cultural standards. These researchers provide good examples of the fine-grained assessment and analysis of religiousness and spirituality needed to explore the nuanced associations between religious and spiritual worldviews and the potential for adverse impact on mental health outcomes among emerging adults.

### In-Group, Out-Group, or No Group at All

The self-authoring and iconoclastic strand of the emerging-adult cohort raises the appeal of a religion without religion today, that is, religiousness without systems and ideology. With historical events, such as 9/11 and the sexual scandal in the Catholic Church, the emerging adult need not look far for examples of destructive religiousness. These painful events only compound an already existing aversion toward traditional religion and religiousness in general.

To the extent that religious issues exist in the global culture for the emerging adult, they typically do so in the form of the value of tolerance, the idea that religious beliefs should not be a source of discrimination or conflict (Smith, 2009). Despite the fact that emerging adults generally espouse this acceptance for others' choices in determining religious and spiritual, moral, and ethical views (Smith, 2009, 2011), religious discrimination is still rampant in American society (Gallup, 2009). How might religious and spiritual emerging adults respond to their own experience of religious discrimination? In a recent study of 134 Muslim American immigrant emerging adults, aged 18–28 years, Sirin and Katsiaficas (2011) found that the majority (61%) of the sample perceived discrimination, which they attributed to their Muslim identity. The authors also found that for young women, but not for young men, perceived religious discrimination by the larger society was related to more community engagement in one's *own* community. Thus, it seems religious discrimination from the larger society can serve to strengthen emerging adults' involvement and ties to their faith community. What we do not know, however, is whether this strengthening of connection to faith communities by way of societal discrimination contributes to a healthy integration of faith into other domains of life (i.e., work and family). Additionally, how does having been discriminated against impact perceptions of religious and spiritual in-group and out-group dynamics? For instance, perhaps being discriminated against on the basis of religion might influence some emerging adults to discourage interfaith dating and marriage for both themselves and others.

In a study of emerging adults in college, Johnson, Rowatt, and Lebouff (2012) found that self-reported religiousness and spirituality was associated positively with increased prejudice toward out-groups compared to in-groups. These researchers also found that individuals primed with religious words (vs. neutral words) showed larger increases in negative attitudes toward value-violating out-groups (atheists, gay men, Muslims). Similarly, in a series of experimental studies by Galen and colleagues (2011), the moral and social judgments of emerging adults enrolled in college were impacted by in-group bias. Specifically, participants high in religious fundamentalism consistently rated a religious "target" more favorably than the nonreligious "target" (target refers to the experimentally manipulated religious identity of the same individual in a videotaped interview shown to participants).

There is also the more rare, but nevertheless real, danger that individuals hold and keep a particular set of religious and spiritual beliefs and practices because they are socially and/or psychologically useful, particularly to assert power (Kressel, 2007), reinforce out-group hate, and justify acts of aggression. As the world knows well from violent acts of religious extremism, there can truly be a detrimental aspect to religious and spiritual worldviews, one that we hope to prevent emerging adults from entering. Kressel (2007) notes that "to understand the origins of destructive faith, it is not enough to scrutinize the religious ideologies themselves, but one must understand the role played by faith in the individual's psychological makeup" (p. 201).

Empirical studies offer further insight into destructive faith and the potential etiology of dangerous religious and spiritual worldviews. In their seminal work with university students, Altemeyer and Hunsberger (1992) found that religious fundamentalism and nonquesting were linked to authoritarianism and prejudice toward minority groups. Also working with college students, Pargament and colleagues (2007) and Raiya and colleagues (2008) found that perceptions of Jews and Muslims (respectively) as desecrators (violators of the sacred) of Christian values and teachings were linked to greater anti-Semitism and greater anti-Muslim attitudes (respectively). Moreover, in both studies, perceptions of the minority religious group (Jews or Muslims) as desecrators were predicted by higher levels of authoritarianism and religious fundamentalism. Thus, while strong religious affiliation can offer grounding for some individuals, if taken to extremes or misinterpreted, religiousness and spirituality can serve harmful ends. Research exploring the *function* of religion in the lives of individuals who report authoritarian and prejudicial views of minority groups would provide possible avenues for prevention of these appraisals during the crucial developmental period of emerging adulthood.

How do these findings juxtapose with the pervading themes of tolerance and relativism in the emerging-adult cohort (Smith, 2009, 2011)? To a certain extent, belonging to any sort of group, including religious groups, requires a tacit agreement to exclude difference and otherness. Research shows that emerging adults struggle more to tolerate and integrate doubt than their much older counterparts (Galek, Krause, Ellison, Kudler, & Flannely, 2008). In a study performed by Ingersoll-Dayton, Krause, and Morgan (2002), older age brought greater tolerance of differing religious beliefs and a budding emphasis on caring for others through prayer. Tornstam (2005) also found positive correlations between age and the development of a more *cosmic* dimension of awareness, which included a sense of being connected with the entire universe as well as a greater sense of *coherence* or meaning in life. Thematically, aging beyond emerging adulthood through the seventh decade of life is associated with an increased concern for others and a decrease in psychopathology (Galek et al., 2008).

## ▲ *How* Do Religiousness and Spirituality Influence Outcomes?

All of these findings beg the question, then, *how* is it that religiousness and spirituality influence these outcomes? There is, of course, great debate about the answer to this question for individuals of all ages (for a review of the issue, see Pargament, Magyar-Russell, & Murray-Swank, 2005a). Among emerging adults, we turn to the idea of seeking a home; that is, searching for belonging in a safe, communal sphere that provides an established worldview and access to peers, mentors, and elders (Good, Willoughby, & Fritjers, 2009). Religious spaces provide venues for important issues to be discussed, including politics, sexual behavior, social justice, education, ethics, and the environment (Smith, 2003). Moreover, religious communities often foster values that are consistent with being personally and socially responsible, which logically extend to the protective outcomes and positive effects found in the empirical literature (Good et al., 2009; Smith, 2003). In other words, religiousness and spirituality provide shelter—a communal dwelling place for emerging adults who might otherwise wander aimlessly in search of a place to rest their spirit. Indeed, as discussed earlier, for a variety of compelling reasons scholars have posited that many emerging adults may lack the necessary resources to overcome normative existential challenges during this developmental stage (such as religious doubt and rites of passage into adulthood) and "emerge" on the other side as healthy, fruitful adults (Eliade, 1958; Scott, 1998).

In their innovative psychospiritual group intervention for college students' spiritual struggles, Oemig Dworksy and colleagues (2013) provide rich qualitative findings regarding how personal religiousness and spirituality may contribute to health outcomes. Participants pointed to the nonjudgmental atmosphere of the peer group, reported a shift toward accepting spiritual struggles as a natural part of life, and described learning something new from peers and leaders in the group that could be integrated into their own lives as key factors facilitating a greater sense of self-acceptance and less stigmatization for struggling with spiritual and religious questions. In other words, the group provided a communal place where these emerging adults could explore difficult issues, acquire religious and spiritual support and resources, and build a sense of self conducive to greater health and well-being— similar assets to belonging to a religious or spiritual community.

## ▲ Missed Opportunities and Benefits Lost in the Coming-of-Age Process

*Reenvisioning Rites of Passage and Spiritual Role Models*

Emerging adulthood is marked by an ideological hunger (King & Boyatzis, 2004) to anchor autonomy and personal choice within a meaning-making context. Scholars have argued that emerging adulthood is chiefly an eschatological period (Eliade, 1958). Many emerging adults tend to reckon alone with their own existential fragility and commonly pursue individualized beliefs and worldviews at the expense of community-centered and religious involvement, which they often perceive as constraints on their quest for an individualized meaning-making framework (Arnett & Jensen, 2002; Hardy, Pratt, Pancer, Olsen, & Lawford, 2010; see Chapter 2). Relatedly, seminal scholars have argued that the self-styled coming-of-age experiences many emerging adults engage in to actualize the sort of qualities of character that purportedly mark their adult emergence actually inhibit psychospiritual and religious growth (Eliade, 1958; Erikson, 1968; Fowler, 1981; King & Boyatzis, 2004; Oman & Thoresen, 2003). For example, research has shown that men who rely on self-styled ritualization, and therefore lack a reintegration experience, subsequently feel the need to reenact the transformative event continually in order to reaffirm its value (Raphael, 1988). Among some men this induces an unfulfilling cycle of increasingly risky, adventure-seeking behaviors, where the "high" of each new achievement eventually fades into a nagging doubt about its meaningfulness (Ravert, 2009).[1]

Accordingly, at the heart of rites of passage is the awareness that psychospiritual transformation is both an individual as well as a relational and community-centered activity. Raphael (1988) argues that young adults need social validation and role modeling in their initiation rites and adult emergence process. Emerging men and women who intentionally participate in communal coming-of-age experiences, such as the sacrament of Confirmation in the Catholic tradition, may benefit from peer-level validation that affirms psychospiritual change. Additionally, the supportive and instructive influence of mentors whose modeling suggests new ways of being and understanding the numinous (Scott, 1998) provides validation about transitioning into adult roles within faith communities.

Indeed, empirical research demonstrates that spiritual and religious communities and role models represent an enormously significant resource for the value formation and development of religiousness in emerging adults (Arnett, Ramos, & Jensen, 2001; King & Boyatzis,

1. It is worth noting that research has yet to explore adequately whether and how this phenomenon applies to women for whom historically coming of age has been more commonly and consistently associated with pubertal, physical changes, such as the onset of menses (Markstrom & Iborra, 2003).

2004). Spiritual modeling, which has become a robust construct in the psychology of religiousness and spirituality, posits that psychospiritual and religious growth is fostered by illustrative exemplars who function as a "catching force" (Oman & Thoresen, 2003, p. 150). Spiritual modeling does not denote blind obedience, but rather refers to an atmosphere of open encouragement for young adults in mentoring relationships with elders and spiritual and religious exemplars. Such a milieu provides the emerging adult an opportunity to observe and sample a host of behaviors and attitudes (Bandura, 2000), particularly through ritual processes, that may lead to his or her psychospiritual transformation (Oman & Thoresen, 2003). In this way, empirical research is suggesting that community-centered coming-of-age experiences—what anthropologists have customarily described as rites of passage—contribute to the constructive growth of emerging adults' religiousness far more than self-styled approaches.

### Religious Doubt

For many emerging adults—particularly those who have grown up in mainline, liberal traditions—achieving a mature religious identity means deconstructing and differentiating from previously held sources of external institutional authority. As Bellah and colleagues (1985) note, "The self-reliant American is required not only to leave home but to 'leave church' as well" (p. 62). Yet differentiating from one's geographical and philosophical home is not the whole story. Too often, deconstruction is mistakenly understood as a singularly nihilistic exercise leading to the complete rejection and destruction of home-making propositions (Kegan, 1998). Indeed, deconstruction begins with a critical inspection of one's worldview—what Wittgenstein (1991) called the "nest of propositions"—the particular schema or representation of "home" that provides coherence to a person's sense of meaning and being in the world. However, deconstruction involves a double movement of dismantling in order to rebuild, of individuating in order to reintegrate. The point of first inspecting, challenging, and removing certain core propositions of the nest is to rebuild a second nest better equipped to navigate the newly accommodated questions and experiences. For religious and spiritual traditions conversant with doubt, it is a means to a greater end, not the end goal itself. In essence, the goal of leaving is not to become an ideological vagabond, but rather home-leaving is a prerequisite for the homecoming to a more mature and cohesive identity and worldview.

In the modern secular context, emerging adults commonly are expected to differentiate from their communal sources of support; they alone are responsible for the reorganization of their nest (Arnett & Jensen, 2002). A significant decline in group religious practices during the transition from adolescence to emerging adulthood is a well-documented trend (Koenig, McGue, & Iacono, 2008). Without a communal environment, however, emerging adults may lack sufficient continuity to guide them through the rebuilding process. Paralysis in a protracted and internally focused state can ensue (Fowler, 1981), leaving little in reserve for real connection and social reciprocity beyond the self. Without a coherent nest, there is less psychic energy and receptive space from which to hear, attend, and grapple with life-giving questions. Consequently, the doubts aroused by classroom experiences with the sciences, for example, may be experienced as the enemy of faith, rather than an invitation to deepen and mature one's faith (Longest & Smith, 2011). Accordingly, doubt itself is not the culprit of dis-ease; rather, how emerging adults integrate doubt with their spiritual and religious worldviews is of ultimate significance.

## ▲ Conclusions

The existing research findings suggest that dismissing or discarding religiousness and spirituality places emerging adults in the United States at increased risk for poorer mental health, physical health, and well-being. Additionally, emerging adults may also be foregoing the opportunity to struggle, which, according to Exline and Rose (2005), "is actually one of the greatest gifts that religion and spirituality have to offer" (p. 325). Struggling with questions and problems of meaning is a direct and effective way for emerging adults to self-examine as well as to orient themselves, not only existentially, but also communally. Religiousness and spirituality can provide the moral structure and practical ritual (Bellah et al., 1985) against and through which emerging men and women can work out a sense of who they are and to what they belong. The promise of religious and spiritual traditions is in the alternate set of values they bring into conversation with those of our secular and individualized culture. Whether emerging adults ultimately decide to come home to the traditions of their upbringing (if any), convert to a new tradition, work out a self-created hybrid spirituality, or identify as agnostics or atheists, exposure to religious and spiritual traditions makes for life-enriching dialogue within the person. The ability to live in the tension of a conversation between a multiplicity of different voices within the self of the emerging adult births and nurtures the grace and wisdom to engage the many voices of the larger community further down the road into middle and late adulthood.

## ▲ References

Altemeyer, B., & Hunsberger, B. (1992). Authoritarianism, religious fundamentalism, quest, and prejudice. *International Journal for the Psychology of Religion*, 2(2), 113–133. doi: 10.1207/s15327582ijpr0202_5

Arnett, J. J. (2000). Emerging adulthood: A theory of development from the late teens through the twenties. *American Psychologist*, 55, 469–489. doi: 10.1037//0003-066X.55.5.469

Arnett, J. J., & Jensen L. A. (2002). A congregation of one: Individualized religious beliefs among emerging adults. *Journal of Adolescent Research*, 17, 451– 467. doi: 10.1177/0743558402175002

Arnett, J. J., Ramos, K. D., & Jensen, L. A. (2001). Ideological views in emerging adulthood: Balancing autonomy and community. *Journal of Adult Development*, 8, 69–79. doi: 10.1023/A:1026460917338

Bandura, A. (2000). Exercise of human agency through collective efficacy. *Current Directions in Psychological Science*, 9, 75–78. doi: 10.1111/1467-8721.000064

Barry, C. M. & Nelson, L. J. (2005). The role of religion in the transition to adulthood for young emerging adults. *Journal of Youth and Adolescence*, 34, 245– 255. doi: 10.1007/s10964-005-4308-1

Bellah, R. B., Madsen, R., Sullivan, W. M., Swindler, A., & Tipton, S. M. (1985). *Habits of the heart: Individualism and commitment in American life*. Berkley, CA: University of California Press.

Boyatzis, C. J., & McConnell, K. M. (2006). Quest orientation in young women: Age trends during emerging adulthood relations to body image and disordered eating. *The International Journal for the Psychology of Religion*, 16, 197–207. doi: doi:10.1207/s15327582ijpr1603_4

Bryant, A. N., & Astin, H. S. (2008). The correlates of spiritual struggle during the college years. *The Journal of Higher Education*, 79(1), 1–27. https://ohiostatepress.org/index.htm?journals/jhe/jhemain.htm

Burdette, A. M., Hill, T. D., Ellison, C. G., & Glenn, N. D. (2009). "Hooking up" at college: Does religion make a difference? *Journal for the Scientific Study of Religion*, 48(3), 535–551. doi:10.1111/j.1468-5906.2009.01464.x

Cushman, P. (1995). *Constructing the self, constructing America: A cultural history of psychotherapy*. Reading, MA: Addison-Wesley.

Eliade, M. (1958). *Rites and symbols of initiation* (W. R. Trask, Trans.). New York, NY: Harper and Row.

Erikson, E. H. (1968). *Identity, youth, and crises*. New York, NY: Norton.

Exline, J., & Rose, E. (2005). Religious and spiritual struggles. In R. F. Paloutzian, & C. L. Park (Eds.), *Handbook of the psychology of religion and spirituality* (pp. 315–330). New York, NY: Guilford Press.

Exline, J. J., Yali, A., & Sanderson, W. (2000). Guilt, discord, and alienation: The role of religious strain in depression and suicidality. *Journal of Clinical Psychology, 56*(12), 1481–1496. doi: 10.1002/1097-4679(200012)56: 12<1481::AID-1>3.0.CO;2-A

Faigin, C. A., & Pargament, K. I. (2008). *Filling the spiritual void: Spiritual struggles as a risk factor for addiction.* Poster presented at the 20th annual convention of the Association for Psychological Science, Chicago, IL.

Fowler, J. W. (1981). *Stages of faith: The psychology of human development and the quest for meaning.* New York, NY: HarperCollins.

Freud, S. (1927/1961). *The future of an illusion* (J. Strachey, Trans/Ed). New York, NY: Norton.

Galek, K., Krause, N., Ellison, C. G., Kudler, T., & Flannely, K. J. (2008). Religious doubt and mental health across the lifespan. *Journal of Adult Development, 14*, 16–25. doi:10.1007/s10804-007-9027-2

Galen, L. W., Smith, C. M., Knapp, N., & Wyngarden, N. (2011). Perceptions of religious and nonreligious targets: Exploring the effects of perceivers' religious fundamentalism. *Journal of Applied Social Psychology, 41*(9), 2123–2143. doi: 10.1111/j.15591816. 2011.00810.x

Gallup. (August 28, 2009). Religious perceptions in America: With an in-depth analysis of US attitudes toward Muslims and Islam. Retrieved from http:// www.gallup.com/se/ms/ 153434/ENGLISH-First-PDF-Test.aspx

Good, M., Willoughby, T., & Fritjers, J. (2009). Just another club? The distinctiveness of the relation between religious service attendance and adolescent psychosocial adjustment. *Journal of Youth and Adolescence, 38*: 1153–1171. doi: 10.1007/s10964-008-9320-9

Hardy, S. A., Pratt, M. W., Pancer, S. M., Olsen, J. A., & Lawford, H. L. (2010). Community and religious involvement as contexts of identity change across late adolescence and emerging adulthood. *International Journal of Behavioral Development, 35*, 125–135. doi: 10.1177/0615025410375920

Homan, K. J., & Boyatzis, C. J. (2010). The protective role of attachment to God against eating disorder risk factors: Concurrent and prospective evidence. *Eating Disorders, 18*, 239–258. doi: 10.1080/10640261003719534

Ingersoll-Dayton, G., Krause, N., & Morgan, D. (2002). Religious trajectories and transitions over the life course. *International Journal of Aging and Human Development, 55*, 55–70. doi: 10.2190/297Q-MRMV-27TE-VLFK

James, W. (1902/1982). *The varieties of religious experience: A study in human nature* (M. E. Marty, Ed.). New York: NY: Penguin.

Johnson, M. K., Rowatt, W. C., & Lebouff, J. P. (2012). Religiosity and prejudice revisited: In group favoritism, out-group derogation, or both? *Psychology of Religion and Spirituality, 2*, 154–168. doi: 10.1037/a0025107

Kegan, R. (1998). *In over our heads: The mental demands of modern life.* Boston, MA: Harvard University Press.

King, P. E., & Boyatzis, C. J. (2004). Exploring adolescent spiritual and religious development: Current and future theoretical and empirical perspectives. *Applied Developmental Science, 8*, 2–6. doi: 10.1207/S1532480XADS0801_1

Koenig, H., King, D., & Carson, V. B. (2012). *Handbook of religion and health.* New York, NY: Oxford University Press.

Koenig, L. B., McGue, M., & Iacono, W. G. (2008). Stability and change in religiousness during emerging adulthood. *Developmental Psychology, 44*, 532–543. doi: 10.1037/0012-1649.44.2.532

Kressel, N. J. (2007). *Bad faith: The danger of religious extremism*. Amherst, NY: Prometheus.

Lefkowitz, E. S., Gillen, M. M., Shearer, C. L., & Boone, T. L. (2004). Religiosity, sexual behaviors, and sexual attitudes during emerging adulthood. *The Journal of Sex Research, 41*(2), 150–159. doi: 10.1080/00224490409552223

Longest, K. C., & Smith, C. (2011). Conflicting or compatible: Beliefs about religion and science among emerging adults in the United States. *Sociological Forum, 26*, 846–869. doi: 10.1111/j.1573-7861.2011.01287.x

Magyar-Russell, G., & Pargament, K. I. (2006). The darker side of religion: Risk factors for poorer health and well-being. In P. McNamara (Ed.), *Where God and science meet: How brain and evolutionary studies alter our understanding of religion (Vol. 3): The psychology of religious experience* (pp. 105–131). Westport, CT: Praeger Publishers/Greenwood Publishing Group.

Mahoney, A., Pendleton, S., & Ihrke, H. (2006). Religious coping by children and adolescents: Unexplored territory in the realm of spiritual development. In E. C. Roehlkepartain, P. E., Ebstyne, L. Wagener, & P. Benson (Eds.). *The handbook of spiritual development in childhood and adolescence* (pp. 341–354). Thousand Oaks, CA: Sage.

Markstrom, C. A., & Iborra, A. (2003). Adolescent identity formation and rites of passage: The Navajo Kinaaldá ceremony for girls. *Journal of Research on Adolescence, 13*, 399–425. doi: 10.1046/j.1532-7795.2003.01304001.x

Oemig Dworsky, C. K., Pargament, K. I., Gibbel, M. R., Krumrei, E. J., Faigin, C. A., Gear Haugen M. R.,…Warner, H. L. (2013). Winding road: Preliminary support for a spiritually integrated intervention addressing college students' spiritual struggles. *Research in the Social Scientific Study of Religion, 24*, 309–339.

Oman, D., & Thoresen, C. E. (2003). The many frontiers of spiritual modeling. *The International Journal for the Psychology of Religion, 13*, 197–213. doi: 10.1207/S15327582IJPR1303_04

Pargament, K. I., Magyar-Russell, G. M., & Murray-Swank, N. A. (2005a). The sacred and the search for significance: Religion as a unique process. *Journal of Social Issues, 61*(4), 665–687. doi: 10.1111/j.1540-4560.2005.00426.x

Pargament, K. I., Murray-Swank, N. A., Magyar, G. M., & Ano, G. (2005b). Spiritual struggle: A phenomenon of interest to psychology and religion. In W. R. Miller & H. D. Delaney (Eds.), *Judeo-Christian perspectives on psychology: Human nature, motivation, and change* (pp. 245–268). Washington, DC: American Psychological Association.

Pargament, K. I., Trevino, K., Mahoney, A., & Silberman, I. (2007). They killed our Lord: The perception of Jews as desecrators of Christianity as a predictor of anti-semitism. *Journal for the Scientific Study of Religion, 46*, 143–158. doi: 10.1111/j.1468-5906.2007.00347.x

Raiya, A. H., Pargament K. I., Mahoney, A., & Trevino, K. (2008). When Muslims are perceived as a religious threat: Examining the connection between desecration, religious coping, and anti-Muslim attitudes. *Basic & Applied Social Psychology, 30*(4), 311–325. doi: 10.1080/01973530802502234

Raphael, R. (1988). *The men from the boys: Rites of passage in male America*. Lincoln, NE: University of Nebraska Press.

Ravert, R. D. (2009). "You're only young once": Things college students report doing now before it is too late. *Journal of Adolescent Research, 24*(3), 376–396. doi: 10.1177/0743558409334254

Regnerus, M. D. (2003). Religion and positive adolescent outcomes: A review of research and theory. *Review of Religious Research, 44*(4), 394–413. doi: 10.2307/3512217

Scott, D. G. (1998). Rites of passage in adolescent development: A reappreciation. *Child & Youth Care Forum, 27*, 317–335. doi: 10.1023/A:1022349312391

Sirin, S. R., & Katsiaficas, D. (2011). Religiosity, discrimination, and community engagement: Gendered pathways of Muslim American emerging adults. *Youth and Society, 43*(4), 1528–1546. doi: 10.1177/0044118X10388218

Smith, C. (2003). Theorizing religious effects among American adolescents. *Journal for the Scientific Study of Religion, 42*(1), 17–30. doi: 10.1111/1468-5906.t01-1-00158

Smith, C. (with Snell, P.). (2009). *Souls in transition: The religious and spiritual lives of emerging adults*. New York, NY: Oxford Press.

Smith, C. (2011). *Lost in transition: The dark side of emerging adulthood*. New York, NY: Oxford University Press.

Snell, P. (2009). What difference does youth group make? A longitudinal analysis of religious youth group participation outcomes. *Journal for the Scientific Study of Religion, 48*(3), 572–587. doi: 10.1111/j.1468-5906.2009.01466.x

Taylor, C. (2007). *The secular age*. Cambridge, MA: Belknap Press of Harvard University Press.

Tornstam, L. (2005). *Gerotranscendence: A developmental theory of positive aging*. New York, NY: Springer Publishing Company.

Uecker, J. E., Regnerus, M. D., & Vaaler, M. E. (2007). Losing my religion: The social sources of religious decline in early adulthood. *Social Forces, 85*, 1667– 1692. doi: 10.1353/sof.2007.0083

U.S. Department of Health and Human Services, Centers for Disease Control and Prevention. (2012). *Sexually transmitted disease surveillance 2011*. Retrieved from http://www.cdc.gov/std/stats11/Surv2011.pdf

Wittgenstein, L. (1991). *On certainty*. Boston, MA: Blackwell.

Yonker, J. E., Schnabelrauch, C. A., & DeHaan, L. G. (2012). The relationship between spirituality and religiosity on psychological outcomes in adolescents and emerging adults: A meta-analytic review. *Journal of Adolescence, 35*(2), 299–314. doi: 10.1016/j.adolescence.2011.08.010

Zaleski, E. H., & Schiaffino, K. M. (2000). Religiosity and sexual risk-taking behavior during the transition to college. *Journal of Adolescence, 23*, 223–227. doi: 10.1006/jado.2000.0309

# Part III ▲

## CONTEXTS AND SOCIALIZING AGENTS IN EMERGING ADULTS' RELIGIOUS AND SPIRITUAL LIVES

# 4 ▲

# The Role of Parents in the Religious and Spiritual Development of Emerging Adults

LARRY J. NELSON

*As a child, I grew up knowing that my father had postponed his career and family ambitions in order to give 2½ years of missionary service for his religion, and that the same was expected for me. Years later, I distinctly remember when as an adolescent this abstract notion of "one day" maybe being a missionary myself turned into a very specific goal and a real and personal part of my developing identity. While fishing with my dad one day, our discussion turned to his years in Japan as a missionary. His words and feelings regarding the people that he met, the things he learned, and the beliefs that he held dear, impacted me differently that day than they had previously. I remember making a personal commitment that day that I would follow in my father's footsteps. Several years later, at the age of 19, I indeed found myself leaving behind a college scholarship, friends, and family to serve a church mission in Switzerland for 2 years.*

This personal vignette illustrates the numerous ways in which parents may affect their children's religious and spiritual development well into emerging adulthood, including serving as religious models, sending direct messages about beliefs and behaviors, and providing the climate for how the message is received (i.e., parenting styles and the relationship they have with their children). Although this is just one account, there is a growing body of literature that points to parents playing a significant role in the complex and changing nature of their emerging-adult children's religiousness and spirituality. The role of parents in this regard is complex because of the evolving nature of both the religious and spiritual beliefs of emerging adults as well as the role that parents appear to play in their children's lives generally and in this domain (religious and spiritual) of development specifically during emerging adulthood.

There are numerous challenges in identifying the possible role of parents in the religious and spiritual development of emerging adults, but two seem particularly salient. First, it is difficult to know whether the influence of parents on their emerging-adult children is just "spill-over" from parental religious socialization during childhood and adolescence. In other words, it is unclear whether parents have a direct influence on emerging adults' religious and spiritual development or if any influence that they have in emerging adulthood is just the residual effect of earlier religious socialization. The second challenge to identifying the possible role of parents in emerging adults' religious and spiritual development is uncertainty as to whether religious socialization is distinct from broader family socialization practices. For example, Smith (2005) found that adolescents' religious faith and practices tend to be influenced by aspects of parent religiousness (e.g., religious beliefs, attending religious services) but also by parenting (e.g., parental warmth, parenting styles) and the parent–child relationship. In sum, it is challenging to extricate the role that parents play in emerging adulthood from the role that they played when their children were younger (i.e., spillover effect), and the role that parental religious socialization plays, if any, that might be unique from parenting in general.

Therefore, to understand the role of parents in emerging adults' religious and spiritual development fully, it is requisite, and therefore the purpose of this chapter, to examine (a) what parents do earlier in children's lives that may be linked to emerging adults' religious and spiritual development; (b) what, if any, direct influence parents have on religious and spiritual development during emerging adulthood; (c) what role parenting and the parent–child relationship more broadly may play in emerging adults' religious and spiritual development; and (d) what areas of future work are needed, including study of the bidirectional nature of the parent–child relationship and how contextual factors (e.g., culture) play in the associations between parents and the religious and spiritual development of emerging adults. It should be noted from the outset that most of the extant research that is reviewed is based on and assumes a two-parent biological parent structure, but that the broader conceptual issues addressed in this chapter might apply to whomever those primary caregivers are to a given child.

## ▲ Early Parental Religious Socialization

In order to understand fully the role of parents in the religious and spiritual development of their emerging-adult children, it is important to examine aspects of parental religiousness, parenting, and the parent–child relationship during earlier developmental periods that have been linked to their children's religious and spiritual development (e.g., Smith, 2005). The goal in doing this is to identify parental factors that have been linked to religious socialization in childhood and adolescence in order to identify the factors that also might be important in religious socialization in emerging adulthood.

### Parental Religiousness

Parents' own religiousness has been found to be related to their children's religious development (e.g., Myers, 2006; Smith, 2005). One direct way in which parents influence their children is via modeling religious behaviors. Both theory (Oman & Thoresen, 2003) and research (e.g., Schwartz, 2006) suggest that children engage in "observational spiritual learning," in which they learn through observing other people (i.e., parents) who are their "spiritual models" (Silberman, 2003). Parents also convey religious messages directly to their children via family religious practices. A number of studies, mostly with adolescents, have shown that various aspects of young people's own religiousness (e.g., strength of religious beliefs, affiliation, personal religious practices) are tied to formal family religious practices, such as attending church, praying, and reading scriptures as a family (e.g., Dollahite & Marks, 2009; Loser, Hill, Klein, & Dollahite, 2009). Child religious outcomes also are linked to informal, less structured family religious practices, such as praying together as well as engaging in discussions with parents about God, scriptures, or religion in general (e.g., Dollahite & Thatcher, 2008).

Parents also appear to influence the religious and spiritual lives of children and adolescents indirectly. For example, it has been found that the impact of religious socialization (e.g., modeling, dialogue) of parents on their adolescents is partially mediated by the religious socialization of friends (Schwartz, 2006). Thus, when taking their children to religious services and other settings in which religious young people interact, parents may be fostering religiousness in their children indirectly via the influence they have on their children's peer group. Furthermore, by immersing their children in a religious community, parents expose them to religious mentors (Smith, 2005). Parents also may direct their children's use of media, which conveys a wide range of views regarding values generally and religion specifically. By monitoring the messages and images to which their children are exposed, media may be an important way in which parents indirectly influence the religious and spiritual development of their children. Other indirect influences of parents may include the decision of what type of school (public versus religious-private) in which to enroll their children, the neighborhood and larger community in which they live, and the places that they visit on family excursions and vacations (e.g., religious sites and museums; see Chapters 5, 6, 8, and 9).

Taken together, the mounting evidence shows that parents' religious socialization is linked to their children's and adolescents' religious and spiritual lives. There is even a growing body of work showing how this early socialization may be related to religious and spiritual development in emerging adulthood, as suggested in the vignette that opened this chapter. For example, adolescents' reports of parental religiousness have been found to be strong predictors of emerging adults' religiousness (e.g., Gunnoe & Moore, 2002; Milevsky, Szuchman, & Milevsky, 2008; Smith, 2009). The question that is still to be addressed is whether parents have any direct or indirect influence on the religious and spiritual development once their children prepare to and enter the third decade of life.

## ▲ Parental Religious Socialization of Emerging-Adult Children

There are studies, albeit few, that have examined the *direct* association between parent religiousness and emerging adults' religious beliefs and practices (e.g., Smith, 2009). However, nearly all of this research is subject to the limitations outlined previously, namely that it does not control for the influence of earlier (childhood and adolescence) parental socialization. Furthermore, the work examining the *indirect* links of parenting and emerging adults' religious and spiritual development is nearly nonexistent. Therefore, the state of the literature still requires us to ask *how* parents matter in the religious and spiritual lives of emerging adults because, although it is possible that they play a rather influential part, especially in certain cultures that emphasize and value elders (e.g., collectivistic cultures), it is also possible that they do not or that they play a significantly smaller role. Consequently, we must look at the developmental shifts that occur across emerging adulthood in order to understand the changing, even diminishing, role of parents as religious socializers.

Aquilino (2006) points out that changing interests, abilities, transitions, and behaviors of emerging adults lead to a "shake up" (p. 193) within the parent–child relationship. Foremost, many young people leave their parents' home for college and/or work where they often live with acquaintances, friends, or romantic partners. This developmental change alone severely alters the influence that parents can have on their emerging-adult children. Another important developmental shift is the child's own desire to make decisions independently, without the input of parents (e.g., Nelson & Barry, 2005). In other words, young people tend to believe that parents should have less of a direct role in their lives, which may include reducing the role of parents as religious socializers. Finally, this period of life is one of exploration (Erikson, 1968), in which young people examine and internalize their worldviews as they solidify their identity (Arnett, 2004). Due to declines in emerging adults' religious *practices* (e.g., Koenig, McGue, & Iacono, 2008), some might think that the exploration and internalization of beliefs typical of this age might not include religious and spiritual beliefs. However, the data suggest otherwise. Numerous studies (e.g., Lee, 2002; Lefkowitz, 2005) show that a rather large percentage of emerging adults, especially college students, experience a strengthening of religious beliefs, suggesting a period of exploration of religious beliefs that results in stronger internalization of their religious identity (see Chapter 2).

Taken together, the developmental transitions that occur in emerging adulthood suggest a diminishing direct role of parents as religious and spiritual socializers. It is much more challenging for parents of emerging adults to serve as models of religiousness and spirituality if their children cannot see them (e.g., do not live at home). Likewise, if their children do not live in the home, parents cannot directly socialize their children on a daily basis via participating together in attendance at religious services, family prayer, or other family religious rituals. Even if emerging adults live in the home, the autonomy that is appropriate for this age, and expected by emerging adults, might lead to emerging adults choosing not to participate in their family's religious activities.

As a result, although ways still exist (as will be considered later), there are far fewer opportunities for parents to influence their emerging-adult children's religious and spiritual development directly, as frequently, and in the same ways that they may have when their children were younger.

Given the unique aspects of emerging adulthood, there is a similar decline in the indirect influence that parents might have on their children's religious and spiritual development. Parents have much less control over their emerging-adult children's friendships, romantic partners, and larger peer groups who therefore have the potential to influence developing religious beliefs more than do parents. Indeed, most college students' religious experiences and discussions occur with friends (Montgomery-Goodnough & Gallagher, 2007), and there is very little evidence suggesting that parents have the same influence over their children's peers in emerging adulthood like they did in childhood and adolescence. Similarly, young people are influenced by a broader range of adults (e.g., professors, employers) who might serve as mentors (e.g., Cannister, 1999), and parents have very little influence in this regard. Likewise, parents are much less able to monitor the movies and television shows that their children watch, the Internet sites that they visit, or the video games that they play. In sum, not only does the direct role of parents as religious socializers appear to diminish in emerging adulthood, but so does the indirect influence that they have in the religious and spiritual lives of their children.

This is not to suggest that parents do not matter in any way in emerging adulthood, but the role that they play may become more complex and be centered on broader aspects of the parent–child relationship. As noted previously, Smith (2005) found that not only was adolescents' religiousness influenced by aspects of parent religiousness but also by parenting (e.g., parenting styles) and the parent–child relationship. In other words, as captured in the opening vignette, it appears that the context for and content of religious socialization matters.

## ▲ The Role of Parenting and the Parent–Child Relationship

The type of parenting and the quality of the parent–child relationship have been shown to be important factors in the religious development of children and adolescents. For instance, Bao, Whitbeck, Hoyt, and Conger (1999) documented that the relation between parent religiousness and child outcomes may be moderated by the way in which children are parented, such that the links between parents' and adolescents' religious beliefs and practices diminished when parental acceptance was low and increased when it was moderate or high. The impact of how parents "packaged" their religious beliefs (i.e., acceptance vs. force) also may last into emerging adulthood in influencing whether emerging-adult children continue on the religious path of their parents. For example, Hoge and colleagues (1993) found emerging adults who perceived the use of coercive techniques for parental socialization (e.g., "Did parents force you to go [to church]?") were less likely to report church involvement in adulthood. Similarly, Gunnoe and Moore (2002) found that the presence of religious models (especially religious mothers) who engaged in authoritative parenting during childhood and adolescence best predicted emerging adults' religiousness. Finally, Petts (2009) found that parental engagement and affection during adolescence predicted children's religious participation in emerging adulthood. In sum, the way in which parents socialize their children and adolescents appears to be related to the religious and spiritual development of emerging adults. It may be that while their role as direct socializers of religiousness and spirituality diminishes as their children enter the third decade of life, parents may still play an important role via their broader parenting practices and the overall quality of the parent–child relationships during this period of development.

Indeed, there is a burgeoning body of research showing that positive parenting is just as important in emerging adulthood as it is with younger children and adolescents (Nelson, Padilla-Walker, Christensen, Evans, & Carroll, 2011). For example, there is a body of work, mostly with college students, showing that positive parenting (e.g., parental acceptance, support, warmth, open communication) is linked to emerging adults' adjustment, including emotional adjustment (McKinney & Renk, 2008), overall well-being (e.g., Holahan, Valentiner, & Moos, 1994), and academic performance (e.g., Turner, Chandler, & Heffer, 2009). In addition to aspects of parenting, the overall quality of the parent–child relationship appears to matter to emerging adults' well-being. For example, a higher quality parent–child relationship or attachment has been found to be associated with higher levels of emerging adults' adjustment (e.g., psychological well-being, Van Wel, Ter Bogt, & Raaijmakers, 2002; internal regulation, Barry, Padilla-Walker, Madsen, & Nelson, 2008) and lower levels of maladjustment (e.g., fewer risk behaviors, Padilla-Walker, Nelson, Madsen, & Barry, 2008).

In sum, the extant evidence suggests that parenting still matters to emerging adults given that positive parenting and the overall quality of the parent–child relationship are key factors in whether emerging adults flourish or flounder as they transition to adulthood (Nelson & Padilla-Walker, 2013). However, the evidence that parenting and the parent–child relationship has an effect on emerging adults' religious and spiritual beliefs and practices is itself just beginning to emerge (e.g., Barry, Padilla-Walker, & Nelson, 2012).

## ▲ Summary of Existing Work

Based on the research reviewed to this point, we know the following regarding the role of parents in their emerging-adult children's religious and spiritual development. We know that several aspects of the time period (i.e., desire for greater autonomy, exploration of personal beliefs, greater frequency of emerging-adult children living outside the home) might explain the role that parents play as religious socializers. Despite these developmental changes, we know that parental behaviors and parent–child relationships still appear to matter in emerging adults' over-all well-being generally as well as their religious and spiritual develop-mental specifically. We know that parents play both a direct (e.g., models, family religious practices) and indirect (e.g., monitoring of peer groups and media) role as religious socializers in childhood and adolescence, and these effects appear to be linked to children's religious and spiritual devel-opment as they enter the third decade of life (e.g., Smith, 2009). However, we know much less about the direct and indirect roles that parents play *in* emerging adulthood because the work is relatively scant and the exist-ing work seldom controls for either religious socialization at earlier ages or broader parental socialization. We also do not know what child factors might be contributing to the bidirectional nature of this process. Finally, we know little regarding the role that the cultural context might play in parental socialization in emerging adulthood. Therefore, the remainder of this chapter outlines areas for future research that might help us to address these gaps in our understanding of the possible role of parents in the religious and spiritual lives of their emerging-adult children.

## ▲ Directions for Future Work

### *Direct Effects*

To explore whether parents have any direct effects on their emerging adults' religious and spiritual development, more longitudinal work is needed, wherein early religious (e.g., modeling, family religious practices) and general (e.g., warmth, support) socialization practices are controlled for in order to identify which parental socialization attempts provide a direct role in emerging adults' religious and spiritual development. By doing this, we can not only begin to see the unique role that parents have, but it might allow us (a) to see what religious socialization practices, if any, parents may employ for their emerging adults that are similar to what they have done in the past, or (b) to identify practices that might emerge to meet the changing nature of the time period and the parent–child relationship. For example, researchers might examine whether parents still serve as models in some way and how that happens if the children do not live at home. One possible avenue through which this might happen is by parents sharing their own narratives as emerging adults with their children. For example, the opening personal vignette of my father's choice to serve a church mission in his twenties served as a religious model for what I might do in my twenties. In this way, choices and experiences both positive and negative that parents had as emerging adults might serve as models.

Another possible way in which parents might have a direct effect religiously or spiritually on their children is via the use of technology. There is much to be explored regarding parental use of texting, e-mail, and social networking sites in continuing to socialize their children's religious and spiritual beliefs and practices. Some parents might send spiritual thoughts or passages of scriptures electronically to support and encourage their children. Parents might attempt to include young people living away from home (or in some cases in which it is the parent who is the one away from home such as being in the military) in some family rituals via electronic communication, such as Skype. Religious socialization practices that have been identified as important with children and adolescents (e.g., family prayer, attending religious services as a family) might become less frequent, and possibly less influential, but they might be replaced with new practices that researchers have yet to identify and explore as avenues for religious socialization in emerging adulthood.

On the other hand, if emerging adults are living at home and parents maintain socialization practices (e.g., family prayer, attending religious services as a family), it would be important to know whether they have the same effects as they did in adolescence. It may be that parental attempts to socialize differ, diminish, or even become a source of contention in the home because many emerging adults (especially those from individualistic cultures, e.g., mainstream Christians in the United States) now want more autonomous exploration of beliefs (Smith, 2009), but such exploration is less common and welcome by parents in more religious conservative faith traditions. It is essential that more work in this area is done in order to ascertain whether parents have any direct effect on religious and spiritual development once their children reach emerging adulthood.

### Indirect Effects

Likewise, more work is needed to examine how, in the current context of emerging adulthood, parents might influence indirectly their emerging-adult children's religious and spiritual development. In order to do this, researchers may need to examine the landscape with a broader lens. For example, as noted previously, in childhood and adolescence parents might influence their children's peer group via involvement in a religious community. Parents of emerging adults may do the same thing via directing children to a particular college or university that is either affiliated with a particular religious denomination or has on its campus a strong presence (e.g., clubs, youth ministries, course offerings, religious institutes) of a preferred religious group or value system. Parents might not only encourage a particular choice of college or university but may even tie financial support to their children's decision (or, for example, their attending church or joining a religious club or organization). This is not intended to suggest that these are appropriate parental socialization strategies; rather, they serve as examples of ways in which parents might still indirectly influence the religious and spiritual development of young people. It behooves researchers to take a more developmental approach in identifying ways in which direct and indirect parental socialization strategies might still be efficacious in their emerging-adult children's religious and spiritual development.

### Parenting and the Parent–Child Relationship

The reviewed literature demonstrates that parenting and the parent–child relationship are important factors in whether emerging adults flourish or flounder. However, few studies have specifically examined religious and spiritual outcomes associated with various types of parenting or levels of quality in the relationship; thus, more work is needed. In regard to parenting, for example, there is evidence that if parents engage in warm, authoritative parenting when their children are adolescents, the more likely it is that those children adopt the religious beliefs of their parents in emerging adulthood (e.g., Gunnoe & Moore, 2002). However, it might be important to explore whether young people purposefully abandon their parents' religious affiliation, possibly to spite their parents, as emerging adults, if their parents have been or are harsh, punitive, and controlling.

Similarly, it may be that the controlling nature of some parents causes their children to limit communication with parents in general and communication about religious topics specifically. Conversely, if parents are more open and supportive in their parenting, and a positive relationship exists, it may be that young people are more likely to engage their parents (particularly mothers; Gunnoe & Moore, 2002) in religious discussions directly, and to be open to continued parental religious socialization via technology (e.g., use Skype, e-mail, or texts to communicate religious messages). In other words, parenting appears to affect child behaviors directly but also may affect whether young people engage parents in discussions about religion and disclose information regarding their religious explorations and behaviors (e.g., attending worship services). Unfortunately, work in this area is limited at best.

### Child Characteristics and Contextual Factors

Scholars also need to understand the bidirectionality of the parent–child relationship as they examine the role of parents in emerging adults' spiritual and religious development. Specifically, there are numerous child characteristics that will either enhance or diminish the potential effects of parental socialization attempts. For example, it has been shown that children (children ages 3–12 years) are the ones to initiate about half of all family conversations about religion (Boyatzis & Janicki, 2003). As noted previously, emerging adults' willingness or desire to initiate conversations with parents centering on religious topics might be a significant factor in how much influence parents are able to have during this time. The bidirectionality of the process also might be affected by the level or extent that emerging adults perceive, accurately or not, that their parents have the ability to answer their religious questions.

Gender also might play a role in the bidirectional nature of this link between parental influence and emerging adults' religiousness and spirituality. Significant evidence exists that emerging-adult men and women tend to differ in the strength of religious beliefs, engagement in religious practices, and the importance of religion in their lives (e.g., Barry & Nelson, 2005; Smith, Denton, Faris, & Regnerus, 2002). There is also evidence from work with adolescents that the effects of parental socialization differ for sons and daughters (e.g., Flor & Knapp, 2001), perhaps as a function of the religious or spiritual values themselves. As a result, scholars need to examine the role that gender plays in the direct and indirect effects that parents might have on religious and spiritual development, as well as the complex intersection of gender and culture (see Chapters 10 and 13).

Individual differences in emerging adults' characteristics also might include genetics (e.g., Koenig et al., 2008), personality traits (e.g., shy individuals may have a smaller peer network and therefore might rely on the parent–child relationship to a greater extent than their peers), age (younger emerging adults may be more eager to distance themselves from parents, whereas the parent–child relationship might have matured to one more of equals to a point where older emerging adults might again seek input and advice from parents), and whether the child is working and/or going to school (i.e., the extent to which children might still be financially dependent on parents might influence the extent to which they might concede to parents the right to still play a role in their religious and spiritual lives). Individual life events also may affect the emerging adults' openness to parental input on religion, including death of friends or relatives, divorce, illness, or accidents. These are just a few examples of the type of characteristics that future research needs to explore in order to understand better the complex, bidirectional nature of the parent–child relationship as it relates to the domain of religion and spirituality.

Culture provides an important context for the socialization process. Culture not only shapes how parents parent, but how in turn parenting affects the development of children through direct and indirect opportunities to socialize emerging-adult children in religiousness and spirituality. Culture can include specific religious subcultures (e.g., specific faith traditions, religious denominations and their affiliated values, beliefs, and practices of such communities in which the parent–child relationship resides). Indeed, there may be certain religious groups or communities that provide specific roles to parents for this time period and/or information on how to interact with their emerging-adult children. For instance, even within the very hierarchical Catholic Church, families who attend a mass that is designed to involve young people in the liturgy have a different religious and spiritual experience than do those who attend mass at an alternate time.

Similarly, certain religions and religious communities may provide structure and expectations for emerging adults that make religion and spirituality a more prominent part of their lives. For example, certain religions/religious cultures place a greater emphasis on marrying young (e.g., evangelical Christian, Xu, Hudspeth, & Bartowski, 2005), engaging in missionary service (e.g., Mormons), receiving specific religious training (e.g., Orthodox Jewish men attending rabbinical school), being involved in humanitarian service, or establishing expectations for dress and behavior (e.g., wearing hijab). In communities where these types of expectations exist, parents might play a greater role in helping to establish and maintain behavioral expectations that inform the context and lives of their emerging adults' religious and spiritual development.

The role of parents may vary not only from one religious subculture to another but from one country to another and across ethnic subcultures as well. Ethnic differences within the United States have been found in religiousness and spirituality among emerging adults (e.g., Boyd-Franklin, 2003; Sanchez & Carter, 2005) but little work has been done to examine ethnic differences in parenting that might help to account for these differences. Furthermore, as a result of the wide variability in religious and spiritual beliefs of people worldwide (Inglehart, Basañez, Díez-Medrano, Halman, & Luijkx, 2004), it is essential to explore how parents' socialization of their emerging adults' religiousness and spirituality is likely to vary both in degree and process across cultures (e.g., from mostly nonreligious or spiritual to state-sanctioned or majority religions including the minority groups, e.g., China vs. Egypt). Again, because the preponderance of research is in the United States, and to a lesser extent in Canada, these are just a few examples used to highlight the need to study contextual factors in examining the role of parents in the religious and spiritual lives of emerging adults.

A final contextual factor that has received little if any attention is the role that family structure and parental figures, other than parents, might play. There is great variability in family structures in today's society and little work has examined how various family structures and parental figures might impact religious socialization in emerging adulthood. For example, work is needed to examine the role that grandparents, step-parents, or godparents might play in the religious and spiritual lives of emerging adults. Indeed, a growing number of grandparents, especially among African American and low-income households, are raising youth today (Fuller-Thomson, Minkler, & Driver, 1997). Likewise, work is needed to examine potential differences in the socialization processes in homes headed by single parents, a mother and a father, or two parents of the same gender. And, finally, all of these issues may become even more complex if the parents or parent figures in a family have differing religious affiliations/beliefs. Such situations are deserving of scholarly attention as well.

## ▲ Conclusion

The current state of the literature regarding the parental role in the religious and spiritual development of emerging adults is itself only beginning to emerge. There is growing evidence that early religious socialization, both direct and indirect, is related to the religious and spiritual lives of emerging adults. We know much less about the direct and indirect roles that parents play *in* emerging adulthood because the work is relatively scant and the existing work seldom controls for either religious socialization at earlier ages or broader parental socialization (e.g., parenting, parent–child relationship). In order to understand the potential role of parents, it is important to understand the unique features of emerging adulthood (e.g., desire for independent decision making, exploration of personal beliefs and identity) and the changing nature of the parent–child relationship (e.g., need for greater autonomy granting, greater frequency of emerging-adult children living outside the home). In doing so, we can see that there is reason to believe that the ways in which parents might still be involved in the religious and spiritual lives of their children change, and become more complex and tied to the emotional climate and quality of the parent–child relationship fostered by parenting styles and practices. Therefore, there is a need for researchers to examine this important topic in emerging adulthood, but in doing so we must utilize a developmental and contextual approach. Developmental designs (e.g., longitudinal, sequential) are needed so the effects of socialization attempts in emerging adulthood can be parceled out from the effects of earlier socialization. We need to examine new ways, consistent with the characteristics of the time period, that parents might be socializing their emerging-adult children.

Just as "emerging adulthood" is an umbrella term for a period of life that captures a variety of paths to adulthood, the study of parenting and emerging adults' religiousness needs to capture the vast variance that exists in child characteristics, parent characteristics, contexts, and socialization strategies and processes that might account for the variance in the role that parents play in the religious and spiritual lives of their emerging-adult children.

## ▲ References

Aquilino, W. S. (2006). Family relationships and support systems in emerging adulthood. In J. J. Arnett & J. L. Tanner (Eds.), *Emerging adults in America: Coming of age in the 21st century* (pp. 193–217). Washington, DC: American Psychological Association. doi: 10.1037/11381-008

Arnett, J. J. (2004). *Emerging adulthood: The winding road from the late teens through the twenties.* New York, NY: Oxford University Press.

Bao, W., Whitbeck, L. B., Hoyt, D. R., & Conger, R. D. (1999). Perceived parental acceptance as a moderator of religious transmission among adolescents and boys. *Journal of Marriage and the Family, 61*, 362–374.

Barry, C. M., & Nelson, L. J. (2005). The role of religion in the transition to adulthood for young emerging adults. *Journal of Youth and Adolescence, 34*, 245– 255. doi: 10.1007/s10964-005-4308-1

Barry, C. M., Padilla-Walker, L. M., Madsen, S. D., & Nelson, L. J. (2008). Impact of maternal relationship quality on emerging adults' prosocial tendencies: Indirect effects via regulation of prosocial values. *Journal of Youth & Adolescence, 37*, 581–591. doi: 10.1007/s10964-007-9238-7

Barry, C. M., Padilla-Walker, L. M., & Nelson, L. J. (2012). The role of mothers and media on emerging adults' religious faith and practices by way of internalization of prosocial values. *Journal of Adult Development, 19*, 66–78. doi: 10.1007/s10804-011-9135-x

Boyatzis, C. J., & Janicki, D. (2003). Parent-child communication about religion: Survey and diary data on unilateral transmission and bi-directional reciprocity styles. *Review of Religious Research, 44*, 252–270.

Boyd-Franklin, N. (2003). *Black families in therapy: Understanding the African-American experience* (2nd ed.). New York, NY: Guilford Press.

Cannister, M. W. (1999). Mentoring and the spiritual well-being of late adolescents. *Adolescence, 34*, 769–779.

Dollahite, D. C., & Marks, L. D. (2009). A conceptual model of family and religious processes in highly religious families. *Review of Religious Research, 50*, 373–391.

Dollahite, D. C., & Thatcher, J. Y. (2008). Talking about religion: How religious youth and parents discuss their faith. *Journal of Adolescent Research, 23*, 611– 641. doi: 10.1177/0743558408322141

Erikson, E. (1968). *Identity: Youth and crisis.* New York, NY: Norton.

Flor, D. L., & Knapp, N. F. (2001). Transmission and transaction: Predicting adolescents' internalization of parental religious values. *Journal of Family Psychology, 15*, 627–645. doi: 10.1037/0893-3200.15.4.627

Fuller-Thomson, E., Minkler, M., & Driver, D. (1997). A profile of grandparents raising grandchildren in the United States. *The Gerontologist, 37*, 406–411.

Gunnoe, M. L., & Moore, K.A. (2002). Predictors of religiousness among youth aged 17-22: A longitudinal study of the National Survey of Children. *Journal for the Scientific Study of Religion, 41*, 613–622. doi: 10.1111/1468-5906.00141

Hoge, D., Johnson, B., & Luidens, D. A. (1993). Determinants of church involvement of young adults who grew up in Presbyterian churches. *Journal of the Scientific Study of Religion, 32*, 242–255. doi: 10.1177/0272431699019002004

Holahan, C. J., Valentiner, D. P., & Moos, R. H. (1994). Parental support and psychological adjustment during the transition to young adulthood in a college sample. *Journal of Family Psychology, 8*, 215–223. doi: 10.1037/0893-3200.8.2.215

Inglehart, R., Basañez, M., Díez-Medrano, J., Halman, L., & Luijkx, R. (2004). *Human beliefs and values: A cross-cultural sourcebook based upon the 1999–2002 Values Surveys*. Mexico City, MX: Siglo Veintiuno Editores.

Koenig, L. B., McGue, M., & Iacono, W. G. (2008). Stability and change in religiousness during emerging adulthood. *Developmental Psychology, 44*, 532–543. doi: 10.1037/0012-1649.44.2.532

Lee, J. J. (2002). Religion and college attendance: Change among students. *The Review of Higher Education, 25*, 369–384. doi: *10.1353/rhe.2002.0020*

Lefkowitz, E. S. (2005). "Things have gotten better": Developmental changes among emerging adults after the transition to university. *Journal of Adolescent Research, 20*, 40–63. doi:10.1177/0743558404271236

Loser, R. W., Hill, E. J., Klein, S. R., & Dollahite, D. C. (2009). Perceived benefits of religious rituals in the Latter-day Saint home. *Review of Religious Research, 50*, 345–362.

McKinney, C., & Renk, K. (2008). Multivariate models of parent-late adolescent gender dyads: The importance of parenting processes in predicting adjustment. *Child Psychiatry & Human Development, 39*, 147–170. doi: 10.1007/s10578-007-0078-1

Milevsky, I. M., Szuchman, L., & Milevsky, A. (2008). Transmission of religious beliefs in college students. *Mental Health, Religion and Culture, 11*, 423–434. doi: 10.1080/13674670701507541

Montgomery-Goodnough, A., & Gallagher, S. J. (2007). Review of research on spiritual and religious formation in higher education. In S. M. Nielsen & M. S. Plakhotnik (Eds.), *Proceedings of the sixth annual College of Education Research Conference: Urban and international education section* (pp. 60–65). Miami, FL: Florida International University. http://coeweb.fiu.edu/research_conference/

Myers, S. M. (2006). Religious homogamy and marital quality: Historical and generational patterns, 1980-1997. *Journal of Marriage and Family, 68*, 292–304. doi: 10.1111/j.1741-3737.2006.00253.x

Nelson, L. J., & Barry, C. M. (2005). Distinguishing features of emerging adulthood: The role of self-classification as an adult. *Journal of Adolescent Research, 20*, 242–262. doi:10.1177/0743558404273074

Nelson, L. J., & Padilla-Walker, L. M. (2013). Flourishing and floundering in emerging-adult college students. *Emerging Adulthood, 1*, 67–78.

Nelson, L. J., Padilla-Walker, L. M., Christensen, K. J., Evans, C. A., & Carroll, J. S. (2011) Parenting in emerging adulthood: An examination of parenting clusters and correlates. *Journal of Youth and Adolescence, 40*, 730–743. doi: 10.1007/s10964-010-9584-8

Oman, D., & Thoresen, C. E. (2003). Spiritual modeling: A key to spiritual and religious growth. *International Journal for the Psychology of Religion, 13*, 149– 166. doi: 10.1207/S15327582IJPR1303_01

Padilla-Walker, L. M., Nelson, L. J., Madsen, S., & Barry, C. M. (2008). The role of perceived parental knowledge on emerging adults' risk behaviors. *Journal of Youth and Adolescence, 37*, 847–859.

Petts, R. J. (2009). Family and religious characteristics' influence on delinquency trajectories from adolescence to young adulthood. *American Sociological Review, 74*, 465–483. doi: 10.1177/000312240907400307

Sanchez, D., & Carter, R. T. (2005). Exploring the relationship between racial identity and religious orientation among African American college students. *Journal of College Student Development, 46*, 280–295. doi: 10.1353/csd.2005.0031

Schwartz, K. D. (2006). Transformations in parent and friend faith support predicting adolescents' religious faith. *The International Journal for the Psychology of Religion, 16*, 311–326. doi: 10.1207/s15327582ijpr1604_5

Silberman, I. (2003). Spiritual role modeling: The teaching of meaning systems. *International Journal for the Psychology of Religion, 13*, 175–195. doi: 10.1207/S15327582IJPR1303_03

Smith, C. (with Denton, M. L.). (2005). *Soul searching: The religious and spiritual lives of American teenagers.* New York, NY: Oxford University Press.

Smith, C., Denton, M.L., Faris, F., & Regnerus, M. (2002). Mapping American adolescent religious participation. *Journal for the Scientific Study of Religion, 41*, 397–612. doi: 10.1111/1468-5906.00148

Smith, C. (with Snell, P.). (2009). *Souls in transition: The religious and spiritual lives of emerging adults.* New York, NY: Oxford University Press.

Turner, E. A., Chandler, M., Heffer, R. W. (2009). The influence of parenting styles, achievement motivation, and self-efficacy on academic performance in college students. *Journal of College Student Development, 50*, 337–346.

Van Wek, F., Ter Bogt, T., & Raaijmakers, Q. (2002). Changes in the parental bond and the well-being of adolescents and young adults. *Adolescence, 37*, 317–333.

Xu, X., Hudspeth, C. D., & Bartowski, J. P. (2005). The timing of first marriage: Are there religious variations? *Journal of Family Issues, 26*, 584–618. doi: 10.1177/0192513X04272398

# 5 ▲

# The Role of Peer Relationships in Emerging Adults' Religiousness and Spirituality

CAROLYN MCNAMARA BARRY AND
JENNIFER L. CHRISTOFFERSON

> *Sharon, age 22, moved to a new city to take a job, and*
> *shared an apartment with an acquaintance, Elena, a*
> *devout Roman Catholic (e.g., she attended mass and*
> *participated in other young adult Church activities*
> *weekly). Elena talked about her beliefs openly, yet in a*
> *nonthreatening way. Although Sharon was raised Roman*
> *Catholic, she became distanced from her faith during*
> *college. Elena regularly invited Sharon to Theology on Tap*
> *(i.e., happy hour at a local bar for young adult Catholics*
> *including a short sermon typically by an energizing*
> *priest), and eventually Sharon decided to attend since she*
> *was eager to meet other young people. The two roommates*
> *formed a strong friendship, had regular and open dialogue*
> *about their religious beliefs, and over time Sharon*
> *recommitted to and deepened her faith.*

As illustrated in this vignette, peers can have an important role in religious and spiritual socialization since these relationships become even more prominent and numerous for emerging adults than for adolescents (Hartup & Stevens, 1999). Given their high levels of residential and job instability relative to other age groups (Tanner & Arnett, 2011), emerging adults' peer relationships tend to be fluid. Nevertheless, their close relationships tend to be of higher quality than what they previously experienced (Barry & Madsen, 2010). As they derive important social and personal benefits (e.g., instrumental aid) not just from parents, but from peers (Carbery & Buhrmester, 1998), active participation in social media may increase interaction with those who have differing values and beliefs (Watkins, 2010), and become immersed in new contexts (e.g., work). Thus, peer relationships at both the dyadic or group level can afford opportunities for co-construction of meaning-making, which in turn can promote identity solidification (Schwartz, 2001). However, cognitive dissonance may result when such beliefs and practices differ substantially among peers, which in turn, may promote deeper exploration and commitment to their beliefs and practices or an adoption of differing beliefs and practices. Alternatively, such dissonance might result in rejection of opposing viewpoints. Moreover, peer interactions can shape the formation of emerging adults' religiousness and spirituality (Zhang, Du, & Zhen, 2012). In this chapter, therefore, we focus on the role of emerging adults' peer relationships in religious and spiritual socialization. First, we provide an overview of types of peer relationships and the peer socialization process. Then, we review scholarship on the relation between religiousness and spirituality for each of the four types of peer relationships: siblings, friends, romantic partners, and other peer relationships. Finally, we discuss limitations, future research directions, and implications.

## ▲ Peer Relationships and Socialization Processes

There are four types of peer relationships. Given the shared family experiences, *sibling relationships* are the primary peer socialization agent, even though they are not chosen, and may involve persons whose ages range widely (Scharf, Shulman, & Avigad-Spitz, 2005). In contrast, individuals select their *friends*, often who are like them on a wide variety of characteristics (Hartup & Stevens, 1999). *Friendships* can vary in quality like sibling relationships but also may be unreciprocated (i.e., only one person views the other as a friend; Carbery & Buhrmester, 1998). Typically, *romantic relationships* in Western countries are a matter of choice; however, opposites tend not to attract as homophily is the norm (Luo, 2009). Lastly, *peers other than close relationships* can vary from one-time encounters (e.g., chance meeting at a party) to more ongoing interactions (e.g., classmate or coworker), and those with more sustained interactions are likely to be more influential (Brown, Bakken, Ameringer, & Mahon, 2008) than are those with less frequent interactions.

Regardless of how these four relationships are formed, they each have the potential to influence emerging adults' religiousness and spirituality. However, parents serve as children's primary religious and spiritual socializing agents (Erikson, 1963; see Chapter 4), with peer relationships situated amid other contexts as secondary agents in religious and spiritual socialization, particularly from adolescence onward. While children choose their nonfamilial peers, parents have the potential still to influence their children directly and indirectly (by channeling their children into particular peer contexts; Himmelfarb, 1980).

Beyond this multicontextual approach to the study of peer socialization, there are other theoretical frameworks and constructs that have focused on the peer context, such as social learning theory and the socializers' resultant operant conditioning (Silberman, 2003). Further, Brown et al.'s (2008) conceptual model for peer influence processes specifies that a given event among peers has the potential to activate peer influence depending upon the timing, mode, intensity, and consistency. Such influence yields a response (i.e., accede/accept, ignore/reject, or counter) followed by an outcome. Modifying factors further explain the process by which activation of peer influence results in a response, and they range from individual (i.e., openness to influence, salience of influencers) to contextual (i.e., relationship dynamics, ability/opportunity to perform). As applied to religiousness and spirituality, the opening vignette illustrates how numerous factors can account for religious and spiritual socialization on the part of the target (previous experience with Roman Catholic faith), the peer (friendly, but not pushy about faith), and the environmental conditions of the target (new to a community, warm and close friendship forming with roommate, high motivation to make friends). Indeed, peer influence is a complicated process, which we now review as it pertains to sibling, friend, romantic, and other peer relationships.

## ▲ Siblings

As the most enduring (Scharf et al., 2005) of all familial relationships, sibling relationships play a very important role in emerging adults' development. Given their shared developmental and affective history, sibling relationships have been characterized with warmth and involvement yet also with conflict and power struggles (Scharf et al., 2005). Scholars who investigate sibling relationships primarily have focused on adolescents, and to a lesser extent those in late adulthood (Aquilino, 2006). With age, sibling relationships undergo developmental shifts, becoming more equal in power and status, yet more intimate and emotionally attached, with less conflict. As emerging adults in the United States often become geographically distant from their siblings (Arnett, 2004), these relationships can become more voluntary and greater sources of social, scholastic, and familial support (Aquilino, 2006). With emerging adults' increased sense of maturity, increases in emotional exchanges between siblings (e.g., seeking advice) also are likely to occur (Scharf et al., 2005).

Family has been noted to be important in the formation and choice of one's religious and spiritual values and ideals (Snarey & Dollahite, 2001), but scholarly attention has focused on parents' influence (see Chapter 4). While parental religious affiliation and faith serve as "cognitive anchors" for adolescents' evolving beliefs (Ozorak, 1989), siblings also can be seen as spiritual role models for religious practices (Silberman, 2003). Yet emerging adults may feel that they can relate more to siblings than to parents and may turn to siblings for guidance and support. Not surprisingly then, emerging adults who reported high levels of religious importance and practices tended to report having very close family relationships, including siblings (Ellison, Burdette, & Glenn, 2011). Further, Wilson and Sandomirsky (1991) noted that family relationships are important determinants of religious affiliation. Since collectivistic groups both within and outside the United States emphasize family cohesiveness (Konstam, 2007), extended family members, including grandparents, aunts, uncles, and cousins, are likely to be prominent in such emerging adults' religious and spiritual socialization as well. Particularly when including extended family, more than one religious affiliation (e.g., Lutheran, Unitarian Universalist, Jehovah's Witness, and nones) may be present due to interfaith marriages or life experiences that resulted in conversions away from the faith of origin (e.g., Roman Catholic). Thus, this limited research documents the importance of this relationship to emerging adults and the potential of the relationship to shape emerging adults' developing religiousness and spirituality.

## ▲ Friendships

Emerging adults' friendships provide unique opportunities to tackle developmental tasks (Barry, Madsen, Nelson, Carroll, & Badger, 2009), and emerging adults who are socially skilled with their friends also tend to display such skills with peers from work and romantic partners (Roisman, Masten, Coatsworth, & Tellegen, 2004). Further, the number of friends remains stable across the emerging-adult years, and the characteristics of these relationships, including warmth, intimacy, and loyalty, are highly valuable to them (Samter, 2003) yet vary by religious affiliation and culture (Smith, 2009). For instance, friendship quality is associated positively with happiness by way of need satisfaction (Demir & Özdemir, 2010). Friendships do, however, differ by gender; men's friendships are focused on companionship, whereas women's friendships are more focused on emotional intimacy (Monsour, 2002).

The centrality of friendships relative to other close relationships depends upon one's roles (Carbery & Buhrmester, 1998), with friendships taking precedence over parents until a romantic partner becomes prominent. Although opposite-sex friendships are more common for emerging adults than for adolescents and provide unique benefits (e.g., emotional intimacy is greater for men with their female friends; Monsour, 2002), some more conservative religions may limit opportunities for opposite-sex friendship formation (Xu, Hudsperth, & Bartowski, 2005). Regardless of affiliation, same-sex friendships remain the most preferred (Demir & Özdemir, 2010). Moreover, while simultaneously seeking friendships that provide opportunities for self-exploration (Hartup & Stevens, 1999), close friends in turn are likely to be salient socialization agents for the formation of their religious and spiritual worldviews.

## Concordance of Religiousness and Spirituality Among Friends

Prior to addressing friend influence, we first discuss the characteristics of emerging adults' friends concerning their religiousness and spirituality. In the National Survey of Youth and Religion (NSYR; Smith, 2009), 53% of American 18- to 23-year-olds reported their close friends to be religious, which varies by ethnicity and religious affiliation (e.g., Black Protestants, 67%; Jews, 33%). Further, 63% of emerging adults perceived their close friends to hold similar religious beliefs to their own. Despite this homophily of close friends' religious beliefs, only 17% of young emerging adults overall had close friends who were involved in the same religious group, with a few exceptions (e.g., Mormons, 48%). In sum, emerging adults tend to have friends who share their religious beliefs, even though most do not participate in religious groups together.

## Role of Friends in Emerging Adults' Religiousness and Spirituality

Scholars have conducted limited research on how friends serve as religious and spiritual socialization agents. Friends with similar religious practices have been shown to affirm one's religious beliefs (Roberts, Koch, & Johnson, 2001). Also, friends' self-reported religious attendance explained middle adolescents' own religious attendance a year later beyond what was explained by parents as well as school peers (Regnerus, Smith, & Smith, 2004). Panel data from the National Youth Survey (1977–1987; Desmond, Morgan, & Kikuchi, 2010) also revealed that adolescents who had delinquent friends were less likely to engage in public forms of religious behaviors (e.g., religious service attendance) as emerging adults. Further, they found that adolescents of diverse religious backgrounds who had the highest friendship quality levels reported greater levels of religious attendance and importance as emerging adults regardless of affiliation but had the greatest rates of decline in religiousness relative to those with lower levels of friendship quality. These scholars reason that having such strong friendship ties may result in greater conformity to friends' behaviors (i.e., decrease in religiousness). In sum, this literature documents the relation between friends' and emerging adults' religiousness beyond the effect of homophily. This research, however, has yet to consider the extent of same versus interfaith friendship dyads, which likely contributes to friend influence; thus, in the future, scholars should assess more friend characteristics with respect to religiousness and spirituality.

## Conversations

Scholars have investigated the role of dialogue in friends' religious and spiritual socialization. Although the religious communities for emerging adults and their friends often do not overlap, 49% of Smith's (2009) NSYR overall sample of emerging adults (and 68% of Mormons and 58% Black Protestants) reported conversing with their close friends concerning religious beliefs and experiences. Such affiliation differences are likely due to the centrality of their faith in their overall identity. Therefore, this finding supports the age-old adage that religion can be divisive like politics, in that those emerging adults who are less certain about their beliefs are less inclined to "go there" (i.e., discuss religious beliefs) even with close friends (Smith, 2009). However, when online, they are more willing, in that, most emerging adults indicate religion in their profile, and that conversation among existing friends increases on social networking sites (Pempek, Yermolayeva, & Calvert, 2009). Thus, in the future scholars should explore the extent to which dialogue through social networking shapes emerging adults' religiousness.

In contrast to religious socialization patterns, the role of spiritual dialogue among friends has been shown to promote emerging adults' spiritual development. Indeed, Kelley, Athan, and Miller (2007) documented that dialogue concerning spirituality promotes young adults' spiritual development. Relatedly, African-American men's spirituality was related positively to their affective sharing with and social support from same-sex friends (Mattis et al., 2001). Further, university students seek out spiritual discourse, especially with friends (Astin & Astin, 2004), and friends provide the spiritual support that, in turn, promotes their spiritual individuation (Desrosiers, Kelley, & Miller, 2011). Collectively, these findings underscore the importance that friendship plays in sharing and potentially reaffirming one's religious and spiritual beliefs but also in discussing such beliefs with close friends, some of whom may share value systems. Because friendships foster empathy and forgiveness, which have been related to spiritual development (McCullough, Thoresen, & Pargament, 2000), dialogue is an important mechanism to explain the process of both religious and spiritual socialization among friends.

### Religious Friend Influence on Behavior

Beyond the opportunity for conversations that promote meaning-making, friends have the potential to shape emerging adults' religiousness and spirituality by way of shaping their behavior. For instance, Smith (2009) found that the most religious emerging adults volunteered for community service at higher rates than did their less religious peers due in part to their strong friendship networks. Further, he found that religious emerging adults were least likely to have their five closest friends engage in drug use or binge drinking compared to religiously disengaged emerging adults, half of whom had such friends.

### Summary

Many emerging-adult friends share similar levels of religiousness and spirituality, and engage in conversations that promote meaning-making, which in turn may promote their religiousness and spirituality. Since these young people vary widely in the amount of such discourse, scholars should investigate the conditions under which such dialogue is likely to occur. Moreover, friends' religiousness has been shown to reduce risk behavior and promote positive behaviors such as community service. In the future scholars should separate the effect of friend selection (i.e., choosing friends from church) from influence on emerging adults' religiousness and spirituality but also on their influence on behaviors as well.

## ▲ Romantic Relationships

Romantic relationships are central to emerging adults' lives as they identify qualities of a romantic partner and, in turn, select a mate (typically by the late twenties for those in United States; Kan & Cares, 2006). These relationships also are longer, more serious (Kan & Cares, 2006), intimate, and deeper than are those in adolescence (Beyers & Seiffge-Krenke, 2010). Compared to family and friend relationships, romantic relationships are comprised of heightened levels of intimacy, communication, emotionality, exclusivity, and commitment (Fisher, 2006), and they serve as an important reference and source of support and guidance (Reiter & Gee, 2008). In fact, emerging adults spend considerably more time with romantic partners than friends and family (especially if the relationship is stable and involves high levels of commitment; Carbery & Buhrmester, 1998), which results in their potential to supersede familial and friend influence (Collins & van Dulmen, 2006). Lastly, although not all romantic partners share the same religious views, Luo (2009) has noted that men who are dating and share the same religion with their partner report higher levels of relationship satisfaction and often show strong similarity in values and attitudes. Given the characteristics of romantic relationships for emerging adults, there is an increased potential for religious and spiritual socialization by romantic partners.

Beyond the characteristics of romantic partners, mechanisms for influence also are important in understanding the role of romantic partners in religious and spiritual socialization. For instance, emerging adults develop skills and values from their surrounding models, including romantic partners (Collins & van Dulmen, 2006). Emerging adults' identity can be in part influenced and formed based on romantic partners' actions, values, and beliefs, including those concerning religiousness and spirituality (Luo, 2009). Because romantic relationships allow for open communication about important factors such as values and beliefs, while providing advice and offering comfort, they can support the exploration of emerging adults' religious and spiritual beliefs, thereby promoting the formation of their moral and religious values (Reiter & Gee, 2008). Although there is scant research on this type of peer relationship, it arguably may be the most important peer relationship for emerging adults' religious and spiritual socialization, and therefore worthy of additional scholarly attention. Indeed, as emerging adults' romantic partners often can become marital partners, it is important for scholars to investigate how such partners navigate their own religious and spiritual backgrounds in forming a mature and potentially lifelong relationship. For example, Reiter and Gee (2008) found that open communication about religious beliefs and practices within romantic relationships allows for greater relationship satisfaction and maintenance. Scholars also should investigate how to maintain these relationships as interfaith marriages have been found to experience higher divorce rates, as compared to their intrafaith counterparts (Reiter & Gee, 2008). In particular, attention should be paid to those couples with differing beliefs systems as well as those from religions with strict doctrine concerning premarital sex (e.g., Evangelical Christian) as the couple negotiates sexual intimacy issues.

### Friends With Benefits

While some emerging adults are searching for long-term, high-quality, stable romantic relationships, others are playing the field by just "hooking up" or establishing friendships with benefits (FWB). According to Burdette, Ellison, Hill, and Glenn (2009), for some FWB relationships, mostly physical encounters between two people without the romantic connection involved, have come to replace traditional dating. Moreover, young adults with FWBs prior to having a romantic relationship reported lower levels of relationship satisfaction than did those who did not have an FWB relationship; yet after accounting for salient predictors of having an FWB, no differences in relationship length and functioning existed between FWB and romantic relationships (Owen & Fincham, 2012). Moreover, they found that 25% of men and 40% of women in FWB relationships hoped that these relationships would become romantically exclusive.

Due to the variability that exists in FWBs ranging from a lack of emotional intimacy to a more satisfying and functional relationship that may become a romantic relationship, it is unclear whether they would have the same impact on emerging adults' religiousness and spirituality. Given the lack of clear definition of this relationship type, emerging adults with FWBs, particularly those whose religious affiliation prohibits premarital sex, may report feelings of cognitive dissonance (Freitas, 2008). Not surprisingly then, Burdette, Ellison, Hill, and Glenn (2009) found that college students with religious involvement are more likely to attend religious services and in turn less likely to "hook up" and be involved in FWB relationships compared to those with less immersion in a religious context. Women who are conservative Protestants were found to be the less likely to "hook up" and be involved in FWB relationships compared to Catholic women, who were more likely. Conversely, they found that religious affiliation in and of itself has few protective factors in terms of "hooking up;" it depends more on involvement and attendance in religious services. One last interesting finding is that college students attending religiously affiliated schools have higher levels of "hooking up" than do those at non–religiously affiliated schools. Overall, religious emerging adults' involvement in FWB relationships may depend more on regular church attendance than religious affiliation. Women who are active participants in their religious services are more protected from "hooking up" and FWB relationships than are those who do not regularly attend religious services. Therefore, religiousness is a protective factor in individuals' participation in FWB relationships; spirituality needs to be investigated in future work to determine whether it also serves a protective function.

## ▲ Other Peer Relationships

Emerging adults are immersed in contexts (e.g., faculty and peers at a public institution vs. orthodox Christian university, Catholic Charities aid worker vs. Costco store clerk) that may embody unique values and beliefs. Such contexts afford emerging adults' encounters and discussions with peers, some of whom may hold discrepant worldviews from their own. These experiences, in turn, may influence emerging adults' evolving religiousness and spirituality.

Much of what is known about peers beyond that of close relationships is derived from structured contexts, such as religious congregations (see Chapter 8), organizations (e.g., military, GED tutoring program), clubs, campus ministry offices, and classes from which to meet peers (see Chapter 9). In so doing, they can form mentoring communities that promote the habits of the mind (i.e., dialogue, critical thought, connective-holistic awareness, and the cultivation of a contemplative mind), and in turn meaning-making (Parks, 2000). For instance, 58% of US college students report having spiritual discussions during class time (Astin & Astin, 2004).

However, Smith (2009) found a surprising paucity (15%) of NSYR young emerging adults who participate in religious groups (e.g., Bible study), which typically meet weekly and are affiliated with denominations. Yet for this minority, a third of them are involved in two or more such groups. Among the subsample of young emerging adults who have attended college, conservative Protestants and Mormons are most likely to have joined a religious group. Further, Erickson (1992) found that high levels of church program involvement were associated with high levels of religious worship behavior for 16 to 18 year olds. In other words, some emerging adults select themselves into these contexts, wherein they are likely to explore and perhaps strengthen their religious and spiritual beliefs to a greater extent, while others do not seek such formalized socialization mechanisms.

The ways in which the religious groups or religious communities (see Chapter 8) are run also have the potential to shape emerging adults' religiousness and spirituality. For instance, Quaker community-sponsored events for young adults are often planned and run by emerging adults and afford a welcoming environment that is associated with internalization of their religious values and beliefs (Best, 2007). In sum, religious groups run by and for peers are one context for further religious and spiritual socialization, which can be structured in ways that promote such socialization; however, most emerging adults in the United States do not choose to be part of this setting.

Peer relationships that are formed in religious contexts have been associated with reduced affiliation with peers who engage in risk behavior as well as less participation themselves in risk behaviors (Schreck, Burek, & Clark-Miller, 2007). These relationships also explain the relation between their religious involvement and adjustment outcomes of purpose and well-being (Suárez-Orozco, Singh, Abo-Zena, Du, & Roeser, 2012). Religious congregations form an additional benefit when they are multiracial in composition, namely through peer interaction with high levels of ethnic diversity, and they are associated with high rates of interracial friendships (especially for men; Tavares, 2011). In cases of more homogeneity, it is plausible that other benefits (e.g., high levels of emotional intimacy that promotes rich faith dialogue) as well as some detriments (e.g., less multicultural competence) may prevail.

In contrast, emerging adults with more commitment to their religious beliefs and participation in religious campus organizations become less likely over the 4 years of college to form cross-race friendships (Park, 2012). Thus, it depends upon the emerging adults, and particularly their own degree of religiousness and spirituality, as to how useful such peer groups may be in their religious and spiritual formation.

## ▲ Limitations and Future Directions

While the literature on the role of emerging adults' peer relationships as religious and spiritual socializers features many strengths, clear limitations exist. For instance, although peers' relationship quality has been related to personality factors (Festa, Barry, Sherman, & Grover, 2012) and shyness (Christofferson, 2012; Nelson et al., 2008), we know little about how individual characteristics can affect emerging adults' receptivity to peer religious and spiritual socialization. Most research has been conducted on European-American, Christian, university students and ignores the reality that religiousness differs by age, ethnicity, culture, religious affiliation, geographical region (Smith, 2009), and country (Inglehart, Basañex, Dåez-Medrano, Halman, & Luijkx, 2004), let alone that the university context affords unique opportunities for peer religious and spiritual socialization (Astin & Astin, 2004), to which those outside this context are not privy. Therefore, in the future, scholars should examine religious and spiritual socialization within different religious communities where more instances of group polarization could occur, given that the findings may be different compared to communities that are not as spiritual or religious. Lastly, understanding these peer relationships needs to be situated amid other socializing agents such as parents, media, religious communities, and universities (see Chapters 4, 6, 8, and 9); therefore, consideration of how these various contexts may intersect to shape emerging adults' religiousness and spirituality is needed.

## ▲ Conclusion

In conclusion, research on emerging adults' peer religious and spiritual socialization is in its infancy, but it does suggest that different peer groups can play an important role in emerging adults' religiousness and spirituality. While much of the research on mechanisms of influence has explored friendships or peers within university contexts, there is reason to believe that future research on siblings and romantic relationships will demonstrate their important role in emerging adults' religious and spiritual development. Practitioners at youth development agencies, universities, and parents and emerging adults themselves should carefully consider the company that emerging adults keep, given their potential to shape emerging adults' evolving worldviews on religiousness and spirituality.

## ▲ Acknowledgments

We wish to thank Bill Bukowski who provided helpful comments on an earlier draft of this chapter.

## ▲ References

Aquilino, W. (2006). Family relationships and support systems in emerging adulthood. In J. J. Arnett & J. L. Tanner (Eds.), *Emerging adults in America: Coming of age in the 21st century* (pp. 193–217). Washington, DC: American Psychological Association.

Arnett, J. J. (2004). *Emerging adulthood: The winding road from the late teens through the twenties.* New York, NY: Oxford University Press.

Astin, A. W., & Astin, H. (2004). *Spirituality development and the college experience* (Research Report). Los Angeles, CA: University of California, Higher Education Research Institute.

Barry, C. M., & Madsen, S. D. (2010). Friends and friendships. In T. Clydesdale (Ed.), *Who are emerging adults?* Washington, DC: Changing Spirituality of Emerging Adults Project. Retrieved from http://changingsea.org/barry.htm

Barry, C. M., Madsen, S. D., Nelson, L. J., Carroll, J. S., & Badger, S. (2009). Friendship and romantic relationship qualities in emerging adulthood: Differential association with progress on identity development and societal tasks. *Journal of Adult Development, 16*(4), 209–222. doi: 10.1007/s10804-009-9067-x

Best, S. (2007). Quaker events for young people: Informal education and faith transmission. *Quaker Studies, 11,* 259–281.

Beyers, W., & Seiffge-Krenke, I. (2010). Does identity precede intimacy? Testing Erikson's theory on romantic development in emerging adults of the 21st century. *Journal of Adolescent Research, 25,* 287–415. doi: 10.1177/0743558410361370

Brown, B. B., Bakken, J. P., Ameringer, S. W., & Mahon, S. D. (2008). A comprehensive conceptualization of the peer influence process in adolescence.

In M. J. Prinstein & K. A. Dodge (Eds.), *Understanding peer influence in children and adolescents* (pp. 17–44). New York, NY: Guilford Press.

Burdette, A., Ellison, C., Hill, T., & Glenn, N. (2009). "Hooking up" at college: Does religion make a difference? *Journal for the Scientific Study of Religion, 48*, 535–551.

Carbery, J., & Buhrmester, D. (1998). Friendship and need fulfillment during the phases of young adulthood. *Journal of Social and Personal Relationships, 15*, 393–409. doi: 10.1177/0265407598153005

Christofferson, J. L. (2012). *The role of identity as a moderator in the relation between social withdrawal subtypes and emerging adults' romantic relationship characteristics*. Unpublished master's thesis. Loyola University Maryland, Baltimore, MD.

Collins, W. A., & van Dulmen, M. (2006). Friendships and romance in emerging adulthood: Assessing distinctiveness in close relationships. In J. J. Arnett & J. L. Tanner (Eds.), *Emerging adults in America: Coming of age in the 21st century* (pp. 219–234). Washington, DC: American Psychological Association. doi:10.1037/11381-009

Demir, M., & Özdemir, M. (2010). Friendship, need satisfaction and happiness. *Journal of Happiness Studies, 11*, 243–259. doi: 10.1007/s10902-009-9138-5

Desrosiers, A., Kelley, B. S., & Miller, L. (2011). Parent and peer relationships and relational spirituality in adolescents and young adults. *Psychology of Religion and Spirituality, 3*, 39–54. doi: 10.1037/a0020037

Desmond, S. A., Morgan, K. H., & Kikuchi, G. (2010). Religious development: How (and why) does religiosity change from adolescence to young adulthood? *Sociological Perspectives, 53*, 247–270. doi: 10.1525/sop.2010.53.2.247

Ellison, C. G., Burdette, A. M., & Glenn, N. D. (2011). Praying for Mr. Right? Religion, family background, and marital expectations among college women. *Journal of Family Issues, 32*, 906–931. doi: 10.1177/0192513X10393143

Erickson, J. A. (1992). Adolescent religious development and commitment: A structural equation model of the role of family, peer group, and educational influences. *Journal for the Scientific Study of Religion, 31*, 131–152. doi: 10.2307/1387004

Erikson, E. H. (1963). *Childhood and society* (2nd ed.). New York, NY: Norton.

Festa, C. C., Barry, C. M., Sherman, M. F., & Grover, R. L. (2012). Quality of college students' same-sex friendships as a function of personality and interpersonal competence. *Psychological Reports, 110*, 283–296. doi: 10.2466/04.09.10.21.PR0.110.1.283-296

Fisher, H. (2006). Broken hearts: The nature and risks of romantic rejection. In A. C. Crouter & A. Booth (Eds.), *Romance and sex in adolescence and emerging adulthood: Risks and opportunities* (pp. 3–28). Mahwah, NJ: Lawrence Erlbaum.

Freitas, D. (2008). *Sex and the soul: Juggling sexuality, spirituality, romance, and religion on America's college campuses*. New York, NY: Oxford University Press.

Hartup, W. W., & Stevens, N. (1999). Friendships and adaptation across the life span. *Current Directions in Psychological Science, 8*, 76–79. doi: 10.1111/1467-8721.00018

Himmelfarb, H. S. (1980). The study of American Jewish identification: How it is defined, measured, obtained, sustained, and lost. *Journal for the Scientific Study of Religion, 19*, 48–60.

Inglehart, R., Basañez, M., Dåez-Medrano, J., Halman, L., & Luijkx, D. A. (2004). *Human beliefs and values: A cross-cultural sourcebook based upon the 1999-2002 values surveys*. Mexico City, MX: Siglo Veintiuno Editores.

Kan, M. L., & Cares, A. C. (2006). From "friends with benefits" to "going steady:" New directions in understanding romance and sex in adolescence and emerging adulthood. In A. C. Crouter & A. Booth (Eds.), *Romance and sex in adolescence and emerging adulthood: Risks and opportunities* (pp. 241–258). Mahwah, NJ: Lawrence Erlbaum.

Kelley, B. S., Athan, A. M., & Miller, K. F. (2007). Openness and spiritual development in adolescents. *Research in the Social Scientific Study of Religion, 18*, 3–33.

Konstam, V. (2007). *Emerging and young adulthood: Multiple perspectives, diverse narratives*. New York, NY: Springer.

Luo, S. (2009). Partner selection and relationship satisfaction in early dating couples: The role of couple similarity. *Personality and Individual Differences, 47*, 133–138. doi:10.1016/j.paid.2009.02.012

Mattis, J. S., Murray, Y. F., Hatcher, C. A., Hearn, K. D., Lawhon, G. D., Murphy, E. J., & Washington, T. A. (2001). Religiosity, spirituality, and the subjective quality of African American men's friendships: An exploratory study. *Journal of Adult Development, 8*, 221–230. doi: 10.1023/A:1011338511989

McCullough, M. E., Thoresen, C. E., & Pargament, K. I. (2000). *Forgiveness: Theory, research, and practice*. New York, NY: Guilford.

Monsour, M. (2002). *Women and men as friends: Relationships across the life span in the 21st century*. Mahwah, NJ: Lawrence Erlbaum.

Nelson, L. J., Padilla-Walker, L.M., Badger, S., Barry, C. M., Carroll, J., & Madsen, S. (2008). Associations between shyness and internalizing behaviors, externalizing behaviors, and relationships during emerging adulthood. *Journal of Youth and Adolescence, 37*, 605–615. doi: 10.1007/s10964-007-9203-5

Owen, J., & Fincham, F. (2012). Friends with benefits relationships as a start to exclusive romantic relationships. *Journal of Social and Personal Relationships, 29*, 982–996.

Ozorak, E. W. (1989). Social and cognitive influences on the development of religious beliefs and commitment in adolescence. *Journal for the Scientific Study of Religion, 28*, 448–463. doi: 10.2307/1386576

Park, J. (2012). When race and religion collide: The effect of religion on interracial friendship during college. *Journal of Diversity in Higher Education, 5*, 8–21. doi: 10.1037/a0026960

Parks, S. D. (2000). *Big questions, worthy dreams: Mentoring young adults in their search for meaning, purpose, and faith*. San Francisco, CA: Jossey-Bass.

Pempek, T. A., Yermolayeva, Y. A., & Calvert, S. L. (2009). College students' social networking experiences on Facebook. *Journal of Applied Developmental Psychology, 30*, 227–238. doi: 10.1016/j.appdev.2008.12.010

Regnerus, M. D., Smith, C., & Smith, B. (2004). Social context in the development of adolescent religiosity. *Applied Developmental Science, 8*, 27–38. doi: 10.1207/S1532480XADS0801_4

Reiter, M., & Gee, C. (2008). Open communication and partner support in intercultural and interfaith romantic relationships: A relational maintenance approach. *Journal of Social and Personal Relationships, 25,* 539– 559. doi: 10.1177/0265407508090872

Roberts, A. E., Koch, J. R., & Johnson, D. P. (2001). Religious reference groups and the persistence of normative behavior: An empirical test. *Sociological Spectrum, 21,* 81–98. doi: 10.1080/02732170150201829

Roisman, G. I., Masten, A. S., Coatsworth, J. D., & Tellegen, A. (2004). Salient and emerging developmental tasks in the transition to adulthood. *Child Development, 75,* 123–133. doi: 10.1111/j.1467-8624.2004.00658.x

Samter, W. (2003). Friendship interaction skills across the lifespan. In J. O. Greene & B. R. Burleson (Eds.), *Handbook of communication and social interaction skills* (pp. 637–684). Mahwah, NJ: Erlbaum.

Scharf, M., Shulman, S., & Avigad-Spitz, L. (2005). Sibling relationships in emerging adulthood and in adolescence. *Journal of Adolescent Research, 20,* 64–90. doi: 10.1177/0743558404271133.

Schreck, C. J., Burek, M. W., & Clark-Miller, J. (2007). He sends rain upon the wicked: A panel study of the influence of religiosity on violent victimization. *Journal of Interpersonal Violence, 22,* 872–893. doi: 10.1177/0886260507301233

Schwartz, S. J. (2001). The evolution of Eriksonian and neo-Eriksonian identity theory and research: A review and integration. *Identity: An International Journal of Theory and Research, 1,* 7–58. doi: 10.1207/S1532706XSCHWARTZ

Silberman, I. (2003). Spiritual role modeling: The teaching of meaning systems. The *International Journal for the Psychology of Religion, 13,* 175–195. doi: 10.1207/S15327582IJPR1303_03

Smith, C. (with Snell, P.). (2009). *Souls in transition: The religious and spiritual lives of emerging adults.* New York, NY: Oxford University Press.

Snarey, J., & Dollahite, D. (2001). Varieties of religion-family linkages. *Journal of Family Psychology, 15,* 646–651. doi: 10.1037//0893-3200.15.4.646

Suárez-Orozco, C., Singh, S., Abo-Zena, M. M., Du, D., & Roeser, R. W. (2012). The role of religion and worship communities in positive development in immigrant youth. In A. E. A. Warren, R. M. Lerner, & E. Phelps (Eds.), *Thriving and spirituality among youth: Research perspectives and future possibilities* (pp. 255–288). Hoboken, NJ: Wiley.

Tanner, J. L., & Arnett, J. J. (2011). Presenting "emerging adulthood": What makes it developmentally distinctive? In J. J. Arnett, M. Kloep, L. B. Hendry, & J. L. Tanner (Eds.), *Debating emerging adulthood: Stage or process?* (pp. 13–30). New York, NY: Oxford University Press.

Tavares, C. D. (2011). Why can't we be friends: The role of religious congregation-based social contact for close interracial adolescent friendships. *Review of Religious Research, 52,* 439–453.

Watkins, S. C. (2010). *The young and the digital: What the migration to social network sites, games, and anytime, anywhere media means for our future.* Boston, MA: Beacon Press.

Wilson, J., & Sandomirsky, S. (1991). Religious affiliation and the family. *Sociological Forum, 6,* 289–309.

Xu, X., Hudspeth, C. D., & Bartowski, J. P. (2005). The timing of first marriage: Are there religious variations? *Journal of Family Issues, 26,* 584–618. doi: 10.1177/0192513X04272398

Zhang, W., Du, D., & Zhen, S. (2012). Belief systems and positive youth development among Chinese and American youth. In A. E. A. Warren, R. M. Lerner, & E. Phelps (Eds.), *Thriving and spirituality among youth: Research perspectives and future possibilities* (pp. 309–331). Hoboken, NJ: Wiley.

# 6 ▲

# Faith in the Digital Age: Emerging Adults' Religious Mosaics and Media Practices

PIOTR S. BOBKOWSKI

Emerging adults' worlds are über-saturated with media, to borrow a qualifier recently made popular with this cohort. Young people use digital media to connect to information, to entertainment, and to connect with each other. They increasingly access media digitally via mobile devices such as smartphones, tablets, or laptop computers, with the Internet often serving as the conduit for all media (i.e., television, radio, magazines, Web sites; Zickuhr & Smith, 2012).

Emerging adults stand at the forefront of the mobile and digital media revolutions. Recent figures show that 94% of US emerging adults (18 to 29 years old) use the Internet, and two-thirds (66%) own a smartphone (Zickuhr & Smith, 2012). Older US adolescents (15 to 18 years old) are exposed to an average of more than 11 hours of media each day outside of school (Rideout, Foehr, & Roberts, 2010). To fit all these media into their days, adolescents often use more than one medium simultaneously. Media use peaks during mid-adolescence (11 to 14 years old) and then decreases slightly in late adolescence (Rideout et al., 2010). Emerging adults who take on demanding college and work obligations may further curtail their media use. For instance, a study that tracked college students' time online using text message surveys found students use the Internet approximately 1 hour a day (Moreno et al., 2012). Other emerging adults, however, may increase their media habits as they enjoy less structured schedules than they did during adolescence, or as they rely on media to maintain contacts with geographically distant family and friends.

Given the prominent role of media in the lives of emerging adults, this chapter focuses on the intersections between emerging adults' media experiences and their personal religious mosaics. The religious mosaics metaphor (Pearce & Denton, 2011) conveys the complex, dynamic, and sometimes contradictory nature of emerging adults' religiousness and spiritualities. According to Pearce and Denton (2011), individuals' religious mosaics are composed of variously colored, shaped, and sized tiles that represent religious and spiritual beliefs and ideas, conduct and practices, and the centrality of these elements within individuals' lives. Tiles may also represent religious disengagement, agnosticism, or lack of religious belief. The tiles may vary in intensity, overlap, and fragment or expand over time in correspondence with individuals' religious and spiritual development. In this chapter, the mosaics metaphor is used conceptually as an alternative to preconceived categories of emerging adults' religiousness and spirituality. Specific measures of religiousness (e.g., affiliation, attendance frequency, salience) are used when the design and results of particular studies are discussed.

The Media Practice Model (Brown, 2000, 2006; Shafer, Bobkowski, & Brown, 2012) provides a tool for identifying and organizing how emerging adults' religious mosaics affect media practices, and the ways in which these practices, in turn, shape religious mosaics. The Model reflects an active audience perspective, conceiving of individuals as having agency to regulate their media practices and how media affect them. When Mel Gibson's *The Passion of the Christ* debuted in theaters, news reports said that the movie evoked religious experiences and even inspired Christian conversions (e.g., Ward, 2004). Such reports called to mind a powerful media directly and uniformly affecting passive audiences. By contrast, the viewpoint espoused by the Model concedes that a media message may influence *some* members of an audience to take specific and immediate actions, but it holds that such powerful effects are unusual on a large scale. Adopting a sociocultural theory perspective (Vygotsky, 1978), the Model positions the media's influence within a broader developmental context of individuals' unique backgrounds and experiences. How individuals approach media such as *The Passion*, what they do with it, and how *The Passion*, in turn, affects them, depends on a host of cultural, social, and personal circumstances that they bring to the experience.

The Media Practice Model is structured around three "moments" that correspond to three sets of media practices: selection, engagement, and application (Shafer et al., 2012). A key principle of the Model is that individuals "choose media and interact with media based on who they are and who they want to be" (Brown, 2000, p. 35). Reflecting individuals' religious and spiritual "who they are and who they want to be," the religious mosaic may constitute the cause, effect, or moderator of media practice, depending on the phenomena and variables of interest. During media *selection*, for example, religious mosaics may play a causal role, dictating whether emerging adults tune in to the inspirational *Joel Osteen* or the sexually charged *The Bachelor Pad*. The Model itself does not impose a directional expectation on individual viewers' media choice, leaving open the possibility that they will view one show or the other, neither, or both, depending on the idiosyncratic nature of their religious mosaic. Once emerging adults are exposed to a media message, the religious mosaic may shape *engagement* with this message. The religious mosaic may cause or moderate the level of attention devoted to a *Bachelor Pad* contest or the amount of counterarguing with the Rev. Osteen's sermon, for example.

The selection and processing of media content influence media *application*, the extent to which media users subsume content into their identities. Emerging adults who watch *Joel Osteen*, who attend to the program, and do not engage in counterarguing, for instance, may appropriate tenets of Osteen's theology into their religious mosaics. Those who watch attentively but disagree with Osteen's message, meanwhile, may reinforce those elements of their mosaics that resist the type of religious influence that Osteen represents. Those who watch *The Bachelor Pad* without counterarguing may align their religious mosaics with the worldviews of that show's characters. Those who watch the show but actively argue against the characters' moral standards may reinforce their own principles. Those who watch both *Joel Osteen* and *The Bachelor Pad*, and who process these shows attentively and in agreement, may adjust their religious mosaics to accommodate both perspectives. In the age of social sharing of media, religious mosaics combined with exposure and processing of media also may determine the extent to which emerging adults identify with media messages in online social venues like Facebook or engage in the production of original content using YouTube, for example.

The remainder of this chapter discusses in greater depth each of the media practice moments vis-à-vis emerging adults' religious mosaics. The first moment, selection, concerns the determinants of media use. The following discussion focuses on the influence of religious mosaics to select religious media and nonreligious, potentially unhealthy media.

## ▲ Selecting Media

### *Religious Media*

Ample research documents the availability and variety of religious content in popular television programs (e.g., Winston, 2009), movies (e.g., Hendershot, 2004), music (e.g., Banjo & Williams, 2011), video games (e.g., Wagner, 2012), marketing (e.g., Einstein, 2008), and online venues such as Christian blogs (Cheong, Halavais, & Kwon, 2008). Considerably less work examines motivations for using or not using these media. Individuals whose religious mosaics include engagement in religious traditions are most likely to use religious media (e.g., McFarland, 1996). Indeed, a central component of the reinforcing spirals theory of media effects (Slater, 2007) is that individuals choose media that echo and reinforce their prior tendencies and behaviors.

Research has shown, thus, that those who search the Internet for religious information tend to call themselves religious and spiritual, and attend religious services with some regularity (Clark, Hoover, & Rainie, 2004). Conversely, it found that those who do not attend religious services, meanwhile, are least likely to search for religious information. In another study, Muslim-American emerging adults reported that they turn to Internet sites hosted both within the United States and abroad to learn about proper religious practices and conduct (Mishra & Semaan, 2010). Some young Muslims use YouTube videos to practice Arabic, while others search Muslim-oriented Web sites for teachings on the religious appropriateness of specific foods, clothing, music, and abortion (Mishra & Semaan, 2010). These Muslim Americans thus illustrate the tendency of the religiously engaged to reinforce their religious mosaics through online media.

There is little evidence that emerging adults who lack salient religious mosaics, or who are not open to religious development, use religious media to explore religious options or to enrich their mosaics. In fact, it may be unlikely for emerging adults to engage in religious and spiritual exploration in general, whether it be media-aided or conventional. Smith (2009) found that emerging adults in the United States tend to focus on the temporal circumstances of transitioning into independence and adulthood, tasks that converge on educations, jobs, finances, and living situations. Many emerging adults also devote considerable nonmedia and media time to developing and maintaining social and romantic connections. These preoccupations, Smith (2009) argued, distract emerging adults from religious and spiritual seeking, and little expansion in religious and spiritual mosaics occurs among people in this age group. In most instances, emerging adults who are not invested in a religious tradition already are unlikely to seek religious media to enrich their religious mosaics. Emerging adults' use of religious media may be best predicted by salient mosaics that these media support and strengthen.

## Nonreligious Media

Outside the domain of explicitly religious media, religiousness inter-sects with media research in the area of health-related media effects. This literature focuses on the public health implications of media use, specifically issues such as aggression, obesity, body image, sexual health, and substance use (e.g., Brown & Bobkowski, 2011). Religious mosaics influence the selection of media in general and potentially unhealthy media in particular. "Potentially unhealthy media" refers to media that may have detrimental effects on young people's well-being. According to Smith (2005), religiously devoted adolescents consume less media than do youth who are religiously disengaged. This may be because religious youth tend to engage in more organized activities than do nonreligious youth (Smith, 2005), leaving less unorganized time for consuming media. Highly religious adolescents also consume less potentially unhealthy media. Specifically, religiously devoted adoles-cents play fewer action video games and watch fewer R-rated television and movies (Bobkowski, 2009; Smith, 2005), and consume less pornog-raphy and other explicitly sexual media content (Smith, 2005) than do their religiously disengaged peers.

In all, we know that religiousness plays a protective role against adolescents' and emerging adults' risk behaviors such as sexual pro-miscuity, aggression, and substance abuse (e.g., Smith, 2005, 2009; Yonker, Schnabelrauch, & DeHaan, 2012). The media are socialization agents that, along with parents, peers, and schools, educate youth about healthy and unhealthy behaviors (e.g., Brown & Bobkowski, 2011). Among adolescents, exposure to unhealthy media seems to mediate the relation between religiousness and the detrimental socializing effects of the media. Religious youth expose themselves to less unhealthy media than do their less religious peers, muting the potentially negative impact of these media on their behaviors and well-being.

It is unclear whether the link between religiousness and unhealthy media is as strong in emerging adulthood as it is in adolescence. Some emerging adults certainly maintain their adolescent media-use pat-terns. Indeed, religiously devoted emerging adults continue consum-ing less pornography than their religiously disengaged peers (Smith, 2009). But experiencing greater independence and less parental sanc-tion also may lead some religious emerging adults to consume more unhealthy programs, games, and Web sites than they would have in adolescence. In a study of male students at a Mormon university, even though all participants agreed that pornography "was an unacceptable way to express sexuality," 35% viewed pornography at least once in the previous year and nearly 9% viewed it every other day or daily (Nelson, Padilla-Walker, & Carroll, 2010, p. 140). Emerging adults especially may be able to reconcile such counterintuitive attitudes and behaviors because cognitively, many of them are predisposed to rejecting universal standards in favor of individual and situational norms (Labouvie-Vief, 2006; Smith, 2009).

At the other end of the religious spectrum, as less religious individuals move into emerging adulthood, they may consume less unhealthy media than they did in adolescence. Some emerging adults engage in fewer risk behaviors than they did in adolescence (e.g., smoking marijuana) because they view these behaviors as artifacts of an earlier, more rebellious stage in life (Smith, 2009). The use of potentially unhealthy media may follow a similar pattern, with emerging adults who indulged in such media during adolescence consuming less unhealthy media in emerging adulthood. In all, evidence suggests that the association between religiousness and unhealthy media use is less linear in emerging adulthood than in adolescence.

Further research is needed to examine the associations between religious mosaics and media selection. Most broadly, it remains unclear how much religious media, on average, emerging adults consume, or what proportions of emerging adults' media diets are devoted to religious, nonreligous, and potentially unhealthy media. More specifically, our understanding continues to be imprecise about the mechanisms that underlie selective exposure to religious and nonreligious media.

## ▲ Engaging Media

The second moment of the Media Practice Model focuses on individuals' processing of media messages, encompassing mechanisms such as attention and involvement, counterarguing and reactance. Attention refers to the cognitive resources that users dedicate to a media message, while involvement concerns their interest in the message (Lang, 2000; Petty, Cacioppo, & Goldman, 1981). Both of these may be shaped by the religious mosaic. Emerging adults whose religious mosaics include interest in religious messages, regardless of whether they agree with those messages, may pay attention to the messages and be involved in them. Alternately, those whose religious experiences or beliefs match the media messages may treat them as background noise and not attend to or process them.

For example, if three Catholic friends watch news coverage of the papal election together, each may attend to the news report and be involved in it differently, depending on the characteristics of their individual religious mosaics. One friend may pay close attention and process the news carefully and positively because the Pope's spiritual leadership plays an important role within her religious mosaic. Another friend may watch the same program but not attend to its details because cultural and family traditions, not church rituals, shape the Catholic component of his religious mosaic. The third friend may carefully attend to the news report but process it using a cynical lens because despite identifying as Catholic, her religious mosaic includes a critical attitude about the Catholic Church's all-male hierarchy. This third friend may engage in counterarguing, which consists of experiencing thoughts that contradict and oppose a message (Cacioppo, 1979).

Another negative response is reactance, which entails reacting to a message that appears to curtail one's sense of independence (Dillard & Shen, 2005). An emerging adult with an established set of religiously based morals that devalue sexual promiscuity may counterargue through her exposure to a music video that glamorizes sexual behavior, for instance. She may also counterargue or experience reactance when exposed to a message that is hostile or degrading to her religious tradition. An emerging adult without a salient religious mosaic, meanwhile, may experience reactance while viewing a message that encourages religion-based lifestyle changes.

Developmentally, emerging adults may be more likely than adolescents to engage meaningfully in media messages that challenge or threaten their religious mosaics because cognitive development enables many emerging adults to "deal with contradiction, diversity, and the individual's own role in the process of knowledge" (Labouvie-Vief, 2006, p. 65). Many individuals report feeling more open-minded as emerging adults than they felt during adolescence (Smith, 2009), suggesting that emerging adults may be willing to process a wider range of media messages than their younger peers. Because they feel more secure in their identities (Smith, 2009), however, emerging adults also may be less persuaded than adolescents by the media messages they consume.

The literature on emerging adults, religion, and media tends not to refer to the specific engagement processes discussed here, but it does provide examples of emerging adults processing media. Some of the Muslim-American emerging adults who used the Internet for religious purposes said that they carefully evaluated the Islam-related media messages they found and the Web sites on which they found this information (Mishra & Semaan, 2010). This suggests high involvement and, for some, counterarguing with the messages they thought to be less authoritative. A study of Wiccan practitioners showed that some emerging adults identified with the portrayals of Wiccan spirituality and ethics in "witchy" television shows such as *Bewitched* and *Charmed* (Berger & Ezzy, 2009). Others reacted against such portrayals, perceiving them to be overly simplistic and inaccurate depictions of their religious tradition.

Substantial gaps remain in our understanding of how processing mechanisms mediate the relation between religious mosaics and media effects. It is unclear, for instance, whether religious emerging adults employ religion-related resistance strategies to prevent attending to or getting involved in media content that endorses risk behaviors such as aggression, sexual promiscuity, or substance abuse. Engagement processes underscore the need for media researchers to measure more than the effects of media exposure. Better understanding of these processes requires researchers to probe what happens in media users at the time of exposure.

## ▲ Applying Media to the Religious Self

The third moment in the Media Practice Model concerns the extent to which individuals incorporate into their religious mosaics the media messages they encounter. Alternately, emerging adults may shape their mosaics to contrast the prevalent media messages. In the era of social media, emerging adults also may express their religious mosaics by producing and distributing media messages that contain elements of their religious identities.

### Incorporating Media

Emerging adults may manifest the religious elements they glean from media in their beliefs, attitudes, and behaviors. To a large degree, media application depends on the previous two moments in the emerging adults' media practice—the extent to which they have exposed themselves to specific media, and the ways in which they processed the media messages. Media messages may reinforce or weaken religious beliefs or attitudes held by emerging adults about the faiths in which they were raised. Exposure to faith-affirming messages may reinforce emerging adults' religious beliefs. Alternately, the level of reactance against religious messages may lead emerging adults to reorganize their religious mosaics to contrast those messages.

Although many of the examples used in this chapter reference single exposures to media content, media effects generally accumulate over time and multiple exposures. Cultivation theory (Gerbner & Gross, 1976; Shrum, 1996) suggests that by viewing the same, or similar, media content over and over again, individuals develop a worldview that parallels the world presented in the media, which tends to be different than the "real" world. Thus, the news media may consistently portray a specific set of ideas about Christianity, drawing a link between Christians and opposition to gay marriage, for example. This equation may become most salient in the minds of individuals who consume a large volume of news media messages (e.g., Putnam & Campbell, 2010). The world portrayed in violent video games, meanwhile, may be replete with images of threat, aggression, and the objectification of women (e.g., Scharrer, 2004). Heavy gamers may absorb such images and ideals, which may result in the gamers endorsing fewer prosocial values (Barry, Padilla-Walker, & Nelson, 2012). Cultivation theory thus emphasizes the cumulative effects of the media on users, underscoring the need for longitudinal studies to assess such effects.

Research illustrates how media messages are correlated with media users' religious mosaics. A study of Mormon college-aged men showed that those who use pornography despite their religious tradition's opposition to pornography engage in fewer religious practices, both formerly and currently, than do their peers who do not use pornography (Nelson et al., 2010). Although this study did not make causal assertions linking pornography use with religious practice, its findings suggest that using media that contradicts the values espoused by individuals' religious tradition may loosen their connections to that religious tradition.

Media also may have a flourishing effect on emerging adults' religious mosaics. In a study of an online fantasy role-playing game structured around players' interactions with divine beings and the performance of ritual, some participants reported that their game experiences prompted them to be "better people" in their offline lives

(Feltmate, 2010). In another study, frequent involvement in online religious discussion groups was associated with an increased sense of a religious identity, which, in turn, accrued social benefits such as increased support, connection to others, and purpose in life (McKenna & West, 2007). In both cases, engagement in online religious activities was associated positively with individuals' religious mosaics.

### Producing Media

In recent years, increased access to media production and dissemination platforms (e.g., YouTube) has allowed many individuals to become "produsers"—both users and producers—of media (Bruns, 2008). In the United States, conflicting social standards about public religiousness complicate individuals' digital disclosure of their religious mosaics. Although the proportion of the US population without a specific religious affiliation is increasing (Kosmin & Keysar, 2009), it is still socially disadvantageous in this country to identify as agnostic or atheist (Edgell et al., 2006; see Chapter 14). Paradoxically, while most younger and adult Americans share a general sense that being religious is beneficial (Smith, 2005), overt religious self-disclosure also appears to be socially undesirable. This may be at least partly because the fusion of conservative Christianity with specific positions on social issues (e.g., abortion and gay rights) by religious and political leaders that have pushed some individuals away from religious institutions (Hout & Fischer, 2002; Putnam & Campbell, 2010). Many nonevangelical young adults hold unfavorable perceptions of Christians, believing them to be judgmental and hypocritical (Kinnaman & Lyons, 2007). Adolescents, thus, and members of older cohorts, take great pains to not come across as being "too religious" when discussing their religious mosaics (Smith, 2005). In light of these intricate norms, for many emerging adults producing media messages that communicate religious mosaics may be the result of careful negotiation between personal needs and aspirations, and audience norms and expectations.

A study of emerging adults' disclosure of religious mosaics in MySpace profiles illustrates the nuances of this process (Bobkowski & Pearce, 2011). Researchers coded all textual and visual elements of the profiles for instances of religious disclosure. Nearly two-thirds (62%) of the MySpace users (18 to 23 years old) identified their religious affiliations in their online profiles, but most (70%) did not say anything religious beyond displaying a one-word label in the "Religion" field. This suggests that without being prompted, many emerging adults may not disclose their religious identity (Bobkowski & Pearce, 2011).

The study also examined several identity attributes and attitudes associated with online religious self-disclosure. Emerging adults who were more religious (i.e., attended religious services more frequently, religion was more important in their decision making) were more likely to identify as religious online, regardless of the religious tradition to which they belonged. Evangelical Protestants, however, disclosed more religious information overall than did other Christians and nonreligious young people. Understanding religion to be a private matter or having a negative perception of organized religion moderated the relation between religiousness and disclosure. Individuals who believed religion to be a private matter were less likely to disclose religiously—even if they were highly religious—as compared with those who viewed religion as a public matter. Those who had a negative perception of organized religion were also less likely to communicate about religion—even if they were religious—than were those who had a positive view of organized religion (Bobkowski & Pearce, 2011).

The study also underscored the importance of social norms for religious self-disclosure. MySpace profile owners who had more religious friends were more likely to disclose religiously in their profiles than were those with fewer religious friends (Bobkowski & Pearce, 2011). Even profile owners who scored low on indicators of religiousness were more likely to identify as religious in their profiles if their closest friends were religious. This suggests that profile owners perceived their more religious friends as expecting religious disclosure, and less religious friends as expecting nondisclosure. Overall, these findings suggest that self-presentational concerns shape emerging adults' self-disclosures about religion. Emerging adults adjust what they communicate about religion to balance their religious mosaics with what they want to project and with what they think their friends expect.

Emerging adults also may engage in the production of nonreligious media. One area of concern is the use of social media to model risk behaviors such as aggression, sexual promiscuity, or substance use. Research is equivocal about the link between religious mosaics and producing such messages. One analysis of the identity elements displayed in social media profiles suggested that risk behaviors and being religious are mutually exclusive and tend not to be displayed simultaneously in the same profiles (Moreno, Parks, Zimmerman, Brito, & Christakis, 2009).

A study of emerging adults' online sexual disclosures found, however, that controlling for several potential correlates, religiousness was not associated with sexual disclosure (Bobkowski, Brown, & Neffa, 2012). It remains unclear, therefore, whether there is a link between religious mosaics and the production of potentially detrimental media messages.

Two elements make the presentation of identity in social media worthy of further research. First, the media that emerging adults produce become the media that other young, often impressionable people consume. These media messages, therefore, whether they concern religiousness or other identity characteristics, likely shape other individuals' social norms and identities. Second, the production of a media message about an element of one's identity reinforces the centrality of that element for one's identity. In both offline and online environments, asserting an attitude publicly or enacting a behavior leads to the internalization of that attitude or behavior (Fazio, Effrein, & Falender, 1981; Gonzales & Hancock, 2008). Producing media that reflect elements of one's religious mosaic is likely to strengthen those elements of the mosaic.

Overall, the application moment of emerging adults' media practice vis-à-vis their religious mosaics needs further explication and research. Questions about who incorporates religious media content into their identities, what content triggers shifts in religious mosaics, and how such shifts are manifested remain unanswered. Future research should also further examine the motives for and implications of producing social media messages about religion among emerging adults who produce, as well as among those who consume, the messages.

## ▲ Conclusion

This chapter plotted the various intersections between media and emerging adults' religious mosaics using the framework of the Media Practice Model (Shafer et al., 2012). Religious mosaics may shape emerging adults' motives for selecting or rejecting media content. The mosaics may also influence how young people engage with the media messages they select. Conversely, religious mosaics may intensify and coalesce, or weaken and fragment, in response to the media messages that emerging adults select, process, and produce.

Critics of the media tend to imbue the media with great power to affect media consumers' identities and behaviors. While there is no doubt that the media are important socializing agents, it is often difficult to document exactly when and how the media affect what individuals think or do. In light of this complex interplay between media and the religious mosaic, the Media Practice Model (Shafer et al., 2012) offers a systematic framework for organizing theoretical principles and research findings. The Model also helps to identify research questions that have not been adequately addressed, mapping out a fertile path for researchers who see the need for more robust evidence and clearer theory in this area.

Admittedly, this chapter comes up short on insights about how emerging adults' religious mosaics intersect their media practices around the globe. Cultural norms affect how individuals live their religious mosaics and how they select, engage with, and apply the media. Many of the assumptions and literature discussed in this chapter reflect contemporary, mainstream US norms. In many ways, however, the United States is an outlier in terms of religious diversity, the religiousness of its general population, media access, and media freedoms. The field is clearly ripe for research that deepens our understanding of how religious mosaics and the media overlap and diverge among emerging adults in other cultures.

Over the coming years, the media to which emerging adults attend will evolve in ways that are difficult to predict. The central role of the Internet as the conduit of all media content is likely to increase, as are the options for experiencing the media using portable devices over expansive wireless networks. As ever more nonprofessionals take up media production and dissemination as a hobby, the media messages that individuals consume are likely to become more fragmented and personalized. Despite the continuing evolution of media technologies and content options, emerging adults' media practices will likely continue revolving around selection, engagement, and application, with each of these moments informed by and, in turn, informing, emerging adults' religious mosaics.

## ▲ References

Banjo, O. O., & Williams, K. M. (2011). A house divided? Christian music in black and white. *Journal of Media and Religion, 10,* 115–137. doi: 10.1080/1534842 3.2011.599640

Barry, C. M., Padilla-Walker, L. M., & Nelson, L. J. (2012). The role of mothers and media on emerging adults' religious faith and practices by way of internalization of prosocial values. *Journal of Adult Development, 19,* 66–78. doi: 10.1007/s10804-011-9135-x

Berger, H. A., & Ezzy, D. (2009). Mass media and religious identity: A case study of young witches. *Journal for the Scientific Study of Religion, 48,* 501–514. doi: 10.1111/j.1468-5906.2009.01462.x

Bobkowski, P. S. (2009). Adolescent religiosity and selective exposure to television. *Journal of Media and Religion, 8,* 55–70. doi: 10.1080/15348420802670942

Bobkowski, P. S., Brown, J. D., & Neffa, D. R. (2012). "Hit me up and we can get down:" U.S. youths' risk behaviors and sexual self-disclosure in MySpace profiles. *Journal of Children and Media, 6,* 119–134. doi: 10.1080/17482798.20 11.633412

Bobkowski, P. S., & Pearce, L. D. (2011). Baring their souls in online profiles or not: Religious self-disclosure in social media. *Journal for the Scientific Study of Religion, 50,* 744–762. doi: 10.1111/j.1468-5906.2011.01597.x

Brown, J. D. (2000). Adolescents' sexual media diets. *Journal of Adolescent Health, 27S,* 35–40. doi: 10.1016/S1054-139X(00)00141-5

Brown, J. D. (2006). Emerging adults in a media-saturated world. In J. J. Arnett & J. L. Tanner (Eds.), *Emerging adults in America* (pp. 279–299). Washington, DC: APA.

Brown, J. D., & Bobkowski, P. S. ( 2011). Older and newer media: Patterns of use and effects on adolescents' health and well-being. *Journal of Research on Adolescence, 21,* 95–113. doi: 10.1111/j.1532-7795.2010.00717.x

Bruns, A. ( 2008) . *Blogs, Wikipedia, Second Life, and beyond: From production to produsage* . New York, NY : Peter Lang .

Cacioppo, J. T. (1979). Effects of exogenous changes in heart rate on facilitation of thoughts and resistance to persuasion. *Journal of Personality and Social Psychology, 37,* 489–498. doi: 10.1037/0022-3514.37.4.489

Cheong, P. H., Halavais, A., & Kwon, K. (2008). The chronicles of me: Understanding blogging as a religious practice. *Journal of Media and Religion, 7,* 107–131. doi: 10.1080/15348420802223015

Clark, L. S., Hoover, S. M., & Rainie, L. (2004). Faith online. *Pew Internet and American Life Project.* Available at http://pewinternet.org/Reports/2004/Faith-Online.aspx

Dillard, J. P., & Shen, L. (2005). On the nature of reactance and its role in persuasive health communication. *Communication Monographs, 72,* 144–168. doi: 10.1080/03637750500111815

Edgell, P., Gerteis, J., & Hartmann, D. (2006). Atheists as "other:" Moral boundaries and cultural membership in American society. *American Sociological Review, 71,* 211–234. doi: 10.1177/000312240607100203

Einstein, M. (2008). *Brands of faith: Marketing religion in a commercial age.* New York, NY: Routledge.

Fazio, R. H., Effrein, E. A., & Falender, V. J. (1981). Self-perceptions following social interaction. *Journal of Personality and Social Psychology, 41,* 232–242. doi: 10.1037/0022-3514.41.2.232

Feltmate, D. (2010). "You wince in agony as the hot metal brands you:" Religious behavior in an online role-playing game. *Journal of Contemporary Religion, 25,* 363–377. doi: 10.1080/13537903.2010.516538

Gerbner, G., & Gross, L. (1976). Living with television: The violence profile. *Journal of Communication, 26*(2), 172–199. doi: 10.1111/j.1460-2466.1976.tb01397.x

Gonzales, A. L., & Hancock, J. T. (2008). Identity shift in computer-mediated environments. *Media Psychology, 11*, 167–185. doi: 10.1080/15213260802023433

Hendershot, H. (2004). *Shaking the world for Jesus: Media and conservative evangelical culture.* Chicago, IL: University of Chicago Press.

Hout, M., & Fischer, C. S. (2002). Why more Americans have no religious preference: Politics and generations. *American Sociological Review, 67*, 165–190. Available at http://www.jstor.org. /stable/3088891

Kinnaman, D., & Lyons, G. (2007). *unChristian: What a new generation really things about Christianity and why it matters.* Grand Rapids, MI: Baker Books.

Kosmin, B. A., & Keysar, A. (2009). *American religious identification survey (ARIS 2009): Summary report.* Hartford, CT: Trinity College.

Labouvie-Vief, G. (2006). Emerging structures of adult thought. In J. J. Arnett & J. L. Tanner (Eds.), *Emerging adults in America* (pp. 59–84). Washington, DC: APA.

Lang, A. (2000). The limited capacity model of mediated message processing. *Journal of Communication, 50*, 46–70. doi: 10.1111/j.1460-2466.2000.tb02833.x

McFarland, S. G. (1996). Keeping the faith: The roles of selective exposure and avoidance in maintaining religious beliefs. In D. A. Stout & J. M. Buddenbaum (Eds.), *Religion and mass media: Audiences and adaptations* (pp. 173–182). Thousand Oaks, CA: Sage.

McKenna, K. Y. A., & West, K. J. (2007). Give me that online-time religion: The role of the internet in spiritual life. *Computers in Human Behavior, 23*, 942–954. doi: 10.1016/j.chb.2005.08.007

Mishra, S., & Semaan, G. (2010). Islam in cyberspace: South Asian Muslims in America log in. *Journal of Broadcasting & Electronic Media, 54*(1), 87–101. doi: 10.1080/08838150903550436

Moreno, M. A., Jelenchick, L., Koff, R., Eikoff, J., Diermyer, C., & Christakis, D. A. (2012). Internet use and multitasking among older adolescents: An experience sampling approach. *Computers in Human Behavior, 28*, 1097–1102. doi:10.1016/j.chb.2012.01.016

Moreno, M. A., Parks, M. R., Zimmerman, F. J., Brito, T. E., & Christakis, D. A. (2009). Display of health risk behaviors on MySpace by adolescents: Prevalence and associations. *Archives of Pediatric and Adolescent Medicine, 163*, 27–34. doi: 10.1001/archpediatrics.2008.528

Nelson, L. J., Padilla-Walker, L. M., & Carroll, J. S. (2010). "I believe it is wrong but I still do it:" A comparison of religious young men who do versus do not use pornography. *Psychology of Religion & Spirituality, 2*, 136–147. doi: 10.1037/a0019127

Pearce, L. D., & Denton, M. L. (2011). *A faith of their own: Stability and change in the religiosity of America's adolescents.* New York, NY: Oxford University Press.

Petty, R. E., Cacioppo, J. T., & Goldman, R. (1981). Personal involvement as a determinant of argument-based persuasion. *Journal of Personality and Social Psychology, 41*, 874–855. doi: 10.1037/0022-3514.41.5.847

Putnam, R. D., & Campbell, D. E. (2010). *American grace: How religion divides and unites us.* New York, NY: Simon & Schuster.

Rideout, V., Foehr, U. G., & Roberts, D. F. (2010). *Generation M2: Media in the lives of 8-18 year-olds*. Menlo Park, CA: The Henry J. Kaiser Family Foundation.

Scharrer, E. (2004). Virtual violence: Gender and aggression in video game advertisements. *Mass Communication & Society, 7*, 393–412. doi: 10.1207/s15327825mcs0704_2

Shafer, A., Bobkowski, P. S., & Brown, J. D. (2012). Sexual media practice: How adolescents select, engage with, and are affected by sexual media. In K. Gill (Ed.), *The Oxford handbook of media psychology* (pp. 223–251). New York, NY: Oxford University Press.

Shrum, L. J. (1996). Psychological processes underlying cultivation effects further tests of construct accessibility. *Human Communication Research, 22*, 482–509. doi: 10.1111/j.1468-2958.1996.tb00376.x

Slater, M. D. (2007). Reinforcing spirals: The mutual influence of media selectivity and media effects and their impact on individual behavior and social identity. *Communication Theory, 17*, 281–303. doi: 10.1111/j.1468-2885.2007.00296.x

Smith, C. (with Denton, M. L.) (2005). *Soul searching: The religious and spiritual lives of American teenagers*. New York, NY: Oxford University Press.

Smith, C. (with Snell, P.) (2009). *Souls in transition: The religious and spiritual lives of emerging adults*. New York, NY: Oxford University Press.

Vygotsky, L. S. (1978). *Mind in society: The development of higher psychological processes*. Cambridge, MA: Harvard University Press.

Wagner, R. (2012). *Godwired: Religion, ritual and virtual reality*. New York, NY: Routledge.

Ward, J. (March 7, 2004). Worshippers take "Passion" back to church: Mel Gibson's film is inspiring parishioners to join congregations, go "back to faith." *The Washington Times*, p. A1.

Winston, D. (Ed.) (2009). *Small screen, big picture: Television and lived religion*. Waco, TX: Baylor University Press.

Yonker, J. E., Schnabelrauch, C. A., & DeHaan, L. G. (2012). The relationship between spirituality and religiosity on psychological outcomes in adolescents and emerging adults: A meta-analytic review. *Journal of Adolescence, 35*, 299–314. doi: 10.1016/j.adolescence.2011.08.010

Zickuhr, K., & Smith, A. (2012). Digital differences. *Pew Internet and American Life Project*. Available at http://pewinternet.org/Reports/2012/Digital-differences.aspx

# 7 ▲

# The Law's Promise of Religious Freedom to Support Emerging Adults' Religious Development and Experiences

ROGER J. R. LEVESQUE

Adolescents' transition to adulthood, now conceptualized as emerging adulthood (Arnett, 2004), may involve substantially uneven progress in a variety of developmental domains, but the legal domain makes the transition quite dramatic and with considerable precision. Except for a few exceptions and nuances, the legal system assumes that individuals become adults at the age of 18 years. That transition means that individuals can exercise their own rights in the fullest sense of citizenship. As adults, they can act against their parents' wishes and their parents (generally) no longer are legally responsible for them. As adolescents transition to adulthood, institutions that used to control them, such as schools as well as health, child welfare, and justice systems, no longer can act as paternalistically on their behalf; such institutions no longer can consider them as children in need of care and protection from themselves. Nor can the state so readily fashion rules that would shape their development in ways to benefit their families and broader society; for example, states no longer can require them to engage in child labor to benefit their families and protect them from media influences to foster responsible development (Levesque, 2008). Legally, emerging adults no longer are citizens in the making. Fully considered adults, emerging adults gain nearly all blanket freedoms allowed by society and previously denied to them because they essentially were deemed children in need of care, even though they may not view themselves as fully adults until about a decade later (Arnett, 2004).

Among the many freedoms that the state bestows on emerging adults, the freedom of religion certainly remains one of the most cherished and well-recognized but widely misunderstood. Ideally, that freedom would include the right to practice one's religion, to believe what one wishes to believe, to have a life guided by religious principles if so desired, to share that way of life with others, and to live in a community that respects those freedoms. The firm commitment to religious freedom even ideally would include the freedom to not embrace a religion and to not be influenced by one. Yet the legal system restrains individuals' religious freedom much more than might be suggested by popular sentiments and highly regarded ideals. A dizzying set of principles governs this area of law. Taking a bird's-eye view of these principles reveals considerable contradiction and much less protection than expected from a right that was so instrumental to shaping the nation's founding and that continues to receive intense popular support, even when the legal system marches toward limiting religious freedoms.

Numerous examples illustrate the freedom's limitations. Adults are free to practice their religion, but the law can limit what they practice. For example, the law can ban rituals, prohibit some forms of proselytizing, criminalize the formation of relationships deemed key to a religious practice (e.g., bigamy), and make it difficult to hold and express values deemed unacceptable (such as religiously based hate; Levesque, 2002). Implicitly, the law also can support one's religion's beliefs over those of another. For example, views of contraception and abortion are religiously informed, and different religious groups consider those views in the types of services that they provide individuals. If one religious group finds contraceptives or abortions inappropriate, and another one does not, the government can choose to support the social and medical services provided by one group over those of the other, and actually forbid state support of one of them (Corbin, 2012). The law even permits financial support for the creation of religious institutions specifically devoted to spreading their way of life, such as by funding parochial schools through vouchers (Eberle-Peay, 2012). Such support means, of course, that individuals who hold beliefs contrary to those that the state supports lose out in two important ways: They do not receive preferential treatment, and the state can tax them to support religious groups and beliefs that they do not otherwise support. Lawmakers can run on platforms that put their religious beliefs in action, such as when they use religious justifications to support their political beliefs on abortion, adultery, climate change, evolution, and the death penalty. Lawmakers who overtly profess these justifications may do so at the expense of those who hold contrary religious beliefs (Perlin, 2011). Even the Supreme Court now reflects the dramatic shift in protections, as it now holds that the ideologies of "diversity" and "nondiscrimination" can trump religious freedom (as will be seen below; see also Lendino, 2011). The right to religious freedom clearly no longer enjoys an elevated, untouchable status as it arguably has become, as leading commentators have argued, a second-class right rather than the fundamental right unequivocally enshrined in the US Constitution (see Glendon, 2012). The image of religious freedom, and perhaps even the everyday experience of it for some, simply does not match the reality of laws regulating it.

In the United States, the divergence between image and legal reality mirrors the divergence between emerging adults' apparently high commitment to religion and the law's decline in protecting those commitments. Emerging adults in the United States profess a strong commitment to their religions and practice their faiths (Smith, 2009). Indeed, they are considered to be more observant and religiously committed than are those in other industrialized nations (Inglehart, Basañez, Daez-Medrano, Halman, & Luijicx, 2004). Yet restrictions on religious freedoms continue. The "wall of separation" metaphor driving state actions necessarily has given way to a metaphor of enmeshment between state and religion for the simple reason that the nature of the state itself has changed dramatically over the past centuries, particularly during the past few decades. The state cannot escape religion and its influence, as we will see below. To exacerbate matters, that change has been marked by a changed society, one much more diverse, inclusive, and tolerant than at any other time in the nation's history. This is even true of religion: Despite increased religious diversity, US citizens embrace religion as a civic glue that unites rather than divides (see Campbell & Putnam, 2010). Thus, we now have more and larger religious groups, the state is now much more present in people's lives (e.g., in terms of the support for social services), and a pressing need exists for different models to uphold the values of religious freedom.

Different models likely will be difficult to come by. In the United States, the regulation of religion rests on a central dilemma: At its core, the legal system seeks to not regulate religion. This effort to remove the government from the religious domain relies on the Constitution's apparently simple mandate that "Congress shall make no law respecting an establishment of religion, or prohibiting the free exercise thereof." That language, which is found in the First Amendment and important enough to be the first protection enumerated in the Bill of Rights, may be understood easily on its face. But, in practice, the language quickly becomes considerably complicated and far from clear. The reality is that, although it seeks to remove itself from religious issues, the legal system cannot avoid them. Religion infuses our lives, including the law itself. And it now infuses the law, which is how the government (the "state") exerts its power, even more than ever imagined given the increasing complexity of legal systems and the concomitant increase in the state's powers and obligations. Individuals no longer live with small governments, and we do not live in small insular groups; the government infiltrates our lives and deeply influences how we live and live with one another. The state cannot stay removed from religion and how it operates in modern civil society. When considering intersections among religion, law, and human development, then, the real concern necessarily transforms itself into determining the extent and how the legal system will tolerate a relationship between the state's actions and religion. These concerns may result in abstract doctrine and concepts, but they go to the core of everyone's religious faith, development, and what religion can do for us (e.g., provide meaning-making, a sense of community, and social support) and what we can do for it (e.g., allow it to thrive for itself and for what it can do for the broader society).

This chapter distills foundational doctrine that shapes the law's response to religion in our everyday lives. Although the effort seeks to distill, it still remains remarkably broad in reach, and it does so for several reasons. Understanding the regulation of religion as it relates to any period of human development requires, for example, understanding not only how the law relates directly to that period but also how it relates to any other developmental period. For example, understanding the laws regulating any developmental period requires understanding those regulating marriage, family life, family structure, the rights of parents, the rights of children, and so forth. All of these rights intermesh and are relevant for any given age group. In addition, understanding those laws and rights requires understanding the regulation of social institutions (e.g., educational, medical, social service, economic, law enforcement, employment, media, and personal relationships). All of these laws also happen to be influenced heavily not only by religious beliefs but also by policies that relate directly to religious institutions or by policies that are grounded in religious beliefs themselves (although they may not appear to be so). Thus, understanding how the law affects the lives of individuals, including their religious lives, requires an exceedingly broad sweep and deep look at how the law itself works.

The chapter begins by examining the foundation of laws relating to religion, provides readers with the tools needed to understand laws relating to religion, describes exemplars of how the law works, and ends with lessons learned. Thus, we first examine the Constitution's religious clauses and the messages behind them, as doing so gives us a sense of themes to come, given that the clauses are the driving force behind this area of law and that they can best be understood within its broader constitutional system of rights. We then examine how the Supreme Court has interpreted these mandates, how the interpretations have evolved, and their apparent future directions. That brief overview provides the background for understanding lessons learned. In the end, we conclude that the United States has eschewed adoption of a state religion, but, in a real sense, the United States has adopted a "religion" in that it grounds its faith in the Constitution itself. We also conclude that the Constitution animates much of what we do, can do, and should do; however, institutions like religions and families give those actions and thoughts their full meaning. In that regard, the study of the regulation of religion reveals its peculiar relevance to growing research relating to emerging adulthood and the place of religion in it.

## ▲ The Religion Clauses and Their Messages as the Foundation for Religious Regulation

Voluminous case law and scholarly literature has examined the Free Exercise and Establishment Clauses as well as their relationships with one another (see Levesque, 2002). Simply stated, one clause prohibits the establishment of religion, while the other prohibits efforts that would limit the "exercise" (which some view as practice) of religion. Although there may be tensions between the clauses, several key values underlie both, and those values have to do with the political system's approach to recognizing and protecting rights.

The Constitution concerns itself with seeking to ensure freedom from the government. By seeking to limit the government, the relevant constitutional provisions recognizing the rights of individuals fundamentally adopt a "negative" approach to rights. A negative approach to rights is one in which the government is viewed as in need of restraint rather than, for example, in need of providing resources such as food, shelter, education, and the like (which would be positive rights). What the Constitution seeks to permit is individuals' freedom to seek and keep what would come from positive rights (e.g., again, food, shelter, and education). What this further translates into in this context is a commitment to removing, as much as practicable, the state from religious practice and beliefs. This posture is adopted in lieu of a state that would, for example, financially support a religion for individuals and ensure that the religion is available by providing state-supported programs.

At their core, both the Free Exercise and the Establishment Clauses reflect a commitment to individual free choice in the selection of values and an opposition to government indoctrination. In a real sense, the clauses support (and are supported by) a strong political statement that societies once considered radical. The statement is that people are free, that free people are free to hold diverse thoughts, and governments neither constrain nor direct such freedom. Given that free governments are ones that are "of and for the people," however, it is difficult to escape the influence of religion on government and vice versa. A two-way relationship necessarily exists between "freely" selected and embraced values and governmental actions, as individuals' values inform their political choices and political life influences individuals' thoughts. The civil rights movement serves as the classic example of these recursive relationships. Many participants' religious faiths drove their involvement in the civil rights movement, and images of social justice inevitably had an impact not only on laws but also on participants' faith and, inevitably, those of others. This type of two-way relationship can be seen in a wide variety of socially contentious issues, ranging from abortion to the death penalty and from visions of appropriate medical care to views of evolution and educational standards. The recursive relationship does not vitiate the need for and power of the clauses, as, on its face, the clauses proscribed such relationships. Rather, the relationship highlights their significance as they stand for the law's commitment to fluidity in the manner values form and are embraced, a commitment that resists governmental efforts to freeze certain values into place and compel individuals' adherence to them.

In addition to reflecting a commitment to individual freedom, the clauses reflect a profound political commitment to not having the government be in the business of exclusion and of fostering strife. Thus, the clauses seek to ensure that the state does not create outsiders, that is, that it does not create and designate unequal groups. A government would do so, for example, when it would support one group over another, such as by imposing or denying benefits based on religious beliefs. Such actions would be deemed improper in that they send messages regarding an individual's status as a full citizen, and they create outsiders who are not full members of their political communities. Such messages are deemed particularly problematic as they would foment civic divisiveness. Relatedly, the clauses reflect a view that sectarian groups should not benefit from state resources in a manner that would enhance their competitive positions; the clauses seek to free religions to gain adherents based on their intrinsic merits rather than through state subsidized incentives. Thus, the clauses protect both the integrity of individual conscience in religious matters as well as the integrity of religions themselves from the potential corruption deemed inherent to state subvention. Such protections are meant to avoid both the human suffering intrinsic in coerced violations of conscience and the social conflict that inevitably arises from attempts to inflict such suffering.

The clauses' deep commitment to freedom and ensuring governmental restraint becomes emblematic in its views of religion itself. The clauses fundamentally prohibit inquiring into whether particular religious beliefs are acceptable, logical, consistent, or even comprehensible. Indeed, this area of law seeks not even to define the specific nature of religion or firmly held religious beliefs. This approach further reflects the focus on the sanctity of individual choice, a wish to avoid governmental intrusion, and the strife that would result from it (see Levesque, 2002). The clauses' concerns with protecting all religions, and rejecting calls to determine what religious beliefs count and those that do not, is deemed as critical to avoiding the exploitation of the machinery of the state to enhance a group's position in civil society and impose one group's beliefs on others. When it comes to religion, there is a true sense that government corrupts, and that government should avoid involvement in individuals' religious beliefs as well as religious institutions. Indeed, and to make matters even more complicated if one is trying to identify religions or religious beliefs in order to protect them, the deep commitment to freedom of thought results in the interpretation that the clauses ensure that the government should not prefer one religion to another but also should not prefer religion to irreligion (see Levesque, 2002; see Chapter 14). Turning these views (not defining religion beyond the need to embrace a firmly held belief and not even protecting it against "irreligion" when the state is supposed to protect religion) into practice can be quite mind-boggling; and they make difficult efforts to shape existing principles into predictions of future legal developments. Not having a firm grip on a substantive definition of a problem would seem to be a recipe for disaster, yet this area of law flourishes as it continues to evolve in response to changing times.

## ▲ The Law Emerging From the Religion Clauses

The Constitution emerges from interpretations of it, and those evolve considerably over time. In a real sense, the clauses relating to religion remained dormant for much of the Constitution's history. Most notably, for example, the clauses focus on "Congress," and thus do not apply at all to states and their governments. It took Supreme Court cases in the 1940s to have the clauses "incorporated" (made to apply against the states) so that they applied equally to the federal and state governments (for the Free Exercise Clause, see Cantwell v. Connecticut, 1940; for the Establishment Clause, see Everson v. Board of Education, 1947). Similarly, the clauses relate specifically to "Congress," but they also tie the hands of administrative and judicial branches, since their application of laws must consider that the main governmental source of laws, legislatures, cannot avoid the constitutional mandate. Once the breadth of application was recognized, however, the interpretations developed quite quickly and have undergone important transformations that are best understandable through separating the clauses for the purposes of discussion.

### The Free Exercise Clause

Over a century passed before the Supreme Court would interpret the protections offered by the Constitution's Free Exercise clause. The Court first did so in *Reynolds v. United States* (1878), which addressed the constitutionality of the prosecution of polygamy under federal law. Reynolds, a member of the Church of Jesus Christ of Latter-day Saints (LDS Church), challenged his conviction of the criminal act of bigamy under the federal Morrill Anti-Bigamy Act. Reynolds presented many claims, the most critical for our purposes being his religious duty to marry multiple times, and concomitantly. The Court recognized that Congress could not pass a law that prohibits the free exercise of religion, but it did not view the prohibition of bigamy as falling under this mandate. The Court noted a distinction between religious belief and action that flowed from religious belief and, following that distinction, ruled that Congress could not legislate against opinions for the simple reason that doing otherwise would make the professed doctrines of religious belief superior to the law of the land and would, in effect, permit every citizen to become a law unto himself. This line of reasoning resulted in *Reynolds'* standing for the

Court's commitment to separating what the state and individuals could do in the practice of their religious faiths, and recognizing that doing so awards the state power over religious practices.

The firm separation between church and state for the purposes of the Free Exercise clause could not withstand the test of time and the development of jurisprudence in other areas. Most notably, the 1960s witnessed the development of civil rights, which transformed some of the Court's views of how to interpret the Constitution. The clearest example of this development was the use of the "strict scrutiny" standard to determine whether laws violated fundamental rights enumerated in the Constitution. This standard allowed for the accommodation of religious conduct. That accommodation could be had if the state could show a compelling interest for restricting a particular religious conduct and demonstrate that the limitation was the least restrictive to reach the compelling interests that served as the foundation for the restriction. This way to approach constitutional challenges was used in several leading cases, most notably in *Sherbert v. Verner* (1963), in which the Court overturned the state Employment Security Commission's decision to deny unemployment benefits to a practicing Seventh-day Adventist Church member who was forced out of work after her employer adopted a 6-day work week, which would have required her to work on Saturdays and against the dictates of her religion. In that case, the Court recognized the slippery slope between action and faith, as it found that conditioning the availability of benefits upon the appellant's willingness to violate a cardinal principle of her religious faith effectively penalized the free exercise of her constitutional liberties. Equally notable, the strict scrutiny standard was applied in the landmark case of *Wisconsin v. Yoder* (1972). In that case, several Amish families appealed a decision convicting them of failing to send their children to public school until the age of 16. The Court ruled that a law that "unduly burdens the practice of religion" without a compelling interest, even though it might be "neutral on its face," would be unconstitutional (Wisconsin v. Yoder, 1972, p. 221). *Yoder* would be deemed a victory for the firm protection of religious rights and also the related rights of parents to raise their children as they deem fit, a closely related right that the law has long recognized (see Meyer v. Nebraska, 1923; Pierce v. Society of Sisters, 1925) and *Yoder* affirmed by using modern standards of constitutional interpretation.

Although the above cases seemed to cement a firm protection of religious practices, the "strict scrutiny" standard for evaluating challenges to constitutional rights became much narrower in 1990. That narrowing emerged in *Employment Division v. Smith* (1990), a case that sought to determine whether the state could deny unemployment benefits to a person fired for violating a state prohibition on the use of peyote, even though the use of the drug was part of a religious ritual. The Court ruled that, although states have the power to accommodate otherwise illegal acts done in pursuit of religious beliefs, states were not required to do so. The general principle that emerged was that, as long it does not target a particular religious practice, a law does not violate the Free Exercise Clause. This ruling appeared to contradict *Yoder*, which had upheld the rights of parents, supported by a Free Exercise claim, to be exempt from a general law. But the Court importantly distinguished *Yoder* on the grounds that it presented a hybrid rights case that presented a constitutional right in addition to the Free Exercise right, rendering the latter worthy of greater protection. The Court revisited this approach in *Church of Lukumi Babalu Aye v. City of Hialeah* (1993). In that case, the city of Hialeah had passed an ordinance banning ritual slaughter, a practice central to the Santería religion, while providing exceptions for some practices such as the kosher slaughter of Judaism. Since the ordinance was not "generally applicable," the Court ruled that it was subject to the compelling interest test, which it failed to meet, and was therefore declared unconstitutional. Thus, if the ordinance (law or policy) would have been general (neutral), it would have passed muster. Today, these two cases confirm that the Court had settled on an important interpretation of law and that it has set clear guidelines for determining the power of the state to limit the exercise of religion: General laws trump religious rights.

Beyond setting a clear and useful standard, both *Smith* and *Church of Lukumi Babalu Aye* also are of significance in that they held a controversial view of *Yoder*. Yoder had evaluated the challenged policy on the strict scrutiny standard (requiring a compelling interest) because the right to religion was attached to other important rights (e.g., parental rights). The upshot of the interpretation presented in *Smith* and *Church of Lukumi Babalu Aye* was that the right to exercise religion, on its own, need not require the state to reach such a high standard of scrutiny from the courts. This was seen as a step back in the development of constitutional standards protecting religion. In a real sense, however, even though the Court used modern standards of constitutional interpretation, the Court essentially returned to a time when the state could not allow even firmly held religious beliefs and practices to usurp the law's power. The Court famously had held to that view in *Prince v. Massachusetts* (1944). Prince involved the constitutionality of a statute used to convict a custodian for furnishing to children copies of a religious pamphlet for subsequent sale. The custodian appealed her conviction on two grounds: as an undue interference by the state with her parental right to control the activities of her children and as an undue inhibition of her exercise of religion. The Court found that "against these sacred private interests, basic in a democracy, stand the interest of society to protect the welfare of children, and the State's authority to that end" (Prince v. Massachusetts, 1944, p. 165). Equally significantly, *Prince* established that parental authority was not without limits. It signaled the beginning of the idea that a state can exercise authority over parents' control of their children's upbringing. Indeed, *Prince* retains the status as being the constitutional bedrock of modern child welfare law, as it announced that parents may become martyrs if they like but they are not "free...to make martyrs of their children" (Prince v. Massachusetts, 1944, p. 170). *Prince* had spurred the Court's move toward protection of societal interests as defined and asserted by the State. Together, the cases reveal the Court's move away from providing protections for religious liberty significantly stronger than the protection of belief alone that had been afforded by *Reynolds*. The cases stand for the claim that the government serves as arbiter between religion and the state, and that the state can hold considerable power when it enlists its broad public health and police powers.

The early 1990s cases, then, held the view that the Constitution generally protected religious exercise under the First Amendment, but that this protection did not prevent the government from passing neutral laws that incidentally impact certain religious practices. Religious groups objected to this development, as they became concerned that this line of cases would be cited as precedent for further regulation of common religious practices. Congress responded by passing the Religious Freedom Restoration Act (RFRA), which sought to restore the "strict scrutiny" standard that would be more protective of religion, as it would require a narrowly tailored regulation serving a compelling government interest in any case substantially burdening the free exercise of religion, regardless of the intent and general applicability of the law. By increasing the protection of religion, the RFRA sought to limit the state's power to regulate it.

RFRA itself became victim to the Supreme Court's position. As RFRA related to the states, the Court overturned it in *City of Boerne v. Flores*

(1997). In that case, a dispute arose when the Catholic Archbishop of San Antonio, Patrick Flores, applied for a building permit to enlarge his 1923 mission-style St. Peter's Church in the historic district of Boerne, Texas. His permit was rejected on the grounds of an ordinance that governed additions and new construction in a historic district. Relying on RFRA, Archbishop Flores argued that his congregation had outgrown the existing structure, rendering the court's ruling a substantial burden on the free exercise of religion without a compelling state interest. The Supreme Court struck down the provisions of RFEA that forced state and local governments to provide protections exceeding those required by the First Amendment, which the courts enjoy sole power to interpret. The Court ruled that Congress had exceeded its powers, that the Court alone retains the ability to declare which rights are protected by the Fourteenth Amendment (the Amendment that the Court had used to "incorporate" the First Amendment into state law). By doing so, the Court brought an end to legislative attempts to overturn *Employment Division v. Smith.* According to the Court's ruling in *Gonzales v. UDV* (2006), RFRA remains applicable to federal statutes, which must therefore still meet the "strict scrutiny" standard in free exercise cases. As a result of these cases, *Smith* rules: As long as a law does not target a particular religious practice, it does not violate the Free Exercise Clause.

*Smith* provides the government with a powerful tool previously thought essentially unimaginable. Although it does not require it, the *Smith* rule does give the state considerable power to regulate religion, but that power needs to be, in a real sense, incidental. In addition, and equally notable, *Smith* signaled that the Court would not read the Free Exercise Clause as generally requiring accommodation of religion, but it made clear that legislatures would be permitted to provide accommodation if they so desired. The previously thought firm legal wall separating church and state certainly does not appear to apply much to the government's power to limit people's freedom to practice their religion.

## The Establishment Clause

History books may center on the clause's importance for prohibiting the establishment or declaration of a national religion by Congress, but the clause's reach is much more broad than that and jurisprudence in this area essentially has ignored that narrow issue as it continues to be taken for granted. This development may be ironic to some who view the nation as based on a Christian/Protestant viewpoint, but, at its core, the clause is understood as focusing on prohibiting Congress (and by judicial interpretation, the states; see *Everson v. Board of Education,* 1947) from preferring one religion over another. As noted earlier, given how religion infuses human life and social institutions, this is no easy prohibition. Although this clause has been the subject of much commentary and its interpretation remains highly nuanced (and often context specific), commentators and judicial interpretations tend to coalesce along two polar points of preference to be given to religious beliefs and groups. One end point seeks to create a wall of separation between religions and the state, and thus provide no aid or support. The other end point seeks to accommodate religious beliefs and practices by permitting some support for religious groups or religiously motivated policies. Thus, the former prohibits state interference while the latter permits state entry into religious domains. As expected, adopting either of these approaches can lead to dramatically different outcomes, and both can be found in jurisprudence in this area.

*Everson v. Board of Education* (1947) served as the vehicle for the Supreme Court's modern foray into this area of jurisprudence, as it both used and challenged the metaphor of a wall of separation between church and state that had been established in *Reynolds. Everson* involved a New Jersey taxpayer's challenge to the use of taxes to reimburse parents of both public and private school children who took the public transportation system to school. The challenge rested on the claim that the reimbursement that went to parents of children attending religious schools violated the Establishment Clause. The Court was unanimous in its support of the need for a wall of separation between church and state, but the justices sharply differed on what that meant. The ruling opinion held that the state acted permissibly because the reimbursements were offered to all students regardless of religion and because the payments were made to parents and not any religious institution. The dissenting justices argued the opposite: that the principles of separation required invalidating the challenged law on the grounds, for example, that parents who were getting reimbursed by state funds for sending their children to parochial schools meant that the state aid was supporting religious training and teaching, and thus violated the Constitution's Establishment Clause mandate that there be a wall of separation between church and state. Perhaps because it contained strong dissenting opinions clearly articulating opposite views that highlighted a different vision of establishment, the case would continue to frame

Establishment Clause cases. The case would retain prominence because it reflected not only the broad interpretation of the clause's prohibition but also the challenge of determining what that prohibition meant, with some insisting that the Constitution forbids all forms of public aid or support for religion and others permitting incidental support (which they did not even define as support).

A flurry of cases sought to clarify the parameters of the separation between church and state. These cases are notable for their development of various standards that the Court would announce in an effort to guide lawmakers, and the rhetoric that would support them. A key development was the construction of the rhetoric that religious organizations had beneficial and stabilizing effects, as highlighted in *Walz v. Tax Commission* (1970). In that case, the Court extended the Establishment Clause doctrine considerably as it sustained a state law providing real estate tax exemptions for churches and other religious organizations, just as it does other nonprofits like public schools and universities. It is difficult to play down the significance of such support, but it also is difficult to argue that the Court consistently supported religious institutions. Most notably, the line of cases from *Everson* to this point, which appeared to favor a robust protection of religions, culminated in *Lemon v. Kurtzman* (1971). That case involved a challenge to a law that permitted reimbursement to nonpublic schools (mostly Catholic) for the salaries of teachers who taught secular material in these nonpublic schools, using secular textbooks and secular instructional materials. The Court reasoned that the law violated the Establishment Clause. That result was significant but *Lemon* became more significant for the doctrine it announced. The case provided the leading standard for analyzing establishment challenges. The Court declared that a state action was not establishment if (1) the statute (or practice) has a secular purpose, (2) its principal or primary effect neither advances nor inhibits religion, and (3) it does not foster an excessive government entanglement with religion. Although some justices (and many commentators) have criticized the approach, the Court continues to consider variations of the three-pronged tests and, indeed, adds other prongs to it to address nuances in Establishment Clause challenges.

The establishment clause jurisprudence that followed *Lemon* reflected its broad impact, as revealed in several cases that exemplify the breadth and depth of the factors that the Court considers in Establishment challenges. *Agostini v. Felton* (1997) demoted the entanglement prong of the *Lemon* test simply to being a factor in determining the challenged statute or practice's effect. In that case, the Court ruled that it was permissible for a state-sponsored educational initiative to allow public school teachers to instruct at religious schools, so long as the material was secular and neutral in nature and no "excessive entanglement" between government and religion was apparent. In *Bowen v. Kendrick* (1988), the Court rejected a challenge against using federal funds, under the federal *Adolescent Family Life Act*, to do research and provide services relating to adolescent sexuality. The Act essentially required recipients of the funds to provide services that were more likely to mirror those of religious groups (e.g., focus on abstinence-based sexuality education rather than comprehensive sexuality education), which some viewed as showing preference to religious groups. The Court, however, found that the secular concern simply mirrored those of some religious groups and that the support was merely incidental (rather than meant to direct establishment). The Court was not concerned with excessive entanglement, as it would be simple for the government to monitor where funds were spent. In *Zelman v. Simmons-Harris* (2002), the Court addressed whether school vouchers, the vast majority of which at that point were used to support children's going to religiously affiliated schools, violated the Establishment Clause. The Court used the opportunity to expand the *Lemon* test into a five-point test to evaluate establishment: (1) the program must have a valid secular purpose, (2) aid must go to parents and not to the schools, (3) a broad class of beneficiaries must be covered, (4) the program must be neutral with respect to religion, and (5) there must be adequate nonreligious options. Following this standard, the Court found that the aid went directly to parents and thus the benefit to religious institutions was only incidental; this was unlike in *Lemon* in which the support went directly to the institutions themselves (and not permitted). The Court also would use *Lemon* in *Santa Fe Independent School District v. Doe* (2000), in which it ruled that a policy permitting student-led, student-initiated prayer at high school football games violated the Establishment Clause due to excessive entanglement with the school's policies and practices relating to the prayers. Yet, in *Good News Club v. Milford Central School* (2001), the Court held that a school could not exclude a religious club, one aimed at proselytizing young children, from meeting in the school, after school hours, just because the club is religious in nature; the Court partly ruled in this manner because the government (school) was acting in a neutral manner toward religion. The Court did so even though it famously had rejected school prayers at graduation, in *Lee v. Weisman* (1992, p. 592), on the rationale that "[t]here are heightened concerns with protecting freedom of conscience from subtle coercive pressure in the elementary and secondary public schools... [and] prayer exercises in public schools carry a particular risk of indirect coercion." The group meetings in *Good News Club*, after school and supported by parents, were deemed as not coercive toward children. Lastly, in *Mitchell v. Helms* (2000), the Court rejected a challenge to the use of federal funds to support the purchase of educational materials purchased by religious schools. The Court did more than reject the request to focus on the pervasively sectarian nature of the recipient's religious views; it found such an "inquiry into the recipient's religious views... not only unnecessary but also offensive" (*Mitchell v. Helms*, 2000, p. 828). These general developments tend to show a movement toward developing laws and policies that permit support for religious beliefs so long as they do not favor a particular sect and are consistent with the secular government's goals. In a real sense, we have a switch away from the rhetoric of separation to the rhetoric of equality and neutrality.

### ▲ Lessons Learned From the Regulation of Religion

We have learned that the Constitution reigns, that the Constitution provides the standards on which to evaluate governmental actions, and that the Supreme Court serves as final arbiter of that evaluation. As a result, and in a real sense, the state controls religion in that a secular purpose could override a parochial one. Most notably, this is seen in criminal law, child welfare law, health care law, family law, and essentially all laws that regulate how people treat one another or how an institution should behave. Indeed, a look at all major institutions regulated by the state reveals instances in which the power of the state can override religious beliefs and customs.

The constitutional protections concern themselves with state actions, with what the state can and cannot do. The general goal is to free individuals from state interference, which includes not supporting specific religions and religious beliefs. Importantly and as we have seen, the state may end up supporting some beliefs or religious institutions, which currently is deemed permissible, for example, so long as the benefits are incidental to a secular purpose. This was decisively announced in *Employment Division v. Smith* (1990, p. 879), which noted "that the right of free exercise does not relieve an individual of the obligation to comply with a 'valid and neutral law of general applicability on the ground that the law proscribes (or prescribes) conduct that his religion prescribes (or proscribes).'" The Court held that it would be wise for states to avoid creating religious exemptions to generally applicable laws as a matter of individual entitlement but that, if they wished to create such exemptions, they could do so without running afoul of the Establishment Clause. Although the Court endorsed legislative accommodation, the power to do so clearly remained with the state.

The constitutional protections relating to religion belong to everyone; the law does not recognize periods (or stages) of human development in this area of jurisprudence. This is of significance for two reasons. First, it demonstrates how protections focus on the liberty of the autonomous individual vis-à-vis the state. Thus, when some individuals may not be deemed competent enough to exercise their own rights, such as children and individuals with mentally debilitating conditions, others deemed legally competent serve as proxies for them. Second, it demonstrates how, in a real sense, this area of law (like other areas of First Amendment law) focuses on the liberty of the autonomous individual vis-à-vis the state in the public sphere. What happens in the private sphere (outside of state control, such as much of what happens in families) remains broadly beyond state regulation and, as a result, can be under the control of religious beliefs and institutions. When the state involves itself directly in private life, such as family decision making, it largely does so to protect individuals from harm, such as children from the irreparable harms that would arise from their parents' acting on their faiths (such as through faith healing) in instances that would jeopardize their children's safety (see Levesque, 2008), Absent such extremes, the law protects the rights of parents to direct the religious upbringing of their children and what adults wish to believe and practice as it relates to their consciences and relationships (Levesque, 2002).

Despite the state's immense power to regulate religion, much of the doctrine in this area remains entirely unapplied to large swaths of conduct that occurs at the intersection of religion and government. Across a whole range of government actions, religiously motivated decisions can be made and the Court will remove itself from evaluating claims through the Establishment and Free Exercise clauses. For example, the Court pervasively avoids inquiring deeply into the actual provenance of legislative actions as long as the laws have a legitimate secular legislative purpose. This is not a trivial matter, as it relates squarely to many of the policy controversies dividing along religious lines—abortion, contraception, stem-cell research, same-sex marriage, and end-of-life care—as well as broad policy reforms relating to highly regulated institutions foundational to the state's mission in modern civil society and to the lives of emerging adults: health, education, criminal justice, welfare, social security, and employment. Indeed, in some of these cases, the Court actually does not even examine the actual provenance of government legislation. Abortion likely provides the most litigated, controversial, and obvious example. In *Harris v. McRae* (1980, p. 319), the Court rejected an Establishment Clause challenge to restrictions on abortion funding, holding that it would not assume that religion is being advanced because a law "happens to coincide or harmonize with the tenets of some or all religions." Similar results emerged in *Bowen v. Kendrick* (1988), a case that supported a narrow view of sexuality education and prevention services that paralleled the beliefs of conservative religious groups championing abstinence-based approaches and eschewed more comprehensive responses to sexual activity. In such cases, religiously infused and inspired policy agendas can survive if they can be justified without reference to religion. Even if a law is motivated by a particular belief or religious constituency, the Court will uphold it if a plausible secular criterion can be raised and religious authorities are not formally exercising state powers (see *Board of Education of Kiryas Joel Village School v. Grumet*, 1994, where the Court rejected an effort to draw the boundaries of a school district based on an area occupied by a religious group). Aside from restricting these formal grants of authority to religious groups, however, the Establishment Clause doctrine does not easily reach informal political interactions between religious groups and government officials. Religious organizations and activists can lobby for certain laws on the basis that they are required by their religions, and legislators may vote for such legislation because of their own individual religious commitments. Indeed, the Constitution does not prohibit politicians from making political alliances with specific churches or religious groups, explicitly endorsing their messages, or asking and receiving their financial assistance. These domains of inapplicability are of significance in that they allow courts to avoid putting the state to the burden of providing secular justifications for laws supporting religions and religious beliefs, not even in instances where the laws have a religious provenance or coincide with the tenets of a particular religion.

Despite the above areas of unregulated activity that occur at the intersection of religion and the state, it is important to emphasize the lesson that regulation has real effects. Most notably, we have seen how the Court can seriously limit the free exercise of religion when it contravenes criminal and other laws. Likewise, the Court will not permit civil governments to cede their powers to religious entities, fund religious institutions directly, discriminate among religions in the disbursement of funds, and directly introduce religious practices in schools. These are considerably real and potentially broad limits. Yet we also have seen the importance of an emerging trend toward neutrality and equality that permits states, in indirect ways, to reach ends that would otherwise have been prohibited. Again, the significance of these new developments cannot be understated as they provide important nuances to what have been deemed broad prohibitions.

## ▲ Lessons for the Study of Emerging Adulthood

Despite considerable Supreme Court attention to the laws relating to religion, the breadth of this area of law necessarily means that much actually remains remarkably uncharted. Much significance attaches to the legal developments identified above, but the jurisprudence merely sets broad parameters that guide the future implementation of policies. The developments still leave considerably open how the government actually will consider the place of religion in its policies, including the extent to which the government will enlist religious institutions and beliefs or limit intrusions on them. Notably, for example, just because the government can enact policies that, in a neutral manner, support some religious groups and beliefs over others, it does not follow that governments would enact such policies. At their core, current legal developments merely highlight the increasing flexibility of the government's role in influencing religious development and institutions as well as the factors that might influence them. That flexibility gains significance for research on emerging adulthood for three fundamental reasons.

First, to the extent that emerging adulthood actually constitutes a distinct period of human development, this time period raises important issues for understanding the nature of religious development, religious experience, and support for religious institutions. For example, the leading scholar in the study of emerging adulthood, Jeffrey Arnett, conducted a compelling analysis of religious beliefs among emerging adults (Arnett & Jensen, 2002). His study rightly concluded that emerging adults' religious beliefs were highly individualized in the United States. Importantly, he also found little relation between childhood religious socialization and emerging adults' religious attendance or beliefs, a point emphasizing the importance of social forces shaping emerging adulthood during that period itself and highlighting the peculiar importance of that period. Regardless of whether researchers wish to emphasize continuity or discontinuity in development, religious development and experiences in emerging adulthood appear to present a period important to consider in their own right (see also Barry, Nelson, Davarya, & Urry, 2010).

Second, even if the period of emerging adulthood constitutes a clearly discernible period, existing research still highlights the need to consider variation as well as multiple social influences on its development, including the place of religion in it. For example, Milevsky and Leh (2008) highlighted the significance of simultaneously examining multiple contextual variables in efforts to understand the multidimensional nature of religious expression in emerging adulthood. They found that factors relating to family life influence religiosity, such as parental divorce, parents' marital satisfaction, and family support. In addition, they found that the well-established psychological dimensions of extrinsic versus intrinsic religiosity play prominent roles in influencing healthy adjustment (such as intrinsic religiosity relating to higher levels of self-esteem). Thus, even though the period of emerging adulthood could be regarded as its own distinct developmental period, the understanding of other aspects of human development, particularly of the factors influencing development, necessarily will need to be investigated to shed important light on the nature and experience of emerging adulthood (see also O'Connor et al., 2011). Without doubt, the understanding of religious development, the factors that influence it, and the importance of those factors in shaping healthy development all can serve as important areas of inquiry to understanding emerging adulthood and the place of religion in human development and the broader society.

Third, the above two factors make this area of research ripe for influencing research and policy relating to religion. Constitutional law may need to rest on legal grounds rather than on empirical findings and postulations, but legal frameworks benefit from close empirical analysis (see Levesque, 2002). Empirical analyses are important to consider not only for understanding the potential nature and effect of policies but also to help envision appropriate ones that further governmental interests. For example, much concern centers on the use of tax monies to support school vouchers. Primary among such concerns has been the worry that the vouchers may foster societal divisions for the simple reason that religious groups currently benefit the most from their support. Yet researchers have demonstrated that parochial schools actually appear to produce an opposite effect. In particular, Catholic schools increase students' civic responsibility, concern for communities, and support for the disenfranchised, such as immigrant groups (see, e.g., Minow, 2010). Supporting Catholic schools with public funds, however, may have negative effects to the extent that it can draw funds from other schools, especially state-run public schools. Importantly, as the school voucher example reveals, research findings do not determine policy outcomes. Rather, research provides insights to enlighten policy alternatives; whether to embrace one alternative over another remains a political decision.

The political decisions exemplified by controversies and concerns regarding school vouchers to support parochial schooling have yet to be examined fully in a variety of state-supported services that use voucher systems directly impacting emerging adults. Voucher-like systems can take many forms, and they may be used either when the state intervenes in emerging adults' lives when they do not want interventions or when emerging adults willingly seek out and accept state aid. Examples again range widely to include vouchers for child care, housing, medical treatment, therapeutic interventions, food, family planning, employment training, and higher education. Examples even include court-mandated treatment for substance abuse and other problem behaviors as well as court interventions that remove children from their care to place them in foster care or assist with ailing parents placed in homes for the elderly. Yet empirical efforts have yet to shed light on the role of religion in these voucher systems and those systems' effects on religious institutions, even though religious groups constitute the largest service providers for many voucher systems supported by the state.

The above three points highlight the ripeness of this area of research and its import for emerging adults and society itself. As shown throughout, the legal system regulates religious environments that can influence emerging adults' lives, ranging from their intimate relationships, work environments, health, family lives, and education, to their levels of civic engagement and to their religious experiences themselves. This means that the legal system can influence the systems that give meaning to lives and that serve as the glue that holds society together. Research can play important roles in determining precisely how the legal system can influence these aspects of their lives, how best the legal system could do so, and whether the government actually should do so.

## ▲ Conclusion: The Reshaping of Efforts to Regulate Religion

The Supreme Court's doctrine relating to religion may be famously confused, contested, and confusing, but we have identified important trends. Indeed, the past two decades have witnessed a dramatic reshaping of American law relating to religion. Legislative and executive actions that led to *Employment Division v. Smith* (1990), and what often is viewed as the Supreme Court's reinterpretation of the Free Exercise clause, have resulted in increased governmental endorsement, financial subsidization, and other privileging of religion. This governmental support may not be direct, but it is governmental support nevertheless. Similarly, legislative and executive actions also led to an altering of the Establishment Clause doctrine that has contributed to a noticeable collapse of the "wall of separation" between "church and state," as highlighted by *Zelman v. Simmons-Harris* (2002), and enlarged the social status and power of religious organizations that can benefit from the government's support so long as the government acts neutrally and treats religions (and nonreligious institutions) equally. Lastly, despite the explicit constitutional mandate that governments will not infringe on the free exercise of religion or will not establish it, the Court remains reluctant to regulate large areas of activity that occur at the intersection of religion and the state, including the actual religious provenance of government legislation. That reluctance may be due to the typical reasons for judicial underenforcement (political pragmatism, institutional competence, and privileging democratic-processes), but the result remains. Together, these developments reveal a discernible move toward protecting religious freedom while, at the same time, setting broad parameters that grant the state ultimate authority over the exercise of religion and state support for it. Also together, these developments actualize the general constitutional vision that the state, as much as practicable, must maintain distance from institutions and ways of thinking that give human and societal development their fullest meaning. Considered full adults under law, emerging adults certainly enjoy important religious freedoms, but their freedoms may be much more curtailed than they might expect. These very possibilities provide those who study the place of religion during emerging adulthood with considerable opportunities to inform governmental policies and make incredibly important contributions to research, law, policy, and society.

## ▲ References

Agostini v. Felton. 521 U.S. 203 (1997).

Arnett, J. J. (2004). *Emerging adulthood: The winding road from the late teens through the twenties*. New York, NY: Oxford University Press.

Arnett, J. J., & Jensen, L. J. (2002). A congregation of one: Individualized religious beliefs among emerging adults. *Journal of Adolescent Research, 17*, 451–467.

Barry, C. M., Nelson, L. J., Davarya, S., & Urry, S. (2010). Religiosity and spirituality during the transition to adulthood. *International Journal of Behavioral Development, 34*, 311–324. doi: 10.1177/0165025409350964

Board of Education of Kiryas Joel Village School v. Grumet. 512 U.S. 687 (1994).

Bowen v. Kendrick. 487 U.S. 589 (1988).

Campbell, D. E., & Putnam, R.D. (2010). America's grace: How a tolerant nation bridges its religious divides. *Political Science Quarterly, 126*, 611–640.

Cantwell v. Connecticut. 310 U.S. 296 (1940).

Church of Lukumi Babalu Aye v. City of Hialeah. 508 U.S. 520 (1993).

City of Boerne v. Flores. 521 U.S. 507 (1997).

Corbin, C.M. (2012). The contraception mandate. *Northwestern University Law Review Colloquy, 107*, 151–164.

Eberle-Peay, D. (2012). The federal Constitution versus a state constitution: Revisiting *Zelman v. Simmons-Harris* in Indiana. *Journal of Law & Education, 41*, 709–721.

Employment Division v. Smith. 494 U.S. 872 (1990).

Everson v. Board of Education. 330 U.S. 1 (1947).

Glendon, M. A. (2012). Religious freedom—A second-class right? *Emory Law Journal, 61*, 971–990.

Gonzales v. UDV. 546 U.S. 418 (2006).

Good News Club v. Milford Central School. 533 U.S. 98 (2001).

Harris v. McRae. 448 U.S. 297 (1980).

Inglehart, R. F., Basañez, M., Diez-Medrano, J., Halman, L., & Luijkx, R. (2004). *Human beliefs and values: A cross-cultural sourcebook based on the 1999–2002 value surveys*. Mexico City, MX: Siglo XXI.

Lee v. Weisman. 505 U.S. 577 (1992).

Lemon v. Kurtzman. 403 U.S. 602 (1971).

Lendino, T. P. (2011). From *Rosenberger* to Martinez: Why the rise of hypermodernism is a bad thing for religious freedom. *Campbell Law Review, 33*, 699–722.

Levesque, R. J. R. (2002). *Not by faith alone: Religion, adolescence and the law*. New York, NY: New York University Press.

Levesque, R. J. R. (2008). *Rethinking child maltreatment law: Returning to first principles*. New York, NY: Springer.

Meyer v. Nebraska. 262 U.S. 390 (1923).

Milevsky, A., & Leh, M. (2008). Religiosity in emerging adulthood: Familial variables and adjustment. *Journal of Adult Development, 15*, 47–53.

Minow, M. (2010). *In Brown's Wake: Legacies of America's Educational Landmark*. New York, NY: Oxford University Press.

Mitchell v. Helms. 530 U.S. 793 (2000).

O'Connor, M., Sanson, A., Hawkins, M. T., Letcher, P., Toumbourou, J. W., Smart, D., Vassalla, S., & Olsson, C. A. (2011). Predictors of positive development in emerging adulthood. *Journal of Youth & Adolescence, 40*, 860–874.

Perlin, J. (2011). Religion as a conversation starter: What liberal religious political advocates add to the debate about religion's place in legal and political discourse. *Georgetown Law Journal, 100*, 331–365.

Pierce v. Society of Sisters. 268 U.S. 510 (1925).

Prince v. Massachusetts. 321 U.S. 158 (1944).

Reynolds v. United States. 98 U.S. 145 (1878).

Santa Fe Independent School Dist. v. Doe. 530 U.S. 290 (2000).

Sherbert v. Verner. 374 U.S. 398 (1963).

Smith, C. (with Snell, P.). (2009). *Souls in transition: The religious and spiritual lives of emerging adults*. New York, NY: Oxford University Press.

Walz v. Tax Commission. 397 U.S. 664 (1970).

Wisconsin v. Yoder. 406 U.S. 205 (1972).

Zelman v. Simmons-Harris. 536 U.S. 639 (2002).

# 8 ▲

# Religious Congregations
# and Communities

WILLIAM B. WHITNEY AND PAMELA EBSTYNE KING

*When I go to temple, I do have a strong religious*
*connection and I feel like I'm connected with God*
*because I'm around people who worship and they are*
*abiding by all the morals and doing good.*
                              —King, Ramos, & Clardy, 2013

This quotation, by a practicing Hindu emerging adult, illustrates a number of points discussed in this chapter that demonstrate the significance of religious participation for many emerging adults in the United States. For many emerging adults, religious communities and congregations are an important resource for consolidating identity, and a growing body of research points to spirituality being a key factor in making meaning or constructing a coherent "narrative out of one's life situations" (Barry, Nelson, Davarya, & Urry, 2010, p. 311). Although recent research reveals a rise in emerging adults (18–29 years) who report no affiliation with a specific religious tradition, spirituality and religion still remain important to many emerging adults within the United States (DeHaan, Yonker, & Affholter, 2011; Pew Forum on Religion and Public Life, 2012; Smith, 2009). This chapter examines trends in emerging adults' religious involvement with religious congregations and communities and discusses how their engagement (or lack of engagement) is indicative of the developmental tasks characteristic to their life stage.

First, we begin by discussing general trends in emerging adults' participation in religious congregations and communities and define key terms that relate to religious and spiritual development. Second, we explore emerging adults' various levels of participation in both formal religious congregations and informal religious communities, while considering how both are an important resource for some in meaning-making, discovering a sense of purpose and identity formation. Finally, we examine how identity formation occurs in these religious groups and submit that religious congregations and communities are complex ecological systems that provide opportunities for meaning-making through various *ideological, social,* and *transcendent* contexts.

## ▲ Defining Religious Involvement in Congregations and Communities

For those in industrialized nations who postpone the roles of marriage and parenthood, the years of 18–29 offer an unprecedented state of freedom for emerging adults to rethink religious beliefs and convictions—and this may include participating or choosing not to participate in a religious community or congregation (Arnett, 2004). For some, religious communities provide stability and an opportunity for emerging adults to clarify their own beliefs as well as understand their own identity. For other emerging adults, given expectations to adhere to behavioral norms, religious communities may be seen as compromising their opportunity to think for themselves, involving too much commitment, or compromising their independence.

It is important to define and differentiate what we mean when we speak of spirituality, religiousness, religious participation, and religious development. *Religiousness* and *religious participation* are terms used to describe the extent to which an individual understands and engages the doctrines, practices, rituals, and communities of a religious tradition. *Religious development* refers to the systematic changes in how an individual understands and utilizes the doctrines, practices, and rituals of a religious congregation or community. Religious development generally occurs through affiliation with a religious group and participation in its prescribed rituals and practices—and/or assent to its prescribed beliefs (King et al., 2013). That being said, *congregations* are formal assemblies of individuals who are guided by common doctrines who gather for common religious worship, education, and fellowship, while *religious communities* refer to more informal and diverse forms of gatherings for religious purposes such as faith-based organizations, para-church/congregation organizations, campus ministries, and faith-based singles' groups. *Spirituality* is the broader and more overlapping construct, but it is unique from religiousness in that it may or may not take place within a religious context, congregation, or community. Spirituality is often referred to as the search for the sacred or transcendent (Pargament,

2007). As such, spirituality refers to transcending the self to the extent that one's beliefs and commitments are transformed and one is propelled to live in a manner mindful of others (King et al., 2013). Spirituality may or may not involve religious participation, but it does play a vital role in understanding the worldview of emerging adults. While emerging adults' spirituality is a significant topic, our primary focus is on the role that formal religious congregations and informal religious communities play in the lives of emerging adults and how their participation contributes to their religious development, the ability to make meaning and consolidate their identity.

## ▲ Trends in Participation in Religious Congregations and Communities

Religious beliefs often change during emerging adulthood due to exposure to new ideas, and emerging adults' desire to decide for themselves often results in a moratorium on religious participation. Yet the general trends in the existing research demonstrate that while active religious participation declines during emerging adulthood, religious and spiritual beliefs continue to be important (see Chapter 2). Over half of emerging adults still hold that faith or religion is important or quite important in their daily lives (Arnett, 2004), and yet they may not actively participate in a religious congregation or community. Given this disconnect between religious participation and beliefs, actual attendance in religious groups does not always correspond with the significance that emerging adults claim that religious or spiritual beliefs have in their lives (Koenig, McGue, & Iacono, 2008; Smith, 2005).[1]

---

1. The most recent research data available on these trends is offered by the Pew Research Center's Forum on Religion and Public Life in a survey conducted in 2012. According to the Pew Research, "The growth in the number of religiously unaffiliated Americans—sometimes called the rise of the 'nones'—is largely driven by generational replacement, the gradual supplanting of older generations by newer ones. A third of adults under 30 have no religious affiliation (32%), compared with just one-in-ten who are 65 and older (9%). And young adults today are much more likely to be unaffiliated than previous generations were at a similar stage in their lives." Moreover, this group of the unaffiliated is less "religious than the public at large on many conventional measures, including frequency of attendance at religious services and the degree of importance they attach to religion and their lives" (Pew Forum on Religion and Public Life, 2012, pp. 9–10).

Smith (2009) similarly reports that while belief in God and importance of faith remain more constant during emerging adulthood, religious service attendance declines for most religious traditions, with 1 out of 3 emerging adults attending religious services regularly or semiregularly (two times per month or more).[2] Those identifying as the Church of Jesus Christ of Latter-day Saints (LDS), conservative Protestant, and Black Protestant report the highest level of religious involvement, and in some cases report growth in religious faith during this time (Smith, 2009). Moreover, by examining cultural and ethnic differences, other important distinctions emerge. According to Arnett, 46% of African Americans reported attending services 3–4 times per month compared to 14% of Whites, 20% of Latinos, and 35% of Asian Americans (Arnett, 2004). Not surprisingly then, 54% of African Americans in Arnett's study indicated that they were "very certain" about their religious beliefs, which is significantly higher than any other ethnic group (Arnett, 2004).

Yet the decline in regular participation among emerging adults is not limited to religious congregations. In general, emerging adults are not only less religiously committed but also less involved in and committed to a wide variety of other nonreligious institutional connections, associations, and activities (Smith, 2009). This research points to other broad cultural and contextual factors of emerging adulthood that need to be considered. The contexts in which emerging adults find themselves are constantly changing due to moving, job changes, a diverse and broad network of friends (compared to later in life), and uncertainty in romantic relationships (Barry et al., 2010; Osgood, Ruth, Eccles, Jacobs, & Barber, 2005). These instabilities may contribute to the decline in civic and institutional nonreligious activities, in addition to a decline in religious participation.

## ▲ Regular Participants in Formal Religious Congregations

But what about those emerging adults who *do* participate regularly in religious services or congregations, and what difference does their level

2. The most detailed picture of emerging adults' involvement in religious congregations that we have available is Smith's (2009) research, which draws upon survey data from the National Study of Youth and Religion (NSYR) of emerging adults ages 18–23 years. This 2009 publication on emerging adults followed Smith and Denton's 2005 research on the spiritual lives of adolescents ages 13–17.

of religious engagement make in their lives? According to Smith (2009), within each religious tradition[3] there is a wide range of "personal religious belief, commitment and practice" ranging from the highly committed to the less committed (p. 258). While each religious tradition is comprised of those who are highly engaged as well as those who are less engaged, this scholar notes that the most significant differences appear when emerging adults were categorized according to *actual degrees of religious participation.* Significant differences in social involvement, well-being, and giving are present when the groups were divided up into the following categories:

1. The devoted (reported attending religious services weekly or more often)
2. The regular (reported attending religious services two or three times a month or more)
3. The sporadic (attending services a few times a year to monthly attendance)
4. The disengaged (reported never attending religious services)

Those classified as "devoted" religious participants across the major religious traditions demonstrated that religious faith and practice did make a difference in their life experiences, beliefs, and behaviors, when compared to disengaged emerging adults. As noted previously, civic engagement, volunteering, and giving *generally decline* among emerging adults, but for the minority that remain devoted (and those who regularly attend), these forms of civic engagement do not. Both devoted and regular attendees of religious congregations are more likely to have given monetarily to an organization or cause and volunteered for a nonmandatory community service more than those who sporadically attend religious services or those who are disengaged (Smith, 2009). The groups of the devoted and regular attenders are more likely to participate in face-to-face organized activities (even nonreligious activities) than are the sporadic or disengaged attenders. The devoted and regular attenders of religious services also are much less likely to binge-drink or engage in other similar risk behaviors. In addition, differences emerge when looking at those who regularly attend religious services compared to those who sporadically attend or never attend services on measures of overall well-being and social bonding. The most religiously

3. The categories of "traditions" used by Smith are as follows: conservative Protestant, mainline Protestant, Black Protestant, Catholic, LDS, Jewish, other religions, and those classified as not religious. In addition, Smith's research sample only included the early years of emerging adulthood, ages 18–23 years.

committed reported higher feelings of overall purpose in life with clear goals, and they reported having feelings of gratitude more frequently than do those who are disengaged from any religious participation (Smith, 2009). Consequently, while religious participation dramatically declines for many emerging adults, for the minority group of the "devoted" or "regular" attenders in religious congregations, religious participation does make a difference in behaviors, goals, and measures of well-being.

## ▲ Informal Religious Communities

Having discussed the differences that exist among committed or devoted attenders of religious congregations, this section discusses possible trajectories that enable meaning-making and identity formation within informal religious gatherings. While informal religious groups may be more difficult to define than a formal religious congregation, these groups still play an important role in the lives of emerging adults. While less "formal" than an actual religious congregation, these gatherings still have goals, norms, and beliefs that are central for their particular community and are often connected with a larger, more formal religious congregation, although they might not always be (Maton, Sto. Domingo, & Westin, 2013). Furthermore, while many participants might regularly attend these informal gatherings, there is also effort made to welcome those who might be less religiously committed to explore aspects of faith. Some case examples will help to clarify the importance and function of these groups.

**Case Example 1** In 2003 the Young Adult Ministry of the Archdiocese of Chicago partnered with a Catholic Spiritual Organization (RENEW International) to launch an initiative called "Theology on Tap" with the aim of addressing topics of faith that are of interest to young adults. Although the program had existed in Chicago since 1981, "Theology on Tap" represents an informal community that can be found in many major cities across the United States. The current goal of "Theology on Tap" is to help young adults meet others who have similar faith interests, to help attendees feel welcomed in the Catholic Church, and to serve as an entry point into other Catholic young adult programs (Renew International's Theology on Tap, 2013). As the name implies, drinking and eating are central features of the gathering, and the informal setting in a bar or restaurant creates an environment that is conducive to relationship building. Although faith topics are presented from a Catholic perspective, non-Catholic and the spiritually curious are invited to attend. Each meeting involves a speaker (speakers vary from ordained clergy to other church leaders) who present on a theological topic with time for discussion. The time also includes "faith sharing" and "community building" that focus on the social aspects of religious development and encourage participants to share their own perspective on the topic of discussion (Renew International's Theology on Tap, 2013). An important aspect of this gathering is that while greater commitment to the Catholic Church is encouraged, it is not required. In this way, Theology on Tap seeks to create an atmosphere or environment where faith can be explored and nurtured, and where service to the local neighborhood or community is encouraged.

**Case Example 2** In 2011 the LDS church reorganized its congregational system to create communities (or "wards" in LDS terminology) that are specifically for young single adults ages 18–30 (Kaleem, 2012). Results of these changes are more informal gatherings that occur during the week, specifically for young single adults. Most of the singles wards are close to universities (where emerging adults might be away from their families, or in cities like New York or Washington, DC, where there are large numbers of Mormon emerging adults). The LDS church encourages Monday nights to be a time set aside to be with one's family for a time typically called "Family Home Evenings" (M. Bowman, personal communication, February 9, 2013). However, in these young single adult wards, Monday nights have become a time to take the concept of "Family Home Evenings" and meet for teaching and socializing with other single adults—which occurs in a more relaxed setting than the typical Sunday services. The goal of the LDS young single adult wards was to provide more opportunities for young adults to teach and to lead, to meet others, and to help engage young adults in aspects of service.

These examples highlight several vital features of informal communities, while they do not encompass the full range of possibilities for all informal gatherings. Sometimes led by young adults and unofficial leaders from a religious congregation, many informal gatherings take place on or near college campuses in order to provide students with the opportunity to become involved with others who share similar faith perspectives (see Chapter 9). Yet these informal communities still hold important potential for shaping convictions and beliefs of emerging adults, emphasizing social and relational aspects of faith, as well as encouraging those who might be interested in religion or spirituality to come and explore aspects of a particular faith community. For instance, aspects of vocation, ethics, and sexuality are points of interest for many emerging adults, and informal communities offer an accessible format for young adults to come hear about these topics and find out how a particular faith community might approach these subjects. Moreover, informal communities often have leaders within the group who are interested in mentoring or guiding younger members or those who are exploring their faith. In this way, the relational and social aspects of the religious community are used to help others develop their faith or promote an atmosphere where sharing or dialogue can take place.

## ▲ Identity Formation in the Ecological System of a Congregation

While Erikson (1968) noted that identity formation is the main task of adolescence, contemporary developmental psychologists agree with him that identity achievement is rarely achieved by age 18; and instead, identity exploration and formation actually intensify during emerging adulthood (Waterman, 1999). As Arnett (2001) pointed out, "Emerging adulthood is a period of life in which young people seek to sort through the range of ideological possibilities present in their society and choose an orientation that will provide them with a guide to life" (p. 78). For many emerging adults, this time of exploration enables them to wrestle with ideological or religious convictions that offer a roadmap for them to engage in the world in a meaningful way. Moreover, advances in developmental brain research further demonstrate how brain maturation supports emerging adults' meaning-making ability (Paus, 2009; Bunge & Wright, 2007; see Chapter 2). As a result, there is an increased cognitive ability to engage with a religion's narratives, meaning systems, and moral codes (Lerner, Roeser, & Phelps, 2008).

For most, identity exploration eventually leads to identity commitment in adulthood, suggesting that emerging adults are moving toward consolidating a sense of self and identity in terms of vocational, societal, and familial roles. One's religious worldview and decision to participate in a religious community can be an important part of this identity exploration as emerging adults ask questions about the ultimate meaning of life. Questions about life purpose are the "existential" or "transcendent" elements that local religious congregations attempt to address. In addition, Markstrom and Kalmanir (2001) found in their study of undergraduates that having stable conceptions of the self was associated with the ability to connect life experience to larger questions of life. Religion is linked to a consolidated sense of self or identity, which results in fidelity that enables individuals to commit to productive roles and become contributing members in society (Erikson, 1964, 1965; King et al., 2013; Lerner et al., 2008).

In sum, three things should be considered as we understand the identity formation and the religious congregation or community as an ecological system: (1) with increased cognitive abilities, emerging adults are able to make meaning out of the narratives of a religious group more effectively and to reflect critically on ideologies of a religious congregation or community in a way that they were unable to earlier in the lifespan; (2) religious communities provide an ideologically rich context that has the potential to contribute to identity formation and fidelity, thereby providing opportunities for emerging adults to form religious convictions that assist in religious development, and (3) emerging adults who are further along in the process of identity formation may have an increased ability to commit to a religious congregation or community.

Developmental systems theory (DST) addresses the varied and bidirectional interactions that occur between persons and the social and cultural contexts in which they find themselves (Broffenbrenner, 1979; King et al., 2013; Lerner, 2006). DST helps scholars to conceptualize congregations or religious communities as one of the contexts that incorporate elements of culture, family, role models, social engagement, and transcendent elements (King, 2008). In addition, Roehlkepartain and Patel (2006) argue that congregations should not merely be understood as providers of services; rather, they should be seen as complex cultures and ecologies for development. Drawing upon these two perspectives, we may understand religious congregations and communities as multifaceted ecologies where religious development is influenced by a network of relationships, rituals, and expectations over time.

Given that emerging adults are still in a state of forming their identity through exploration, participation in a religious congregation or community may be seen as contributing to their sense of self and providing a source of stability. Provided that congregations offer emerging adults a wide variety of opportunities and connections, it is little wonder why emerging adults who actively and regularly engage in congregations report significant differences on a wide variety of behaviors and measures of well-being (Smith, 2009). Moreover, identity formation that occurs through participation in religious congregations during emerging adulthood has the potential to impact stages of development after emerging adulthood, including marriage and parenting (Barry et al., 2010). Though the trend in emerging adulthood is one of decline in regular congregational participation, those who choose to stay involved have access to networks of close relationships and resources that can be helpful for identity formation and one's religious and spiritual development. Viewing religious congregations and communities as complex ecologies where development occurs enables one to conceptualize the various developmental pathways.

## ▲ Religious Congregations and Communities as Centers of Meaning-Making

In 2005, Smith suggested nine ways that religion exerts a positive influence on youth. These include moral directives, confirmation of spiritual experiences, role models, community and leadership skills, coping skills, cultural capital, social capital, greater network closure in relationships, and intercommunity links.[4] For the number of emerging adults who participate in a religious congregation or community, these groups still have a constructive role as a developmental resource. This section proposes that meaning-making occurs through three contexts (*ideological, social*, and *transcendent*) that one encounters in religious congregations and communities. Generally speaking, these ideological, social, and transcendent contexts within a congregation or community have the possibility of being accessed by emerging adults in a way that helps them to engage with others and the world around them in a meaningful way (King, 2008; King et al., 2013). Thus, the values of religious congregations and communities provide a context where emerging adults are able to generate a sense of meaning, order, and place in the world that is

4. In his 2009 follow-up survey, Smith concludes that most of these "same mechanisms apply equally well in the lives of emerging adults" (p. 278).

vital to their identity formation. Emerging adults who actively participate in a religious group use the signs, symbols, and rituals of the congregation or community in a way that is *personally* significant. We will briefly outline what each of these ideological, social, and transcendent contexts might include.

## Ideological Context

First, by conceptualizing how religious congregations and communities provide an *ideological* context for meaning-making addresses the ways that a community provides structure and resources to help individuals to develop beliefs and morals. Ideology is essential to young people's identity formation (Erikson, 1968), wherein they strive to make sense of the world and to assert their place in it. The beliefs, worldview, and values of religious traditions provide an ideological context in which emerging adults can generate a sense of purpose, order, and place in the world that is crucial to their development (Damon, 2008; Erikson, 1968; King, 2003). More specifically, religious congregations and communities provide a structure and resources that help emerging adults to make meaning from rituals and practices and to develop and internalize beliefs, values, and morals (Yust, Johnson, Sasso, & Roehlkepartain, 2006). For example, consider the religious community that emphasizes in their teaching that helping others is of great importance and value. This community may not simply espouse this belief but may also provide opportunities to reach out to their local neighborhood, such as rebuilding a house or working a local food bank. In addition, this religious community may provide opportunities for reflection on this experience by allowing time for emerging adults to discuss aspects of the experience that were most meaningful to them; in this way the community helps them to internalize this experience of helping others (Astin, Astin, & Lindholm, 2011). In this way, religion has the potential to provide interpretive value of life experiences that contributes to emerging adults' own identity formation and development. For example, researchers noted that students who participated within a religious context to provide community service adopted religious beliefs and a rationale for their actions that aided in identity formation (Youniss et al., 1999). Thus, religious congregations and communities can provide opportunities for young people to "use their analytical capacities to think through and question beliefs and values, which may be especially helpful in the consolidation of identity" (King, 2003, p. 198). Moreover, by providing access to many levels of emerging adults' developmental system such as peers, family, adults, and potentially ethnic community, religious congregations and communities have the potential of offering a *consistent ideological framework* that can help emerging adults to make sense of the different ideologies available through the broader culture that compete for their attention (Furrow et al., 2004; King, 2003; see Chapter 5).

### Social Context

Second, religious congregations and communities also provide a *social* context where other participants who embody religious and spiritual ideological norms in a community setting may act as role models (Oman, 2013), which are a vital element in identity formation. Although religious groups are not the exclusive providers of these social resources, they may be particularly effective in offering social capital, social support, and mentors (King, 2008; Roehlkepartain & Patel, 2006; Schwartz, Bukowski, & Aoki, 2006). Religious congregations and communities intentionally teach prosocial values, and members may embody values of the congregation, while serving as mentors or role models (King & Furrow, 2004; Oman, 2013; Schwartz et al., 2006). Furthermore, educational, social, and service experiences within congregation or community help to translate beliefs, values, and standards into language, stories, and experiences that help one to form a sense of self and to find meaning and purpose, while also providing a way that emerging adults may understand their current experience. In this way, emerging adults not only have access to people they would consider to be role models, but emerging adults are presented with the prospect of being leaders or role models themselves. An emerging adult has the opportunity within some religious congregations to teach youth in youth programs, act as a small group leader for peers or younger children, and even participate in formal services or ceremonies by reading or playing an instrument. For example, in Jewish communities, emerging adults are often asked to educate younger children in *"Shabbat* school," where children learn about Jewish beliefs, culture, and the heritage of the Judaism. Moreover, many LDS, Catholic, and Protestant churches provide opportunities for emerging adults to participate in service, mission, and/or advocacy. These opportunities provide emerging adults with a supportive context and framework for them to try different roles and expand their own concepts of themselves—thereby creating new capacities within themselves as they might come to understand themselves as a leader or helper (King, 2003).

For example, within the Hindu religion, gurus are teachers who are considered to be self-realized masters and embodiments of the divine (King & Roeser, 2009; Martignetti, 1998). In such relationships, followers of such masters treat devotion or service to this teacher as a major focus of their lives. In some traditions of Judaism, sages serve as role models who illustrate correct living and wisdom. In the Christian tradition, young people are often "discipled" by pastors or adult volunteers at churches. Whether a young person perceives himself or herself as being a follower or being mentored, these individuals serve to connect the young person to a larger whole and enable the individual to identify with a community beyond himself or herself (Schwartz et al., 2006).

### Transcendent Context

Third, religious congregations and communities offer a *transcendent* context that contributes to identity formation. In short, transcendence involves a shifting of people's cognitive and emotional orientation from self to another in such a way that provides ultimate value and meaning beyond the mundane and material and shapes identity (Lerner, Roeser, & Phelps, 2008). Identity formation within spiritual contexts, such as within religious congregations or communities, also encourages emerging adults to transcend the self and promotes devotion and fidelity in a way that fosters individual well-being and the well-being of society at large (King, 2003; Lerner et al., 2008).

Transcendent context differs from the previously discussed social context. While the social context is the potential resources of social influence central to identity formation, the transcendent context refers to opportunities to experience a profound sense of connection with either the divine or human other that does not require physical presence, while also promoting a sense of awareness of self in relation to other (King, Ramos, & Clardy, 2013). This heightened consciousness of others often triggers and inspires an understanding of self that is intertwined and somehow responsible to the other. Both formal religious congregations and more informal religious communities often present poignant opportunities to transcend daily concerns and encounter a supernatural other and a historic and/or local faith community in a meaningful way that affirms a sense of self in relationship with others. It is through these interactions that young people experience something of significance beyond themselves and gain a growing sense of transcendence.

Many activities within religious congregations and communities foster transcendence—rituals, forms of worship, and spiritual practices often heighten individuals' awareness of the greater religious community, common humanity, or knowledge of God. For example, one of the foremost religious practices within Islam is *salat* or prayer. According to this tradition, Muslims pray at five specific times a day. In this repetitive act, believers experience themselves in solidarity with other believers prostrating themselves toward Mecca. Additionally, the Lord's Supper, Eucharist, or Communion provides Christians with a consistent experience of transcendence with the "communion of saints," which refers to all believers past and present. Within the practice of the Lord's Supper it is understood that by eating the bread and drinking the wine that one not only experiences union with Christ, but one also participates in this act with the communion of saints.

Experiences of transcendence often propel commitments or devotion to beliefs (King et al., 2013; Lerner et al., 2008). Religious congregations and communities provide opportunities for such transcendence that contribute to identity formation by providing opportunities for emerging adults to be embedded within a larger context that validates the inherent value of the self, while also promoting a sense of belonging and connectedness to something greater (King, 2003). In this way, emerging adults who regularly participate in religious groups may be able to gain a sense of self as a unique individual, as well as an understanding of themselves as contributing members to a larger whole, and are able to have contact with others who embody similar values (King, 2003). From this perspective, interaction with a religious congregation or community that informs one's beliefs and commitments propels the young person to live in a manner mindful of others. If we take the notion of transcendence seriously and understand how religious communities help to orient persons to consider others, then it comes as no surprise that the research suggests that the most religiously devoted emerging adults are also the most likely to rank the highest in volunteering, community service, and donating to various service organizations (Smith, 2009). While this is noted, further research also is warranted to verify the role of transcendence in promoting such generative behaviors among emerging adults.

Rarely do nonreligious organizations intentionally offer ideological cohesiveness and an intergenerational social network that nurtures and sustains beliefs, meaning, and values—while also providing opportunities for sacred and communal transcendence. The combination of all of these contributions enables religious congregations and communities to serve as a potentially fertile ground for identity formation. Although these resources are most available to those most active in actual religious communities, many of the potential resources remain accessible to less active emerging adults (Maton et al., 2013). Given that research suggests that personal faith and spirituality often remain important to many emerging adults in the United States, it is valuable to consider how religion continues to serve as a developmental resource for them (Smith, 2009). On this account, religious beliefs and values may endure from early-life religious attendance and may function to assist in meaning-making during emerging adulthood despite little or no religious attendance. Similarly, although some emerging adults may not participate consistently with a local religious community, they may be aware of their connection to a broader community of believers. For example, a Jewish emerging adult may not attend the local synagogue but might value his or her connection with the Jewish people. The emerging adult may draw a sense of belonging, strength, and devotion from being a part of this group of people.

Just as faith communities are potentially helpful resources in identity formation, in some cases they also may potentially hinder identity achievement. While communities that are resource-rich in transcendence can aid in religious development and help emerging adults to connect with something beyond themselves, religious communities that do not connect emerging adults with a social group or transcendent elements may not promote a self-concept that fully integrates a moral, civic, and spiritual identity. Taken to the extreme, religious communities that exalt individuals over a greater good can promote a sense of narcissism, entitlement, and lack of connectedness and contribution to society (King, 2008). Some religious communities may espouse beliefs that run counter to a person's identity (e.g., GLBT adults who belong to a religious tradition that condemns their sexual orientation), and in such cases, engagement with a religious community may cause internal and social conflict (see Chapter 12). Another example would be a religious community or congregation where faith is reduced to a series of propositional statements devoid of transcendent and social elements so that questioning of faith is not permitted. Thus, if a religious community emphasizes adherence to group norms over and above questioning and discovering one's own beliefs and roles within society and the community, emerging adults may not have opportunities to explore various roles of leading or helping others. In short, if there is insufficient room to connect with transcendent elements within a religious community, religious communities are at risk of promoting identity foreclosure rather than aiding in identity achievement.

## ▲ Future Directions for Research and Concluding Remarks

In conclusion, both formal religious congregations and informal communities potentially provide an ecologically rich context for emerging adults on their quest for identity achievement. The ideological, social, and transcendent resources available through congregations and communities are especially pertinent to the psychological endeavors of identity formation and meaning-making that characterize emerging adulthood. Consequently, it is not surprising that research demonstrates that the most devoted and regularly attending emerging adults in religious congregations report significant differences on several measures of behaviors and well-being from those who are not regularly a part of a religious community. However, the jury is still out on whether emerging adults will continue to participate actively in religious communities throughout their adulthood. Only with longitudinal research can scholars determine whether this group of devoted emerging adults will remain devoted or regular attenders in religious congregations and communities into adulthood. However, given the rise in attendance of adults in their thirties (Pew Forum on Religion and Public Life, 2012), we may surmise that as individuals begin to commit to adult roles such has marriage, parenting, and a vocation, their religious participation commitments may rise as well.

Further research also is needed to determine the long-term effects of the different aspects of religious congregations and communities on adult development. Additionally, studies that explore the various resources accessible through more traditional congregations and less formal religious communities would shed light on how and for whom various forms of religious participation is most helpful. For example, for those curious emerging adults who are exploring their identity with a particular faith community, informal communities may provide a more conducive setting for emerging adults than a formal religious congregation to access ideological, social, and even transcendent resources. Whereas, for those used to a traditional setting, historic rituals and practices may be more effective.

Whether old or new, formal or informal, congregations and religious communities are potentially fertile ground for development during emerging adulthood. The opportunities to pursue existential issues, to experience a community of fellow believers, and to transcend the mundane concerns of life create an environment conducive to exploring meaning, purpose, and identity. Religious congregations and communities that are attuned to these developmental needs of emerging adults and that are structured to address these needs will be most effective in engaging these searching emerging adults and providing them with essential resources for a productive and meaningful adulthood.

## ▲ References

Arnett, J. J. (2001). Conceptions of the transition to adulthood from adolescence through midlife. *Journal of Adult Development, 8*, 135–145.

Arnett, J. J. (2004). *Emerging adulthood: The winding road from the late teens through the twenties.* New York, NY: Oxford University Press.

Astin, A., W., Astin, H. S., & Lindholm, J. A. (2011). *Cultivating the spirit: How college can enhance students' inner lives.* San Francisco, CA: Wiley.

Barry, C. M., Nelson, L., Davarya, S., & Urry, S. (2010). Religiosity and spirituality during the transition to adulthood. *International Journal of Behavioral Development, 34*, 311–324. doi: 10.1177/0165025409350964

Broffenbrenner, Urie. (1979) *The Ecology of Human Development: Experiments by Nature and Design.* Cambridge, MA: Harvard University Press.

Bunge, S. A., & Wright, S. B. (2007). Neurodevelopmental changes in working memory and cognitive control. *Current Opinion in Neurobiology, 17*, 243–250.

Damon, W. (2008). *The path to purpose: How young people find their calling in life.* New York, NY: Free Press.

DeHaan, L. G., Yonker, J. E., & Affholter, C. (2011). More than enjoying the sunset: Conceptualization and measurement of religiosity for adolescents and emerging adults and its implications for developmental inquiry. *Journal of Psychology and Christianity, 30*, 184–195.

Erikson, E. H. (1964). *Insight and responsibility.* New York, NY: Norton.

Erikson, E. H. (1965). Youth: Fidelity and diversity. In E. H. Erikson (Ed.), *The challenges of youth* (pp. 1–28). Garden City, NY: Anchor Books.

Erikson, E. H. (1968). *Identity: Youth and crisis.* New York, NY: Norton.

Furrow, J., King, P. E., & White, K. (2004). Religiousness and positive youth development: Identity, meaning, and prosocial concerns. *Applied Developmental Science, 8*, 17–26. doi: 10.1207/S1532480XADS0801_3

Kaleem, J. (September 9, 2012). Mormon Singles, LDS Singles Wards Rise as Members Delay Marriage. *Huffington Post*. Retrieved from http://www. huffingtonpost.com/2012/09/14/mormon-singles-lds-singles-wards-marriage_n_1875524.html.

King, P. E. (2003). Religiousness and identity: The role of ideological, social, and spiritual contexts. *Applied Developmental Science, 7*, 196–203.

King, P. E. (2008). Spirituality as fertile ground for positive youth development. In R. M. Lerner, R. W. Roeser, & E. Phelps (Eds.), *Positive youth development and spirituality: From theory to research* (pp. 55–73). West Conshohocken, PA: Templeton Foundation Press.

King, P. E., & Furrow, J. L. (2004). Religion as a resource for positive youth development: Religion, social capital, and moral outcomes. *Developmental Psychology, 40*, 703–713. doi: 10.1037/0012-1649.40.5.703

King, P. E., Ramos, J. S., & Clardy, C. E. (2013). Searching for the sacred: Religion, spirituality and adolescent development. In K. I. Pargament, J. Exline, & J. Jones (Eds.), *APA handbook of psychology, religion, and spirituality: Vol. 1 context, theory, and research* (pp. 513–528). Washington, DC: American Psychological Association. doi: 10.1037/14045-001

King, P. E. & Roeser, R. (2009). Religion & spirituality in adolescent development. In R. M. Lerner & L. Steinberg (Eds.) *Handbook of adolescent psychology, 3rd Edition, Volume 1: Development, relationships and research methods* (pp. 435– 478). Hoboken, NJ: John Wiley & Sons.

Koenig, L. B., McGue, M., & Iacono, W. G. (2008). Stability and change in religiousness during emerging adulthood. *Developmental Psychology, 44*, 532–543.

Lerner, R. M. (2006). Developmental science, developmental systems, and contemporary theories of human development. In R. M. Lerner (Ed.), *Theoretical models of human development* (pp. 1–17). Hoboken, NJ: Wiley.

Lerner, R. M., Roeser, R. W., & Phelps, E. (Eds.). (2008). *Positive youth development and spirituality: From theory to research*. West Conshohocken, PA: Templeton Foundation Press.

Markstrom, C. A., & Kalmanir, H. M. (2001). Linkages between the psychosocial stages of identity and intimacy and the ego strengths of fidelity and love. *Identity: An International Journal of Theory and Research, 1*, 179–196.

Martignetti, C. (1998). Gurus and devotees: Guides or gods? Pathology or faith?. *Pastoral Psychology, 47*(2), 127–144. doi:10.1023/A:1022961613051

Maton, K. I., Sto. Domingo, M. R., & Westin, A. L. (2013). Addressing religion and psychology in communities: The congregation as intervention site, community resource, and community influence. In K. I. Pargament, A. Mahoney, & E. P. Shafranske (Eds.), *APA handbook of psychology, religion, and spirituality (Vol. 2): An applied psychology of religion and spirituality* (pp. 613–632). Washington, DC: American Psychological Association. doi:10.1037/14046-032

Oman, D. (2013). Spiritual modeling and the social learning of spirituality and religion. In K. I. Pargament, J. J. Exline, & J. W. Jones (Eds.), *APA handbook of psychology, religion, and spirituality (Vol. 1): Context, theory, and research* (pp. 187–204). Washington, DC: American Psychological Association. doi:10.1037/14045-010

Osgood, D. W., Ruth, G., Eccles, J. S., Jacobs, J. E., & Barber, B. L. (2005). Six paths to adulthood: Fast starters, parents without careers, educated partners, educated singles, working singles, and slow starters. In R. A. Settersten, Jr., F. F. Furstenberg, Jr., & R. G. Rumbaut (Eds.), *On the frontier of adulthood: Theory, research and public policy* (pp. 320–355). Chicago, IL: The University of Chicago Press.

Pargament, K. I. (2007). *Spiritually integrated psychotherapy: Understanding and addressing the sacred.* New York, NY: Guilford Press.

Paus, T. (2009). Brain development. In R. M. Lerner & L. Steinberg (Eds.), *Handbook of adolescent psychology: Individual bases of adolescent development* (pp. 95–115). Hoboken, NJ: Wiley.

Pew Forum on Religion and Public Life. (2012, October 9). *"Nones" on the rise: One-in-five adults have no religious affiliation.* Retrieved from http://www.pewforum.org/ unaffiliated/nones-on-the-rise.aspx

Renew International's Theology on Tap. (2013). *About RENEW Theology on Tap.* Retrieved from http://www.renewtot.org.

Roehlkepartain, E. C., & Patel, E. (2006). Congregations: Unexamined crucibles for spiritual development. In E. C. Roehlkepartain, P. E. King, L. Wagener, & P. L. Benson (Eds.), *The handbook of spiritual development in childhood and adolescence* (pp. 324–336). Thousand Oaks, CA: Sage.

Schwartz, K. D., Bukowski, W. M., & Aoki, W. T. (2006). Mentors, friends, and gurus: Peer and nonparent influences on spiritual development. In E. C. Roehlkepartain, P. E. King, L. Wagener, & P. L. Benson (Eds.), *The handbook of spiritual development in childhood and adolescence* (pp. 310–323). Thousand Oaks, CA: Sage.

Smith, C. B. (with Denton, M.). (2005). *Soul searching: The religious and spiritual lives of American teenagers.* New York, NY: Oxford University Press.

Smith, C. B. (with Snell, P.). (2009). *Souls in transition: The religious and spiritual lives of emerging adults.* New York, NY: Oxford University Press.

Waterman, A. S. (1999). Issues of identity formation revisited: United States and the Netherlands. *Developmental Review, 19,* 462–479.

Youniss, J., McLellan, J. A., & Yates, M. (1999). Religion, community service, and identity in American youth. *Journal of Adolescence, 22,* 243–253.

Yust, K. M., Johnson, A. N., Sasso, S. E., & Roehlkepartain, E. C. (2006). *Nurturing child and adolescent spirituality: Perspectives from the world's religious traditions.* Lanham, MD: Rowman & Littlefield.

# 9 ▲

# Changing Souls: Higher Education's Influence Upon the Religious Lives of Emerging Adults

PERRY L. GLANZER, JONATHAN HILL,
AND TODD C. REAM

*Abdul attends a secular liberal arts college in the southwestern United States. A Muslim of Pakistani decent, he was raised in Zaire and Houston, Texas, which partly explains his involvement in the Black Student Union instead of a particular Muslim group. In fact, it is largely in class and not in the cocurricular life of the college where he wrestles with larger issues of religion and the meaning of life. He recently read in class Boethius' Consolation of Philosophy, which addresses the debate between how a just God could allow evil, and wrote an essay claiming that the consolation of philosophy was not enough for Boethius because he needed a higher consolation from theology, which he claims, "really helped me understand myself and what consoles me as an individual."*

*Sharmin, a Christian convert from Hinduism, attends a large Southern state research university. There, she finds a great deal of encouragement regarding her religious faith from a Christian group on campus, where she finds opportunities for fellowship, Bible study, and discussions with adult mentors. Since she is a science major, however, she says that she cannot recall one professor or class that discussed issues of meaning or purpose in life, much less issues of spirituality or religion.*

*Anne chose to attend a Jewish university in the Northeast for religious reasons. She appreciates the focus on larger life purpose and religious questions that she finds in her*

*Jewish ethics and philosophy classes, although she does find them "very academic." What she says has helped her to think about the meaning of life have been "the extracurriculars, the activities or speeches, and lecturers that come in." Although she acknowledges that some students joke about the "Jewish bubble" that the campus provides, she finds the atmosphere one that nurtures her growth as a modern Orthodox Jewish woman.*

As these vignettes illustrate, the diverse emerging adults attending higher education institutions today experience a disparate spiritual landscape. Through this chapter we offer an overview and evaluation of some important common elements shaping this uneven terrain and examine what these mean for religious and spiritual growth. In particular, we highlight the changes in four aspects of higher education that may form the religious and spiritual development of emerging adults: (1) the growth of secular higher education; (2) the changing role of religion in the curriculum of secular institutions; (3) the place of religion in the cocurricular offerings of secular campuses; and (4) the unique contributions of faith-based colleges and universities. We conclude with an overview of what we know about the influence of higher education upon students' religious beliefs.

## ▲ From Christian Pluralism to Secular Pluralism

Since its founding, the United States has provided amazingly fertile soil for a wide variety of religious institutions of higher education. Whereas most European countries supported universities affiliated with only one or two Christian traditions, a whole variety of Presbyterian, Methodist, Congregational, and Baptist colleges grew in the United States along with a sprinkling of Roman Catholic, Episcopal, Lutheran, and Quaker institutions (Tewksbury, 2011). When one includes institutions without a religious affiliation, such as the Universities of Virginia and Pennsylvania, one finds that before the Civil War, the United States supported arguably the most religiously robust and diverse system of higher education in the world.

After the Civil War, however, the higher education sector became secularized in a number of important ways. First, all the earliest elite

Christian colleges were transformed into secular research universities (Marsden, 1994). Second, whereas before the Civil War the vast majority of students were educated in private religious colleges and state universities were the outliers (Tewksbury, 2011), the 1862 Morrill Land Grant Act and government's increasing support of research universities after this time drastically changed this reality. By 1952, public institutions began educating more students in the United States than private institutions for the first time in history. Today over three-fourths of students now attend state institutions and emerging adults are attending these increasingly secular postsecondary institutions at higher rates than any previous generation (US Department of Education, National Center for Education Statistics, 2012). Finally, the decline of "sectarian" or "church-related" education, along with the increasing dominance of secular institutions, created legal, professional, and cultural pressures for administrators and faculty to use secular language and categories in scholarly analysis (Marsden, 1997; Sommerville, 2008).

## ▲ Religion in the Curriculum at Secular Institutions

The growing dominance of secular institutions transformed the past role of religion in the curriculum during the 20th century. Normative religious teaching and practice began to be considered something one does in private. The resulting privatization of religion led to less identification by institutions and emerging adults with specific religious traditions and a larger interest in "spirituality"—"a more personal, less institutionalized way of creating meaning and relating to the transcendent" (Jacobsen & Jacobsen, 2012, p. 37). In addition, faculty in secular institutions abandoned confessional religious approaches to subject matter in the name of objectivity or legal concerns (Nord, 2010). In the formal curriculum, both theology and ethics courses, once essential parts of the required curriculum, either disappeared or became marginalized electives at best (Hart, 1999; Reuben, 1996).

All of these changes mean that emerging adults attending higher education are now less likely to be exposed to religion in their general education. One consequence of this development is a declining religious literacy among college-educated emerging adults (Prothero, 2007). Although adults with a college degree perform better on basic religious literacy tests than do adults with no formal education beyond high school, their scores are still remarkably low (Jacobsen & Jacobsen,

2012, pp. 59–62). In addition, larger existential questions appear to have faced the same marginalization as religion. Writing about the question of life's meaning, Kronman (2007) claims, "I have seen this question exiled from the humanities, first as a result of the growing authority of the modern research ideal and then on account of the culture of political correctness that has undermined the legitimacy of the question itself and the authority of humanities teachers to ask it" (p. 7). Longitudinal surveys by the Higher Education Research Institute (HERI) appear to reinforce this reality. In 1971, 73% of first-year students saw developing a meaningful life philosophy as essential or very important to them; in 2010 only 48% affirmed this view. In contrast, 78% saw "wealth and success" as the important outcome in a 2010 survey (Astin, Astin, & Lindholm, 2011).

In the past two decades, however, some evidence exists of a revival of attention to religion or spirituality in the curriculum, although this revival may be limited (Jacobsen & Jacobsen, 2012). For instance, Schmalzbauer and Mahoney (2012) point to the fact that membership in one of the prominent professional societies that studies religion (the American Academy of Religion—AAR) doubled between 1990 and 2006. Furthermore, AAR reports that between 1996 and 2005 religion majors increased by 31% and enrollment in religion courses increased 23%. They also claim that scholars in other fields, such as philosophy, literary studies, history, and political science, have increased their attention to religious matters. Some scholars (Marsden, 1997; Nord, 2010) also argue that we now need to acknowledge the value of teaching students about explicitly religious perspectives. Whether these developments influence emerging adults' religious literacy or academic sophistication in matters of religion or life's meaning remains to be seen.

## ▲ Religion and Spirituality in Secular Universities' Cocurricular Life

While the missions and curricular dimensions of most colleges and universities secularized dramatically during the 20th century, the communal life of students did not. In fact, the growing cocurricular sphere became the domain into which moral and religious concerns were pushed (Reuben, 1996). Early Christian student movements, such as the Young Men's Christian Association (YMCA) and the Young Women's Christian Association (YWCA), significantly shaped the development of cocurricular life in state universities (Alleman & Finnegan, 2009).[1] At secular private universities, the early student personnel movement that eventually became the fully formed professional organization for campus student development staff still encouraged the nurturing of the religious dimensions of student life through religious counseling and chaplaincy programs (see Williamson, 1949).

Today, due to the growth of religious pluralism, many institutions seek to reach students beyond a specific religious denomination or tradition. Thus, older Protestant chapels have been transformed into interfaith worship centers, and dining and housing accommodations are made to support a wider diversity of religious students. Student religious groups on campus also show a similar increase in diversity. Whereas mainline Protestant groups formed and played the dominant role in the cocurricular dimension of student religious life in the mid-20th century, today a whole variety of groups now flourish. Following in the history of the YMCA and YWCA, evangelical college groups, such as InterVarsity, Cru (originally Campus Crusade for Christ), Navigators, and the Fellowship of Christian Athletes, as well as campus groups affiliated with religiously conservative denominations (e.g., Southern Baptist, Reformed/Presbyterian) continue to grow numerically and now total over 210,000 students (Schmalzbauer, 2007). Longitudinally, these groups also demonstrated significant growth over the past decades, although it remains unclear whether their numerical growth has kept pace with the growth of higher education as a whole (Schmalzbauer, 2007). These groups, as many scholars note, play an important role in providing a countercultural identity and community in the midst of what is perceived as a hostile secular university life (Bryant, 2011; Dutton, 2008; Magolda & Gross, 2009).

While the significant presence of evangelical groups is not a new historical phenomenon, due to the growing religious diversity in the United States, Catholic, Jewish, Islamic, Hindu, and other religious groups (e.g., Pagan groups) are burgeoning as well. In some cases, these groups are following the example of their more aggressive evangelical peers. For instance, the conservative Fellowship of Catholic University Students (FOCUS), modeled upon the evangelical approach, has grown

1. Originally founded in 1855 by evangelistically minded students discontent with the existing staid campus religious organizations, YMCA student associations coordinated and proliferated nationally, establishing chapters on 772 college campuses by 1912 (Alleman & Finnegan, 2009).

from 1 campus in 1998 to 74 campuses in 2012 (Focus Campuses, 2012). Schmalzbauer (2007) cites the existence of 1,351 Catholic campus organizations, 251 Jewish Hillel Centers, 600 chapters of Muslim Student Associations, 70 Hindu Student Councils, and 113 pagan student associations as evidence of the religious diversity currently existing among campus student ministries and what Cherry, DeBerg, and Porterfield (2001) describe as the "protean flexibility that has characterized American religion" (p. 5). One also could add the 328 groups affiliated with the Secular Student Alliance (2012), a group supporting naturalistic, secular worldviews (e.g., atheists, agnostics, humanists). What this means for emerging adults is that a much more robust environment exists for communal and personal religious practice than does for the intellectual development of students. In fact, one could perhaps point to the disparity between the curricular and cocurricular as the reason why American college students have a reputation for vibrant religious practice, but not more advanced forms of religious knowledge both of their own and other religious traditions (Jacobsen & Jacobsen, 2012; Prothero, 2007).

Despite an expanding respect for religious and spiritual pluralism in the cocurricular dimension, conflicts continue to emerge over pluralism's limits, particularly in relation to conservative religious student groups. Evangelical, Catholic, and Muslim groups all have been subject to various challenges regarding their official status on secular private and public universities (Glanzer, 2011). The problem in each of the cases involves the groups' attempt to require the groups' leaders to adhere to particular theological beliefs and moral standards and the university's stance that those requirements constitute discrimination. For example, Vanderbilt University recently derecognized evangelical Christian and Roman Catholic groups that insisted upon maintaining theological and behavioral requirements for students in leadership. On these campuses emerging adults from more conservative religious traditions (largely Christian but sometimes Muslim) may increasingly experience the "unease" described as characterizing their present experience due to their different beliefs and practices than do those of the dominant peer culture (Bryant, 2011).

## ▲ The State and Influence of Religious Colleges and Universities

Notwithstanding the secularization of many higher education institutions in the United States, the country still contains one of the most diverse groups of religious colleges and universities in the world (to compare, see Glanzer, Carpenter, & Lantinga, 2011). Today, emerging adults can attend a wider diversity of religious colleges such as Jewish, Mormon, Buddhist, Islamic, Adventist, and fundamentalist Christian institutions (e.g., Yeshiva University, Brigham Young University, Soka University of America, Zaytuna College, Loma Linda University, and Bob Jones University, respectively). Many are growing in prestige and numbers. The Mormon Brigham Young University and Jewish Yeshiva University are both highly regarded research universities. Fundamentalist colleges and universities also continue to grow with Liberty University claiming to be the largest Baptist university in the world with 13,400 students on campus and 60,000 online students. Seventh-Day Adventists also now operate 11 different colleges and universities in America, and, outside of Catholics, have the largest network of faith-based universities around the globe (Glanzer et al., 2011). The two largest groups of faith-based institutions, however, are associated with evangelical Protestantism and Roman Catholicism. These institutions offer emerging adults a unique form of religious education and formation.

## Evangelical

Evangelical Protestant institutions cannot be identified by any one particular denomination and, in fact, associate with a variety of Christian traditions (Wesleyans, Pentecostals, Reformed, and Evangelical Friends, to name only a few). These groups generally hold a high view of the Bible as sacred scripture, emphasize the importance of belief in Christ's sacrifice on the cross as the means of humanity's redemption, and the need to live out one's faith through evangelism and social reform (Bebbington, 1989). Historically, some of these reform efforts included the building of educational institutions. Beginning in 1976, a number of institutions banded together to form the Council for Christian Colleges and Universities (CCCU), an umbrella organization that currently represents the interests of 118 evangelical colleges and universities in North America. Through this partnership and other scholarly conversations, evangelical scholars in almost every discipline began thinking about what came to be known as the "integration of faith and learning." As a result, over the course of about 20 years, a number of these Protestant colleges and universities moved from the academic margins to the center of many conversations in academe (Benne, 2001; Wolfe, 2000).

Emerging adults appear to demonstrate an increasing interest in a higher education that integrates faith and learning. In a report comparing enrollment trends between 1990 and 2004 (drawn from numbers reported by the US Department of Education), the CCCU noted that its member institutions grew 70.6%. In contrast, public 4-year campuses grew 12.8% and independent or private 4-year campuses grew by 28%. Growth in student enrollment on these campuses parallels other critical numbers such as growth in the numbers of faculty members employed and endowment sizes (CCCU, 2005).

## ▲ Roman Catholic

The largest percentage of faith-based colleges and universities in the United States are Catholic, with the Association of Catholic Colleges and Universities (ACCU, 2012) itself boasting 193 college members. Although these institutions all identify as Roman Catholic, they exhibit a great deal of diversity in mission and organization. Historically, this diversity was driven by the variety of religious orders (e.g., Jesuit, Dominican, Franciscan, and Benedictine) that founded almost all of these schools. As a result, Jesuit institutions often now emphasize social justice as a key component of their understanding of Catholic identity. Other schools, such as the Benedictines, emphasize the personal formation that comes with adherence to core spiritual disciplines (ACCU, 2012).

Unlike most evangelical Protestant institutions, a number of Roman Catholic institutions have emerged as academically influential and prestigious (e.g., University of Notre Dame, Boston College, and Georgetown University) and thus now appeal to a wide range of individuals—students, faculty, and administrators alike. Yet Roman Catholics also worry about whether their fate may prove similar to mainline Protestants. Many Roman Catholic colleges and universities underwent processes of secularization in the 1960s and 1970s, and some now question the degree of Catholic commitment of some historically Catholic institutions (Burtchaell, 1998). Catholic educational leaders also worry that the decline among the Roman Catholic orders left largely unprepared lay leaders to carry on the Catholic mission at such universities. Furthermore, they believe the Catholic component to their curriculum and the Catholic culture in the cocurricular lives of students appears to be diminishing (Gleason, 1995; Morey & Piderit, 2006).

In the face of these challenges, a number of Catholic colleges and universities launched efforts to reclaim and/or reinforce their religious identity. Most notably, in 1990 Pope John Paul II issued the Papal encyclical entitled *Ex Corde Ecclesiae*. While covering a wide range of topics, this encyclical's most vexing challenge for some schools in the United States proved to be the expectations the Pontiff had for theologians and the prerogative of the local bishop to grant a mandate conferring the orthodoxy of their views and, in turn, their eligibility for employment. Catholic university professional organizations, as well as individual institutions, developed programming to train faculty on Catholic Intellectual Life as well as established Offices of Mission Integration to ensure ongoing attention to faculty development in this arena. An increasing segment of Catholic colleges and universities now have policies in place for hiring of faculty and even the recruitment of students that favor those most invested in the practices of the Roman Catholic faith (Morey & Piderit, 2006). Yet the extent to which such policies are implemented at the departmental hiring or admissions' counselor levels (given individuals' beliefs about the appropriateness of such policies is likely to vary) as well as oversight and enforcement of such policies likely varies.

Perhaps due to the conversation about Catholic identity sparked by *Ex Corde Ecclesia*, the Catholic higher education sector still shows signs of vitality. New Catholic universities continue to be started with campuses recently appearing in Florida, California, Virginia, and Wyoming. Many of these institutions are more religiously conservative in nature and focus upon studying the Great Books or the Western intellectual tradition as a means of extending what they believe is a time-honored pedagogical tradition. The growth of these schools reflects the growing desire among many Roman Catholic emerging adults to receive an education where their faith is at the core of their intellectual pursuits. One also can find an increasing crossover with Catholic and evangelical Protestant scholars regarding matters of integrating faith and reason. Catholic scholars have joined with some of the Christian professional societies described earlier, while Catholics also continue to nurture their own journals in various fields such as education. Thus, unlike mainline Protestant institutions and similar to the evangelicals, Catholic institutions continue to make a substantial contribution to the life of faith-based higher education.

## ▲ Influence Upon Students

Do these institutions influence the religious beliefs of students in unique ways? Some limited evidence points to the possibility that religious students actually maintain higher levels of traditional beliefs on secular campuses. In one study (albeit nearly 30 years old), evangelical students on a secular campus strengthened their faith, while those attending an evangelical school saw a "slow erosion" of their faith (Hammond & Hunter, 1984). More recent studies, using nationally representative samples, however, find little substantial differences between students attending religious and secular institutions on student religious belief (Hill, 2011), although religious practice in the form of worship service attendance tends to decline more at Catholic and mainline Protestant colleges compared to both evangelical and secular institutions (Hill, 2009).

In addition, several studies pertaining to the spiritual and moral development of emerging adults noted that evangelical Christian campuses are having a greater influence upon the moral and religious lives of their students than secular campuses in certain areas (Astin et al., 2011; Glanzer & Ream, 2009). For example, Freitas (2008) found students at evangelical colleges and universities report much higher rates of being able to connect how their spiritual lives influence their sexual lives than do their peers on other types of campuses. Astin et al. (2011) contend that students at evangelical Christian colleges and universities are often the high-scoring outliers in their studies of spirituality. While further investigation is necessary in order to clarify this picture, these studies, and the recent growth of evangelical and Catholic colleges and universities, indicate these institutions may harbor important lessons for any study of the spiritual development of emerging adults.

## ▲ The Impact of College Upon Students' Religious Beliefs and Practices

What can we say about the overall influence of these developments in higher education on student faith and spirituality? Early studies found that college was corrosive to traditional religious faith. Feldman and Newcomb (1969) summarizing the research from the 1950s and 1960s, concluded that, when first-year college students are compared to graduating seniors, seniors were less orthodox on measures of Christian belief and practiced their faith less frequently than first-year students. But these studies, without a comparison group of young people who did not go to college, cannot tell us if the college experience itself was the source of this change.

More recent studies on college and religion offer a different picture and use a more rigorous methodology. By comparing representative samples of young people enrolled in college to others in the workforce, these studies can specify the impact of college on standard measures of faith and practice. These studies conclude that, overall, college is neither poison nor panacea for most (Clydesdale, 2007; Hill, 2011; Mayrl & Uecker, 2011; Uecker, Regnerus, & Vaaler, 2007). For those emerging adults who attend and graduate from college, the educational experience has little overall impact on religious affiliation, standard religious practices, and the content of religious belief. This is *not* to say that many of these indicators of religiousness are stable as young people move from adolescence to emerging adulthood (Smith, 2009). Rather, these studies find that there is no substantial difference between those who attend and graduate from college and those who do not in the *degree* of this decline. The one clear exception to this generalization is religious service attendance, which is temporarily less frequent among students, but rebounds at a higher level for college graduates when compared to emerging adults of the same age (Hill, 2009).

But, one might wonder, even if college does not change, on average, *what* young people think, perhaps it changes *how* they think. In many ways, this query addresses the turn to the inner, privatized, spiritual experience of students that we referred to at the beginning of this chapter. Scholars with UCLA's Higher Education Research Institute recently undertook an effort to quantify this phenomenon through a national, longitudinal survey (Astin et al., 2011). They found that by the end of their junior years, college students scored modestly higher on spiritual constructs such as questing, ecumenical worldview, ethic of caring, and equanimity. While all of these increases are fairly small (and the majority of students score low on all of these measures), they suggest that at least some students may be thinking about and experiencing their spiritual lives differently as a result of college.

In summary, recent research finds slight increases in spirituality and virtually no overall differences by educational attainment on religiousness indicators (with the exception of an increase in church attendance after graduation) in the overall emerging-adult population. Upon further reflection, we think this finding is actually not very surprising. Most students do not arrive on campus with strong religious commitments. For instance, sociologist Tim Clydesdale (2007) studied students the first year out of high school and found that most tend to take their religious identity and place it in a metaphorical "lockbox." A majority of emerging adults are simply following a script that tells them religion has very little to do with this phase of their life and can be safely set aside for a few years. Donna Freitas (2008) found a similar disconnect in her study of how students who attend public or private (but not evangelical Protestant) institutions think about the relation between their sexual and spiritual lives.

While religious and spiritual privatization may be the default for most students, and thus what is primarily picked up in national survey data, a focus only on the overall impact of college will miss other religious and spiritual shifts occurring for minority students (both religiously and by race or ethnicity; see Chapter 13) and within religious colleges and universities that are not well represented in national surveys. Promising research that addresses some of these complexities is beginning to surface.

A small number of studies took into account the religious identification of the student coming into college to see if the student travels, on average, on different religious and spiritual trajectories. The few findings from these studies suggest that college may have a negative impact on religious practice for Roman Catholics (Hill, 2008) and a positive impact for evangelical Protestants (Schwadel, 2011). Schwadel argues that evangelical Protestants are embedded in communities that strongly promote religious participation as a key marker of identity. Consequently, we should expect evangelical peer networks and parachurch groups to provide more opportunities for public religious practice than do other groups. The opposite also may be true. Religious groups that are not well represented on college campuses may have a difficult time developing strong peer networks or organizations that offer opportunities for public religious practice. Consistent with this, Small and Bowman (2011) find that students belonging to non-Christian faiths (e.g., Jewish, Buddhist, Hindu, Quaker, and Islamic groups), on average, develop greater religious skepticism than do Christian students, and have smaller overall gains in spiritual identification (Bowman & Small, 2010). These findings, they suggest, can be linked to the relative lack of religious experiences that these minority faith adherents have during the college years. This reality points to the need for greater institutional intervention in the spiritual lives of nonprivileged religious groups and more direct support of nonmajority religious organizations (Bowman & Small, 2013).

Clearly, considerable work on student differences still needs to be done. For example, we know little about what happens to students who enter college as practicing adherents of a faith tradition. In many ways, this small minority (perhaps 5%–10% of the population according to measures by Smith, 2009) will shed more light on the impact of college than will surveys of the entire emerging-adult population. We think a study that focuses on students who come to college with strong religious identities, and then compares these students across different institutional contexts and college experiences, is an important next step in untangling the impact of college on religion and spirituality.

## ▲ Conclusion

Emerging adults entering higher education will find a varied landscape when it comes to religion and spirituality. On the one hand, the cross-disciplinary study of religion is expanding, cocurricular support for student religious groups and interfaith dialogue on secular campuses is growing, and certain kinds of Christian colleges are also increasing in both influence and numbers. As a result, students' religious and spiritual beliefs and practices do not necessarily suffer and some may even flourish.

On the other hand, in higher education as a whole, students demonstrate less religious knowledge and show less belief that higher education should help them with big questions. Faculty also demonstrate limited support for giving spirituality attention in classes and, according to students, display limited attention to big questions such as the quest for meaning in life in their classrooms. Thus, while different religious groups and perspectives are provided resources through the student life departments on campus, students striving to integrate what they are learning, both socially and academically, with their own faith commitments will likely receive less support in the curricular arena. Moreover, faith-based universities, while growing and expanding in variety, still remain on the periphery of a market quantitatively dominated by state institutions and new for-profit universities.

Overall, further research is still needed to bring clarity to the field. Empirical forms of research are needed so that a better portrait of students' perceptions of their spiritual identity can emerge. We also need to learn more about what administrators and faculty members think about the place of religion within the context of the collegiate experience.

While those forms of research will prove difficult enough, perhaps the more demanding challenge will come with the normative work needing to be done to reconceptualize how religious commitments will play a role in the contemporary academy. Some lessons can be learned from previous models. Alas, what is needed will prove to be the byproduct of a thoughtful and imaginative dialogue engaging the diverse array of stakeholders present on these campuses. Time will tell whether those models will yield fertile soil or a thorny environment for the religious faith of emerging adults.

## ▲ References

Alleman, N. F., & Finnegan, D. E. (2009). "Believe you have a mission in life and steadily pursue it": Campus YMCAs presage student development theory, 1894–1930. *Higher Education in Review, 6,* 11–45.

Association of Catholic Colleges and Universities (2012). Retrieved October 4, 2012, from http://www.accunet.org/i4a/pages/index.cfm?pageid=3759.

Astin, A. W., Astin, H. S., & Lindholm, J. A. (2011). *Cultivating the spirit: How college can enhance students' inner lives.* San Francisco, CA: Jossey-Bass.

Bebbington, D. W. (1989). *Evangelicalism in modern Britain: A history from the 1730s to the 1980s.* London, UK: Unwin Hyman.

Benne, R. (2001). *Quality with soul: How six premier colleges and universities keep faith with their religious traditions.* Grand Rapids, MI: William B. Eerdmans Publishing.

Bowman, N. A., & Small, J. L. (2010). College experiences, well-being, and spiritual development of religiously privileged and marginalized college students. *Research in Higher Education, 51*(7), 595–614.

Bowman, N. A., & Small, J. L. (2013). The experiences and spiritual growth of religiously privileged and religiously marginalized college students. In A. B. Rockenbach & M. J. Mayhew (Eds.), *Spirituality in college students' lives: Translating research into practice* (pp. 19–34). New York, NY: Routledge.

Bryant, A. N. (2011). Evangelicals on campus: An exploration of culture, faith, and college life. In M. D. Waggoner (Ed.), *Sacred and secular tensions in higher education: Connecting parallel universities* (pp. 108–133). New York, NY: Routledge.

Burtchaell, J. T. (1998). *The dying of the light: The disengagement of the colleges and universities from their Christian churches.* Grand Rapids, MI: Eerdmans.

Cherry, C., DeBerg, B. A., & Porterfield, A. (2001). *Religion on campus.* Chapel Hill, NC: The University of North Carolina Press.

Clydesdale, T. T. (2007). *The first year out: Understanding American teens after high school.* Chicago, IL: University of Chicago Press.

Council for Christian Colleges and Universities (2005). "Explosive Growth for CCCU Schools." Retrieved October 5, 2012 from https://www.cccu.org/filefolder/Enrollment_Growth.xls

Dutton, E. (2008). *Meeting Jesus at university: Rites of passage and student evangelicals*. Burlington, VT: Ashgate.

Feldman, K. A., & Newcomb, T. M. (1969). *The impact of college on students*. San Francisco, CA: Jossey-Bass.

Focus Campuses (2012). Retrieved October 16, 2012, from http://www.focus.org/on-campus/focus-campuses.html

Freitas, D. (2008). *Sex and the soul: Juggling sexuality, spirituality, romance, and religion on America's college campuses*. New York, NY: Oxford.

Glanzer, P. L. (2011). The wall between student affairs and faith-based student organizations: Cautions and considerations regarding Peter Magolda's proposal for an unholy alliance. *Journal of College and Character, 12*(3), 1–8.

Glanzer, P. L., Carpenter, J. A., & Lantinga, N. (2011). Looking for God in the university: Examining trends in global Christian higher education. *Higher Education, 61,* 721–755.

Glanzer, P. L., & Ream, T. C. (2009). *Christianity and moral identity in higher education*. New York, NY: Palgrave Macmillan.

Gleason, P. (1995). *Contending with modernity: Catholic higher education in the twentieth century*. New York, NY: Oxford University Press.

Hammond, P. E., & Hunter, J. D. (1984). On maintaining plausibility: The worldview of evangelical college students. *Journal for the Scientific Study of Religion, 23*(3), 221–238.

Hart, D. G. (1999). *The university gets religion: Religious studies in American higher education*. Baltimore, MD: The Johns Hopkins University Press.

Hill, J. P. (2008). *Religious pathways during the transition to adulthood: A life course approach*. Ph.D. dissertation, Department of Sociology, University of Notre Dame, Notre Dame, IN.

Hill, J. P. (2009). Higher education as moral community: Institutional influences on religious participation during college. *Journal for the Scientific Study of Religion, 48*(3), 515–534.

Hill, J. P. (2011). Faith and understanding: Specifying the impact of higher education on religious belief. *Journal for the Scientific Study of Religion, 50*(3), 533–551.

Jacobsen, D., & Jacobsen, R. H. (2012). *No longer invisible: Religion in university education*. New York, NY: Oxford University Press.

Kronman, A. T. (2007). *Education's end: Why our colleges and universities have given up on the meaning of life*. New Haven, CT: Yale University Press.

Magolda, P., & Gross, K.E. (2009). *It's all about Jesus: Faith as an oppositional collegiate subculture*. Sterling, VA: Stylus Publishing.

Marsden, G.M. (1997). *The outrageous idea of Christian scholarship*. New York: NY: Oxford University Press.

Marsden, G. M. (1994). *The soul of the American university: From Protestant establishment to established nonbelief*. New York, NY: Oxford University Press.

Mayrl, D., & Uecker, J. (2011). Higher education and religious liberalization among young adults. *Social Forces, 90*(1), 181–208.

Morey, M. M., & Piderit, J. J. (2006). *Catholic higher education: A culture in crisis*. New York, NY: Oxford University Press.

Nord, W. A. (2010). *Does God make a difference? Taking religion seriously in our schools and universities*. New York, NY: Oxford University Press.

Prothero, S. (2007). *Religious literacy: What every American needs to know—and doesn't*. San Francisco, CA: Harper One.

Reuben, J. (1996). *The making of the modern university: Intellectual transformation and the marginalization of morality*. Chicago, IL: University of Chicago Press.

Schmalzbauer, J. (2007). *Campus ministry: A statistical portrait*. Social Science Research Council. Retrieved October 15, 2012, from religion.ssrc.org/reforum/Schmalzbauer.pdf.

Schmalzbauer, J., & Mahoney, K. (2012). Religion and knowledge in the post-secular academy. In P. S. Gorski, D. K. Kim, J. Torpey, & J. VanAntwerpen (Eds.), *The post-secular in question: Religion in contemporary society* (pp. 215– 248). New York, NY: New York University Press.

Schwadel, P. (2011). The effects of education on Americans' religious practices, beliefs, and affiliations. *Review of Religious Research*, *53*(2), 161–182.

Secular Student Alliance. (2012). Affiliated campus group list. Retrieved November 20, 2012, from www.secularstudents.org/affiliates.

Small, J. L., & Bowman, N. A. (2011). Religious commitment, skepticism, and struggle among U.S. college students: The impact of majority/minority religious affiliation and institutional type. *Journal for the Scientific Study of Religion*, *50*(1), 154–174.

Smith, C. (with Snell, P.). (2009). *Souls in transition: The religious and spiritual lives of emerging adults*. New York, NY: Oxford University Press.

Sommerville, H. J. (2008). *The decline of the secular university*. New York, NY: Oxford University Press.

Tewksbury, D. G. (2011). *The founding of American colleges and universities before the Civil War*. Mansfield Centre, CT: Martino Publishing. (Original work published 1932)

Uecker, J. E., Regnerus, M. D., & Vaaler, M. L. (2007). Losing my religion: The social sources of religious decline in early adulthood. *Social Forces*, *85*(4), 1667–1692.

U.S. Department of Education, National Center for Education Statistics. (2012). *Digest of Education Statistics, 2011* (NCES 2012-001). Washington, D.C.: U.S. Dept. of Health, Education, and Welfare, Education Division, National Center for Education Statistics.

Williamson, E. G. (Ed.). (1949). *Trends in student personnel work*. Minneapolis, MN: University of Minnesota Press.

Wolfe, A. (2000, October). The opening of the evangelical mind. *The Atlantic Monthly*, *286*(4):55–76.

# Part IV ▲
## VARIATIONS

# 10 ◭

# Gender, Religiousness, and Spirituality in Emerging Adulthood

JACQUELINE S. MATTIS

The assertion that women are more religious and spiritual than their male counterparts is one of the most frequently reified conclusions in empirical social science research. Indeed, that conclusion has been asserted so unambiguously in religion research that it generally has come to be understood as universal and invariant across the developmental span. However, the dearth of empirical research on the gender-religion link among emerging adults raises important questions about the validity of such claims for individuals during this time period. In the absence of such empirical work, I interrogate the gender-religion link among emerging adults. In doing so, I take a deliberately integrative approach. I review empirical work from four streams of literature: (1) research on the meaning of gender; (2) research on religiousness and spirituality among adolescents and adults; (3) research on religiousness in the lives of college students; and (4) work on religiousness and spirituality among emerging adults outside of college contexts. In the latter three bodies of work, I excavate findings related to gender. Using literature from gender and feminist studies as analytic lenses, I assert that, for at least four reasons, these bodies of empirical work offer inadequate treatments of the link between gender and religiousness among emerging adults.

First, in studies of adult religiousness, scholars rarely segment their samples into groups that capture the range of ages that comprise emerging adulthood. Second, while studies involving college students include a large segment of the age group that is defined as emerging adults, college students are an especially highly educated, often well-resourced, and racially and culturally less diverse subset of the populace, many of whom live in contexts (e.g., college campuses) that do not always mirror the complexities of community contexts. Third, in general, the research on religion among college-age adults is not explicitly intended to study emerging adulthood. As such, these studies (and the variables included in these studies) are not conceptualized in relation to theories that are specific to understanding the lived experience of emerging adults. Finally, existing literature is inadequate for interrogating the religiousness-gender link because these studies generally fail to provide analyses or interpretations of findings that are explicitly grounded in feminist or gender theories.

In light of these realities, as in my review of the literature mentioned earlier, I focus on one foundational question: What does it mean to examine critically the link between religion and gender among emerging adults? I imagine this foundational question appears to reflect three crucial constituent questions: (1) What is gender and how does gender operate in the social world? (2) What can scholars learn from feminist, feminist theological, and gender studies literatures about how to study gender in relation to religion? and (3) What can scholars understand about how to study the interplay between gender and religion in the developmental context of emerging adulthood?

## ▲ On Gender

In social science literature the terms "sex" and "gender" often are conflated either conceptually or as a matter of praxis. "Sex" is a biologically grounded, binary construct that distinguishes whether one is either "male" or "female" on the basis of the presence or absence of particular biological markers, including genitalia and chromosomal patterns (Deaux & Major, 1990; Marini, 1990). The term "gender," in contrast, refers to the meanings that are ascribed to "maleness" and "femaleness" in the social world, and to the ways in which those meanings shape identity, beliefs, expectations, perceptions, values, roles, practices, emotions, relationships, opportunities, and the like (see Deaux & Major, 1990). Gender pervades all aspects of our lived experience. Language is gendered (e.g., English speakers talk of sharing knowledge in terms of "dissemination"). Our visual world is gendered such that colors, shapes, and textures often are described as "masculine" or "feminine." Our social organizations (e.g., families, schools, religious institutions) and the relationships that emerge within them are gendered, such that certain roles are seen as appropriate for men (e.g., preaching and the highest reaches of formal leadership in Christian churches is seen as the domain of men), while other roles (e.g., caring for children and providing community outreach service) are seen as appropriate for women. Despite the prevalence of gendered meanings and references in everyday life, the specific meanings and manifestations of gender are not universal—communities and cultures have their own understandings and expectations of gender groups. What is universal is the fact that in every community, culture, and society people's understandings of, responses to, and enactments of maleness and femaleness are so highly codified that gender itself comes to operate as a sociocultural symbol. Indeed, as Stewart and McDermott (2004) note, gender symbolizes power relations, and it catalyzes and reifies these power relations in the public as well as private spheres of life. Gender shapes the expectations that people hold about our ability to succeed at particular tasks and how we are expected to comport ourselves (e.g., how we are expected to dress, speak). Gender informs the social roles that we are expected and able to occupy and the social and monetary value placed on those roles.

Although gender often is treated as a binary identity in which individuals are either male/masculine or female/feminine, the lived experience of gender nonconforming or gender-variant (i.e., "transgender") individuals challenges that binary construction. Scholars in gender studies argue for models that conceive of gender not in "either or" terms, but in terms of a spectrum (Davidson, 2007; McKenzie, 1994; Stryker, 1998). Such a reconceptualization of gender would challenge researchers interested in the gender-religion relation to ask a new range of questions. Scholars might consider, for example, the complex ways in which gender, religiousness, and spirituality may co-construct each other for both gender-conforming and gender-nonconforming young adults. Scholars also might consider the range of ways in which gender nonconformity might manifest for young people (e.g., as violations of scripts regarding appropriate clothing choice or aesthetics, or as the adoption of attitudes, beliefs, or relational practices that are inconsistent with prescribed gender roles), and the ways in which those particular manifestations of gender may inform young adults' religious and spiritual identity and practice. Finally, scholars would be challenged to understand how the study of the relations among religiousness, spirituality, and "gender" (i.e., the meaning of maleness and femaleness) might be different from the study of religiousness, spirituality, and sexual identities or romantic or sexual partner choice. In doing so, it would be necessary to understand that most heterosexuals, lesbians, gay men, and bisexuals are generally gender conforming regardless of their choice of romantic partners.

## ▲ Empirical Findings Regarding Gender and Religion Among Emerging Adults

The evidence for a link between gender and religiousness among emerging adults comes largely from empirical studies of differences in patterns of formal religious organizational involvement and subjective religious identification among individuals (generally Christian individuals) in this age group. The heavily Christian bias in the field underscores the need to appreciate that there are limits to the generalizability of extant findings regarding the religion-gender link. The limits of the research notwithstanding, findings suggest that emerging-adult women are more likely than are men in their age group to attend religious services (e.g., Smith, 2009). Further, while service attendance appears to decline during emerging adulthood, among college students, the decline in religious involvement (e.g., service attendance) appears to occur significantly earlier (i.e., in the second semester of college) for men than for women (Stoppa & Lefkowitz, 2010). Relative to women in their age group, emerging-adult men assign lower personal importance to attending religious services (Arnett & Jensen, 2002) and tend to report that religion is less important in their lives (Arnett & Jensen, 2002; Barry et al., 2010; Desmond, Morgan, & Kikuchi, 2010; Stoppa & Lefkowitz, 2010). As is the case with men in adulthood generally (Pew Forum on Religious and Public Life, 2008), men in this age group are more likely than are women to self-define as agnostic or atheist (Arnett & Jensen, 2002).

Gender also appears to be relevant to the religious socialization of emerging adults. Young men and women tend to emulate the religious practices of their same-gender parent. Ahmed (1992) found, for example, that young Muslim women were likely to wear hijab if their mothers also wore hijab. Young adults' religious beliefs also are differentially associated with their mothers' and fathers' beliefs. For example, college men and women's religious beliefs are correlated strongly with their mothers' religious beliefs, but not with their fathers' (Milevsky, Szuchman, & Milevsky, 2008). Interestingly, Milevsky et al. (2008) found that young people's personal religious beliefs were significantly related to what they *thought* their fathers believed, but not with their fathers' *actual* beliefs. These findings suggest a particularly powerful role for mothers in the religious development of the next generation, so much so that those lessons maintain as individuals transition into adulthood.

Further, studies suggest a role for gender, in the relation between religion, spirituality, and socioemotional outcomes among young adults.

For example, perceived discrimination is associated with an increase in young-adult Muslim women's community engagement, but not for young-adult Muslim men (Sirin & Kastiaficas, 2011). Religiousness also is differentially related to the sexual attitudes and practices of men and women. It more strongly predicts sexually conservative attitudes for college-aged women than for their male counterparts (Ahrold & Meston, 2010). However, greater religiousness is associated with a lower likelihood of using pornography among young men attending a religious university (Nelson, Padilla-Walker, & Carroll, 2010). Taken together, these findings suggest that religion differentially informs the values, choices, and behaviors of men and women who are transitioning from adolescence into adulthood.

Finally, there is some evidence that young-adult Christian men and women in the United States differ in their views of how to understand and resolve key gender differences in their respective churches. Lummis (2004), for example, in his study of Episcopal congregants found that relative to women, men more strongly disagreed with the belief that male church participation would be reduced if there were more women in leadership positions in the church. More than 66% of men and women under age 35 reported that they disagreed with the notion that men's participation in church life would be reduced if there were more women in leadership. Half of the men and women in Lummis's sample endorsed the statement that "Men need to be encouraged to have a meaningful involvement in church life more so than women." Young men were more likely than their older counterparts, and more likely than young women, to report that their participation in the life of the church was appreciated. Relative to their older counterparts, men and women under the age of 35 were more likely to express support for having women serve in the role of bishop of their diocese. The majority of men in Lummis's study indicated that they had never participated in church-related men's groups and that they had no interest in doing so. Men did, however, express an interest in being involved with a specific array of activities, including fundraising, home building, and outreach to local and global communities in need.

## Counterexamples

Importantly, despite the conviction with which scholars assert that women are intrinsically more religious than are their male counterparts, there are non-Christian religious traditions and communities in the United States and worldwide for which this assertion does not hold true. Indeed, Sullins (2006) and Loewenthal, MacLeod, and Cinnirella (2002) have found a gender by religious identity effect for religious involvement, such that Christian women report greater religious activity than do their male counterparts, whereas Hindu, Muslim, and Jewish men appear to be more religiously active than are women in their communities. Importantly, consistent with extant findings, Sullins (2006) notes that whether gender differences in religiousness are observed depends on (1) the religious affiliation of those being studied, and (2) the domain(s) of religiousness being measured.

In Islam and Judaism (as in other religious traditions) there are gendered differences in the religious obligations (particularly the public religious obligations) that are assigned to men and women, and these differences manifest in behaviors and perspectives that challenge the notion that women are intrinsically and universally more religious than are men (Loewenthal et al., 2002; Sullins, 2006). In Islam and Judaism men are required to attend their house of worship, while women have no such requirement placed on them. Indeed, while many women do worship in temples and mosques, many women worship at home. In some religious communities (e.g., Orthodox Jewish communities), women may not enter certain spaces that are considered sacred and may not read from sacred texts. In some religious traditions there also are gendered rules (and gendered interpretations of sacred texts) that guide conditions under which women can and cannot enter places of worship (e.g., in some contexts Muslim women are expected not to enter places of worship while menstruating). Further, in many religious traditions (e.g., many Christian denominations) women are explicitly forbidden from holding certain positions of leadership (i.e., women cannot be ordained as Catholic priests), which then preclude administering critical religious rites (e.g., marriage). Given that the United States is a religiously diverse nation, Sullins's assertion reminds us of a need to broaden research on the religious lives of emerging adults beyond the almost exclusive focus on Christians.

In his effort to account for gender differences in religiousness, Sullins (2006) distinguishes between "affective religiousness" (i.e., subjective or personal aspects of piety) and "active religiousness" (i.e., participation in the formal organizational and ritual aspects of religious life). He demonstrates through analyses of national-level data that in most national contexts, gender differences are more evident in the affective domains of religiousness. Indeed, he notes that in almost 1 in 3 nations studied there are either no gender differences in the active dimensions of religiousness, or men are in fact higher on these dimensions than are their female counterparts. Sullins (2006) found that in 28% of the nations for which they had data, women did not score higher than did men on weekly service attendance, and in 5 nations, men scored higher than did women on this index of active religiousness. In 15 countries there was no relation between gender and weekly service attendance. In 31 nations (44% of the countries sampled in the study) there was no significant relation between gender and the likelihood of membership in a religious institutions, and in 5 nations men were more likely than their female counterparts to hold memberships in religious institutions.

Orthodoxy has particularly important implications for gendered patterns of active religious engagement. In "fundamentalist" Christian communities and in Orthodox Jewish and Muslim communities, men and women tend to be either balanced in their patterns of involvement, or men score higher on measures of active religiousness (e.g., service attendance, membership in religious institutions) than do their liberal counterparts. Sullins's (2006) work on the "identity x activity" interaction suggests that Christian and Hindu women tend to outpace men with regard to the importance they assign to weekly service attendance and to the importance of religion. Christian and Buddhist women outscore their male counterparts on measures of subjective religiosity and on the likelihood of being a member of a religious institution. Sullins also reports that men and women residing in the Middle East do not differ on measures of religiousness, thus demonstrating that region of residency also matters with regard to gendered expressions of devotional life.

## ▲ Explanations for Gender Differences in Religiousness

Sullins (2006) asserts that explanations of gender differences in religiousness can be organized into four general sets of theories: (1) theories that center on social location and sociostructural factors; (2) theories that are grounded in a focus on socialization; (3) personality-centered theories; and (4) theories that emphasize risk-taking as an explanation for gender differences in religiousness. First, social location/structural explanations suggest that men's disproportionate presence in the public sphere of paid work and women's disproportionate presence in the private/domestic sphere of home led to the two gender groups being exposed to different meaning-making systems, differing values (including different degrees of importance assigned to religious involvement), and different opportunities to participate in religious life. Second, there are socialization theories that have posited that within and across cultural contexts, men and women are socialized to embrace different norms of behavior, beliefs, values, and roles that ultimately inform how they experience faith life. Socialization theories posit that men are socialized to attend more closely to autonomy, power, and to instrumental roles, while women are socialized to attend more closely to socioemotional and sociomoral concerns. The heightened focus on religiousness among women is presumed to be a direct result of the relevance of religion to addressing the sociomoral, to which women are required to attend. A third set of explanations proposes that gender differences in religiousness can be explained effectively by gendered personality factors (e.g., femininity, masculinity). Finally, theories of risk suggest that testosterone predisposes men to seek out risk and to minimize engagement in activities (e.g., religious activities) that suggest emotionality and, therefore, weakness. The corollary to this risk-centered theory is the notion that estrogen physiologically predisposes women to avoid risk and to engage in nurturing and emotionally valenced activities. As such, women are "naturally" (i.e., physiologically) inclined to be more religious. It is unclear to what extent these theories are empirically supportable. However, a review of extant literature on gender differences in religiousness among emerging adults suggests a particularly heavy leaning on socialization as an explanation for putative differences.

Sullins (2006) suggests, however, that no one factor can explain gender differences in religiousness. He argues, instead, that gender differences in active and affective religiousness can be explained by a combination of social (i.e., structural factors such as number of hours worked, socialization factors such as whether one's parents attended religious services, and religious network factors such as the number of friends at church) and nonsocial (e.g., personality and physiological) factors. In sum, his work highlights the reality that the gendered roots of religiousness are complex.

## ▲ Investigating the Intersection of Gender and Religion for Emerging Adults

Stewart and McDermott (2004) posit that "an important precondition for using gender as a conceptual tool to full advantage in psychology is having a developed understanding of how to bring factors at different levels of analysis—social structural, individual, and even biological— into a single model" (pp. 522–523). I highlight here the limits of existing work and the value of an integrative model.

As a starting point, it is important to note that much of the evidence for a religion-gender link has come from empirical studies. Indeed, historically, the predominant strategy for exploring gender in research on religion is the "sex differences" approach. In this approach scholars bifurcate samples into men versus women and explore whether there are mean differences between men and women on scores on established measures of religiousness (e.g., service attendance) or in patterns of correlation between variables. This sex differences approach presumes that there are essential differences in religiousness between emerging-adult men and women, and grounds explanations of those sex-linked differences in biology, socialization, social location (e.g., age, socioeconomic status), and relationship (e.g., romantic partner status) to social structures, including the labor market (see Stewart & McDermott, 2004 for a discussion). These approaches are problematic in that they ignore within-group variability and ignore scholarship about gender, development, and religiousness.

An integrative model points us to six important considerations: First, such a model requires that scholars reject the sex-gender binary, and that we (1) recognize the existence of a broader and more fluid range of gender expressions; (2) explore the complex ways in which theologies, and religious and spiritual institutions and adherents understand and respond to emerging adults at various places on the gender identity and expression spectrum; and (3) examine the ways in which emerging adults of various gender identities subjectively construct their own religious and spiritual lives (e.g., their understanding of and relationship with God, religious institutions, theology) as they transition from adolescence to adulthood.

An integrative model also requires that we recognize that all gendered identities and practices are classed, raced, ethnically and developmentally bound, and historically, sociopolitically, and contextually situated. Gender is understood and enacted differently by people of various ages and ethnic, racial, cultural, and class groups. Individuals understand and "do" gender differently in childhood than in adulthood; in urban versus suburban settings; in public spaces (e.g., work) versus in private spaces (e.g., family); and in secular versus sacred spaces. People do not perfectly internalize the rules and codes of their social groupings. Indeed, the larger cultural meanings and enactments of gender exist alongside powerful (and sometimes contradictory) subjective meanings and enactments of gender.

Understanding the role of gender in religious life requires us to acknowledge that in many religious communities gender is highly scripted, and established codes of gender normativity are considered inviolable because they are rooted in sacred texts and/or in the authority of God (Cadge & Wildeman, 2008). As such, adherence to gender normative beliefs, practices, and structures is equated with piety, religious authenticity, respectability and goodness, while violations of such codes and practices are linked to sin, depravity, immorality, and evil as well as to eschatological consequences (Douglass, 1999). Religious communities police gender enactments, and there are social, emotional, physical, and material rewards and consequences for adhering to or violating those gendered expectations. In some instances the consequences of violating gender norms can be quite profound (e.g., consequences range from social marginalization to death).

Second, an integrative model requires that we consider the contexts that are meaningful for young people and the way that gender operates in these contexts. College is certainly one such context. However, how gender is understood and enacted among those who are educated may be different from how it is understood and lived by those who have limited or no access to postsecondary education. As such, we cannot generalize the experience of college students to non-college-educated individuals. There are also variations in college contexts, including Christian versus secular institutions (see Barry & Nelson, 2005), and in the way that gender operates in these settings.

Although college is an important context for many young American men and women, tens of thousands of men and women between the ages of 18 and 30 are incarcerated in state or federal prisons in the United States (Carson & Sabol, 2012). More than 2 million individuals who are 18–29 years old (most of whom are men) are veterans or are actively engaged in military service (Department of Veteran's Affairs, Statistical Abstracts of the United States, 2012). Data from the 2011 Annual Homeless Assessment Report to Congress also reveal that of the individuals who live in shelters for the homeless in urban contexts, 23.5% are between the ages of 18 and 30, and most are women (U.S. Department of Housing and Urban Development, 2011). Further, 8.4% of America's more than 100,000 homeless veterans (most of whom are men) are in this age group. These data point to the need for studies that look beyond college as a context for studying the link between gender, religiousness, and spirituality among emerging adults.

Third, an integrative model must question the ways that religious texts (e.g., the Torah, Guru Granth Shaib) and traditions shape the construction of social identities and social experiences of young men and women. In many political contexts religion shapes the opportunity structure for men and women—informing systems of gender privilege (e.g., gendered differences in access to educational or employment opportunities). Religion and spirituality also play critical roles in men's constructions of their identity as men (Hammond & Mattis, 2005; Satlow, 1996). Although some attention has been paid to the role of religion in men's gender identity construction, it is not clear how religion or spirituality informs gender identity construction for young women. These topics deserve exploration.

Fourth, an integrative model must explore how power and authority are negotiated across gender lines in sacred and secular spaces. Men occupy most public and powerful leadership positions in religious institutions, and the readings of sacred texts in many religious communities continue to reflect male voices and perspectives. Ozorak (1996) found that in order to negotiate gender inequality in religious institutions women use a core set of strategies: (1) cognitive strategies (e.g., they deny the existence of inequality; or reject formal religious involvement or rejection of faith); and (2) behavioral strategies (e.g., participate in women's groups at church). Liberation theologians, particularly feminist and feminist liberation theologians, have issued a call for theologies that more effectively regard and respect the roles of women (and men) in religious and cultural history; that respect the lived experiences and meaning-making systems of women; and that support institutional practices that provide men and women with equal opportunities to live their faith through service and leadership (Ahmed, 1992; Moon, 2008; Schüssler Fiorenza, 1983). Until we achieve these outcomes it will be useful to ask: How do young men and women come to invent "subjective theologies" that help them to live and function more effectively in their religious communities? How do young adults authorize and deauthorize gendered narratives within the theologies and faith communities? How do rationalizations and practices of (de)authorization complicate the landscape of young adults' faith (e.g., their readings of sacred text) and how might they inform theories of adult religious and spiritual development?

Fifth, in keeping with our understanding of gender as a meaning-making system, an integrative model would examine the link between gender and symbolic expressions of faith among emerging adults. Religion is a cultural system (Geertz, 1973) and the symbols (including gendered symbols) of faith life and piety and the meanings assigned to those symbols are continually received, constructed, and contested by individuals within any community. The meanings of gendered symbols of faith are not universal. The meanings of religious symbols are not intrinsic to the symbols themselves, nor are they static (i.e., meanings change across historical moments, sociopolitical contexts, or geographic spaces; Read & Bartowski, 2000). In keeping with this understanding of symbols, it will be critical for scholars to examine points of synthesis and difference in the ways in which men and women use, experience, and understand icons (e.g., religious symbols and images, clothing) in language, music, visual arts, poetry, social media, witness wear (e.g., clothing, jewelry that includes religious sayings or religious images), and in their use of body art (e.g., religious tattoos).

In many faith communities clothing serves as critical, gendered symbols of faith and of the expressive aspects of religious identity. In Sikh communities, for example, the topknot and turban (generally worn by boys and men) are clear public, gendered signs of Sikh identity and piety. Similarly, the kippa/yarmulka serves as a clear public sign of men's identity as orthodox Jews. Gendered symbols of faith and piety are also complex religious and political symbols that may have varying meanings for men and women in public and private contexts. For some Muslim women, for example, the veil/hijab is a powerful symbol of female religious piety, humility, modesty, sexual safety, respectability, cultural distinctiveness, liberation, and empowerment, and an overt symbol that marks the differences between men and women (Read & Bartowski, 2000). For some non-Muslim critics of Islam, and some Muslim feminists, however, the hijab serves as a public symbol of female oppression, of men's inability to manage their sexual urges, and of religious fanaticism and zealotry. When considered in tandem with theories on identity development and theories of faith development, these studies lead us to important questions. How, for example, are emerging-adult men's and women's decisions about whether to wear the public symbols of their faith informed by the developmental demands of this period of life (e.g., the need for connection and autonomy)?

Finally, an integrative model requires us to attend to religious institutions as spaces marked by highly gendered styles and patterns of expression (e.g., dancing, weeping). One important direction of future research will be to explore the ways in which gender norms of expressiveness (e.g., norms of emotional expression) are reified or challenged in religious spaces. These concerns have begun to be addressed in research on the Promise Keepers (an Evangelical Christian group that provides men with an all-male context in which they can intentionally (re)construct masculinity in the framework of Christianity). In their meetings Promise Keepers focus on issues and practices of connectedness, intimacy, and care (foci that are often seen as "feminine"), in the service of finding new ways to embrace and enact their authority and identity as men (Bartkowski, 2000; Heath, 2003). How gender and religiousness combine to shape men's and women's expressiveness should be explored.

## ▲ Conclusion

Scholars have come to fetishize putative gender differences in religiousness. The notion that men are less religious and spiritual than are women has become so ubiquitous that we have come to accept and reify it. Any serious effort to understand the roles of religion and spirituality in the lives of emerging adults of various gender orientations requires a distinctly interdisciplinary approach—one that integrates literature in the psychology and sociology of religion and spirituality, developmental psychology, gender studies, and feminist studies (among others). We must expand our view of gender from one that is binary to one that accommodates a range of gender constructions. We must take a deliberately intersectional approach to the construction of gender so that we can examine the ways in which classed, racialized, nationalized, and cultural constructions of religion inform how emerging adults experience their faith life. In integrating these literatures we must broaden our empirical and methodological foci (e.g., from a focus on sex differences in patterns of religious involvement) to include approaches that are explicitly focused on meaning. Finally, we must explore the ways in which theories of gender, developmental theories centered on emerging adulthood, and theories of spiritual and religious development intersect to shape our understandings of the faith lives of emerging adults.

## ▲ References

Ahmed, L. (1992). *Women and gender in Islam: Historical roots of a modern debate.* New Haven, CT: Yale University Press.

Ahrold, T. K., & Meston, C. M. (2010). Ethnic differences in sexual attitudes of U.S. college students: Gender, acculturation, and religiosity factors. *Archives of Sexual Behavior, 39*, 190–202. doi 10.1007/s10508-008-9406-1

Arnett, J. J., & Jensen, L. A. (2002). A congregation of one: Individualized religious beliefs among emerging adults. *Journal of Adolescent Research, 17*, 451–467. doi: 10.1177/ 0743558402175002

Barry, C. M., & Nelson, L. J. (2005). The role of religion in the transition to adulthood for young emerging adults. *Journal of Youth & Adolescence, 34*, 245–255. doi: 10.1007/s10964-005-4308-1

Barry, C. M., & Nelson, L. J., Davarya, S., & Urry, S. (2010). Religiosity and spirituality during the transition to adulthood. *International Journal of Behavioral Development, 34*, 311–324. doi: 10.1177/0165025409350964

Bartkowski, J. P. (2000). Breaking walls, raising fences: Masculinity, intimacy, and accountability among the Promise Keepers. *Sociology of Religion, 61, Special Issue: [Promise Keepers: A Comment on Religion and Social Movements]*, 33–53.

Cadge, W., & Wildeman, C. (2008). Facilitators and advocates: How mainline Protestant clergy respond to homosexuality. *Sociological Perspectives, 51*, 587–603.

Carson, E. A., & Sabol, W. (2012). Prisoners in 2011. December 2012, NCJ 239808. http://bjs.ojp.usdoj.gov/index.cfm?ty=pbdetail&iid=4559

Davidson, M. (2007). Seeking refuge under the umbrella: Inclusion, exclusion, and organizing within the category transgender. *Sexuality Research & Social Policy, 4*, 60–80.

Deaux, K., & Major, B. (1990). A social-psychological model of gender. In K. Deaux & B. Major (Eds.), *Theoretical perspectives on sexual difference* (pp. 89–99). New Haven, CT: Yale University Press.

Desmond, S. A., Morgan, K. H., & Kikuchi, G. (2010). Religious development: How (and why) does religiosity change from adolescence to young adulthood? *Sociological Perspectives, 53*, 247–270. doi: 10.1525/sop.2010.53.2.247

Douglass, S. (1999). *Sexuality and the Black church: A womanist perspective.* Maryknoll, NY: Orbis Books.

Geertz, C. (1973). *The interpretation of cultures.* New York, NY: Basic Books.

Hammond, W. P., & Mattis, J. S. (2005). Being a man about it: Manhood meaning among African American men. *Psychology of Men & Masculinity, 6*, 114–126. doi: 10.1037/1524-9220.6.2.114

Heath, M. (2003). Soft-boiled masculinity: Renegotiating gender and racial ideologies in the Promise Keepers movement. *Gender and Society, 17*, 423–444.

Loewenthal, K. M., MacLeod, A. K., & Cinnirella, M. (2002). Are women more religious than men? Gender differences in religious activity among different religious groups in the U.K. *Personality and Individual Differences, 32*, 133–139.

Lummis, A. T. (2004). A research note: Real men and church participation. *Review of Religious Research, 45*, 404–414.

Marini, M. M. (1990). Sex and gender: What do we know? *Sociological Forum, 5*, 95–120.

McKenzie, G. O. (1994). *Transgender nation.* Bowling Green, OH: Bowling Green State University Popular Press.

Milevsky, I. M., Szuchman, L., & Milevsky, A. (2008). Transmission of religious beliefs in college students. *Mental Health, Religion & Culture, 11*, 423–434. doi.org/10.1080/13674670701507541

Moon, H. (2008). Women priests: Radical change or more of the same? *Journal of Feminist Studies in Religion, 24*, 115–134.

Nelson, L. J., Padilla-Walker, L. M., & Carroll, J. S. (2010). "I believe it is wrong but I still do it": A comparison of religious young men who do versus do not use pornography. *Psychology of Religion and Spirituality, 2*, 136–147. doi: 10.1037/a0019127

Ozorak, E. W. (1996). The power, but not the glory: How women empower themselves through religion. *Journal for the Scientific Study of Religion, 35*, 17–29.

Pew Forum on Religion and Public Life. (2008). *U.S. religious landscape survey*. Washington, DC: Pew Research Center.

Read, J. G., & Bartkowski, J. P. (2000). To veil or not to veil? A case study of identity negotiation among Muslim women in Austin, Texas. *Gender and Society, 14*, 395–417.

Satlow, M. L. (1996). "Try to be a man": The Rabbinic construction of masculinity. *The Harvard Theological Review, 89*, 19–40.

Schüssler Fiorenza, E. (1983). *In memory of her: A feminist reconstruction of Christian origins*. New York, NY: Crossroads.

Sirin, S. R., & Katsiaficas, D. (2011). Religiosity, discrimination, and community engagement: Gendered pathways of Muslim American emerging adults. *Youth & Society, 43*, 1528–1546.

Smith, C. (with Snell, P.). (2009). *Souls in transition: The religious and spiritual lives of emerging adults*. New York, NY: Oxford University Press.

Stewart, A. J., & McDermott, C. (2004). Gender in psychology. *Annual Review of Psychology, 55*, 519–544. doi 10.1146.

Stoppa, T. M., & Lefkowitz, E. S. (2010). Longitudinal changes in religiosity among emerging adult college students. *Journal of Research on Adolescence, 20*, 23–38. doi: 10.1111/j.1532-7795.2009.00630.x

Stryker, S. (1998). The transgender issue: An introduction. *GLQ: A Journal of Lesbian and Gay Studies, 4*, 145–158.

Sullins, D. P. (2006). Gender and religion: Deconstructing universality, constructing complexity. *American Journal of Sociology, 112*, 838–880. doi: 10.1086/507852

U.S. Department of Housing and Urban Development. (2011). The 2011 point-in-time estimates of homelessness: Supplement to the annual homeless assessment report. Retrieved from http://www.hudhre.info/documents/PIT-HIC_SupplementalAHARReport.pdf

# 11 ▲

# The Roles of Religiousness and Spirituality in the Sexual Lives of Heterosexual Emerging Adults

TARA M. STOPPA, GRACIELA ESPINOSA-HERNANDEZ, AND MEGHAN M. GILLEN

*Being a religious person and believing in what my religion asks of me and what it instructs me to do, I am not allowed to have any sexual relationships with women. The concept of premarital sex is not allowed in Islam. So anything that would lead to it is best left not pursued. So I try to be avoidant to anything that would lead to it ... because it would be inconsistent with who I am and what I believe.*
—Ahmed, age 24, Muslim

*I think for me, I have questions ... sometimes, I'm still uneasy about things with the Catholic Church's teachings and sexuality ... like on abortion and birth control and homosexuality. And I still question like "What's the difference between what I believe and what the Catholic Church says?" I sometimes see those as two different things, even though as a Catholic, it's supposed to be the same thing.... sometimes I see the Catholic Church as like government, you know. And the government is not always right in my view.*
—Mary, age 21, Roman Catholic

These opening excerpts (Stoppa, 2009) highlight the experiences of two emerging adults wrestling with the intersections of their religious and sexual lives. As these vignettes illustrate, emerging adulthood can be a significant time of discernment and meaning-making, which for many young people may involve seeking to establish religious and/

or spiritual identities and integrating these domains with other salient aspects of identity and behavior, such as interpersonal relationships and sexuality (Arnett, 2004; Lefkowitz, 2005).

Many emerging adults experience changes in aspects of their religious and spiritual identities during this period (see Chapter 2). For instance, emerging adults may demonstrate increased skepticism of religious dogma and its applications in their lives relative to previous points in their development. For some emerging adults, such questioning may lead to "picking and choosing" from an array of religious and spiritual identity and behavioral choices (Arnett & Jensen, 2002). A minority of emerging adults also remain highly devoted to the specific tenets of their respective faith traditions, whereas for others, religiousness and spirituality may not be relevant. Religious and spiritual experiences and their roles in individuals' lives vary significantly based upon individuals' personal characteristics and social and cultural contexts (Smith, 2009).

Further, for some emerging adults, religious and spiritual identities and behaviors may be integrated with their intimate and sexual lives in coherent ways, whereas for others, intersections between these domains may pose significant conflict. How emerging adults reconcile religion, spirituality, and sexuality may affect how they view themselves, their relationships, and the attitudes and behaviors they may carry into adulthood. In this chapter, we present an overview of how emerging adults negotiate such important intersections between their religious and spiritual beliefs and practices with their sexual lives. We do so under the assumptions of developmental systems theory (Lerner, Boyd, & Lynch, 2008) with attention to the dynamic nature of emerging adults' development in these domains, as well as to the various contexts which may influence and be influenced by individuals' sexual development. We focus mostly on heterosexual emerging adults' experiences, acknowledging that these experiences may differ in unique ways from sexual minorities' experiences (see Chapter 12).

First, we provide an overview of close relationships and sexuality among emerging adults and second, we describe important findings that highlight the influence of religiousness, spirituality, and religious affiliation on emerging adults' sexual behaviors and beliefs and other specific sex-related issues such as abortion, pornography, and romantic relationships. Next, we describe processes of integration and dissonance between religious identities and sexuality. Finally, we suggest promising directions for future research and practice.

## ▲ Close Relationships and Sexuality in Emerging Adulthood

Exploring intersections between emerging adults' religious experiences and their sexual lives requires a broader understanding of emerging adults' intimate relationships and sexuality. As individuals move from adolescence to emerging adulthood, relationships tend to involve greater physical intimacy and become more serious (Arnett, 2004), yet the role of culture and religion can shape the nature of these developmental trajectories. Many emerging adults report changes in sexual beliefs, such as becoming more accepting of casual sex and feeling less guilt about sexuality as compared to adolescents (e.g., Chara & Kuennen, 1994; Lefkowitz, 2005).

Partnered sexual activities also increase from adolescence to emerging adulthood (Herbenick et al., 2010a), with a majority of 18–24 year olds reporting that they have had some type of oral or penetrative sex (Buhi, Marhefka, & Hoban, 2010; Grello, Welsh, & Harper, 2006). About half of 18–21 year olds indicate that some of this activity may occur with a casual partner (Grello et al., 2006); however, recent intercourse and oral sex is still more likely to occur in the context of a romantic relationship (Herbenick et al., 2010b).

Relative to other adult age groups, emerging adults' frequency of sexual behavior is high. Women ages 18 to 29 report higher frequency rates of intercourse than older women (ages 30 to 92; Herbenick et al., 2010b). Married men ages 18 to 29 report the highest rates of intercourse among adult men; over 95% report intercourse in the last 3 months (Reece et al., 2010). Nearly 50% of married women ages 18–24 have intercourse twice per week or more, a frequency that declines steadily with age among women (ages 25 to 92; Herbenick et al., 2010b). Emerging adulthood is also a peak period for a variety of sexual risk-taking behaviors that may increase risks for acquiring sexually transmitted infections (STIs), including unprotected sexual activity, combining sexual activity with alcohol or drug use, and casual sexual encounters (Centers for Disease Control and Prevention, 2010; Fielder & Carey, 2010; Grello et al., 2006).

### Influence of Religiousness and Spirituality on Close Relationships and Sexuality

Research suggests that religiousness and spirituality matter for many areas of emerging adults' relational and sexual development, but findings depend upon contextual factors and the particular aspects of religiousness/spirituality and relationships/sexuality examined. In this section, we review how religiousness, religious affiliation, and spirituality may impact emerging adults' sexual attitudes and behaviors as well as their attitudes and behaviors with respect to other sex-related issues, including abortion, pornography, dating, cohabitation, and marriage.

### Sexual Attitudes and Behaviors

Based upon the proscriptions of their respective religious traditions or spiritual beliefs, some emerging adults report remaining abstinent of sexual activity in anticipation of marriage (Halpern, Waller, Spriggs, & Hallfors, 2006; Regnerus & Uecker, 2011). In this respect, there is a connection between the perceived influence of religion on individuals' personal lives and sexual abstinence. For example, emerging adults who are sexually abstinent report that religion has more influence on their daily lives and that they adhere more to religious teachings than do sexually active individuals. In addition, considering religion to be more influential is associated with more conservative sexual attitudes about when a sexual behavior is acceptable (Lefkowitz, Gillen, Shearer, & Boone, 2004). Intrinsic religiousness and religious fundamentalism are also associated with more conservative sexual attitudes toward same-sex sexuality, casual sex, and extramarital sex. These associations, however, are stronger among European Americans and Asian Americans as compared to Latino Americans (Ahrold & Meston, 2010).

High levels of religious importance and attendance at religious services also have been associated with guilt about masturbation, decreased likelihood of having sexual intercourse, decreased numbers of sexual partners, more restrictive contraceptive attitudes and behaviors, and reduced sexual risk-taking (Lefkowitz et al., 2004; Regnerus & Uecker, 2011; Rostosky, Regnerus, & Wright, 2003). In fact, religiousness may have a protective role against risky sexual behaviors among emerging adults, including Latino, European, and African Americans (Edwards, Haglund, Fehring, & Pruszynski, 2011; Kogan et al., 2008). Similar associations have been found in non-US samples, including university students in both Germany and Turkey (Brody et al., 1996; Essizoglu, Yasan, Yildirim, Gurgen, & Ozkan, 2011).

Research regarding emerging adults' religious affiliation suggests that it may likewise have some influence in shaping sexual attitudes and behaviors; however, findings are inconsistent. Young people who identify as Muslim, Catholic, and Evangelical Protestant tend to hold more conservative sexual attitudes relative to other emerging adults (e.g., Coleman & Testa, 2008; Lefkowitz et al., 2004). With respect to sexual behavior, in one study, emerging adults who identified as Protestant, Catholic, and nonbelievers (agnostic, atheist, or no religion) were equally likely to be sexually active (Lefkowitz et al., 2004), but in another study, Jews were less likely and Catholics more likely to have had intercourse than nonaffiliated individuals (Pluhar, Frongillo, Stycos, & Dempster-McClain, 1998). In another study, Muslim women were the least likely to engage in intercourse relative to other affiliations (Coleman & Testa, 2008). In terms of lifetime sexual partners, Lefkowitz et al. (2004) report that Catholics have fewer lifetime partners than do Protestants, although nonaffiliated individuals did not differ from either group. Religious affiliation may be a better predictor of sexual activity among women than men. Women with a religious affiliation are less likely to report engaging in sexual intercourse compared to nonreligious women. In contrast, no religious affiliation differences were found among men (Farmer, Trapnell, & Meston, 2009). The inconsistency in these findings may be due to heterogeneity within religious affiliations. Although emerging adults may share a religious faith, other factors may be more important in contributing to their sexual attitudes and behaviors (e.g., extent to which they adhere to religious teachings, attendance at religious services). To that end, it is important to acknowledge the within-group variability that may exist within religious faiths. To capture this variability, research should examine sexual attitudes and behaviors among individuals of the same faith (e.g., oral contraceptive attitudes among Jordanian Muslim women; Kridli & Schott-Baer, 2004).

In addition to religious affiliation, it is important to examine the connection between spirituality and sexual attitudes and behaviors. Spirituality may be associated with more frequent sexual activity among women. In two samples of mostly emerging adults (Brelsford, Luquis, & Murray-Swank, 2011; Burris, Smith, & Carlson, 2009), findings suggest that women who were more spiritual, regardless of religiousness, had more sexual partners, and engaged in more frequent sexual activity and sex without a condom compared to women who identified as less spiritual (Burris et al., 2009). In contrast, men who were more spiritual engaged in less sexual activity and endorsed less permissive sexual attitudes than did less spiritual men (Brelsford et al., 2011; Burris et al.,

2009), suggesting that women may be more likely to find a spiritual connection with self and others through sex than men.

## Contraception

Religiousness and spirituality also may influence emerging adults' attitudes and behaviors regarding other sex-related issues. For example, some religions discourage the use of contraceptives (Brewster, Cooksey, Guilkey, & Rindfuss, 1998); however, research on the association between religion/religiousness and contraceptive use is complex. Some work shows no association (Adamcyzk & Felson, 2008; Brewster et al., 1998), whereas others show that more religious female emerging adults may be less likely to use effective contraceptives (e.g., Coleman & Testa, 2008). Moreover, more religious emerging adults are more likely to use abstinence or withdrawal (Pluhar et al., 1998). Other work suggests that Catholics and Protestants may have greater difficulty discussing contraception relative to their less religious peers (Lefkowitz et al., 2004).

## Abortion

Religiousness also may be related to beliefs and behaviors pertaining to abortion. According to many religions, life begins at conception, making abortion morally wrong. Some studies indicate that traditional-age college students who identify as non-Catholic (vs. Catholic), have no religion (vs. a committed religious affiliation), and who are less religious (vs. more religious) have more favorable attitudes toward abortion (Esposito & Basow, 1995; Hess & Rueb, 2005). Others show that although many young Evangelical Christians hold more liberal views compared to older Evangelicals on issues of sexuality, such as premarital sexual behavior, same-sex sexuality, and cohabitation, both tend to share restrictive views about abortion (Farrell, 2011). With respect to religiousness and actual abortion behavior, among unmarried women who became pregnant as adolescents or emerging adults, Conservative Protestants are less likely to have an abortion than mainline Protestants, Catholics, and those of non-Christian religions, even when accounting for religiousness. There does not appear to be an association between religiousness and obtaining an abortion (Adamczyk, 2008, 2009). However, religiousness may indirectly be associated with unmarried women having an abortion by increasing the chances that they will marry and carry the pregnancy to term (Adamczyk & Felson, 2008).

## Pornography

Pornography viewing is another domain of sexual behavior prevalent among emerging adults with 50% of emerging-adult women and 92% of emerging-adult men reporting ever having viewed sexually explicit material (Morgan, 2011). In spite of many religious groups' prohibitions, it is not clear whether those who are more religious differ in their use of pornography than their less religious peers. Some work shows no association between religiousness and ever using cyberporn (Baltazar, Helm, McBride, Hopkins, & Stevens, 2010), whereas other work shows that students who are more religious report less exposure to sexually explicit materials (Lottes, Weinberg, & Weller, 1993), and that more religious men report using cyberporn less frequently (Baltazar et al., 2010) compared to those who are less religious. In contrast, other research shows that young men who are more religious report more cyberporn use than do those who are less religious (Abell, Steenburgh, & Boivin, 2006). In general, discrepant findings on religiousness and sexual behaviors and attitudes suggest that these associations are complex and may depend on various, and perhaps intersecting, factors such as religious affiliation and adherence to or identification with religious teachings.

## Dating, Cohabitation, and Marriage

Once emerging adults become sexually active and involved in committed romantic relationships, such relationships may affect religious attendance and vice versa. Uecker and colleagues (2007, 2008) found that religious attendance declined more among emerging adults who engaged in premarital sex compared to those who did not. Similarly, married emerging adults who attended religious services weekly or considered religion to be very important (as adolescents) were more likely to abstain from sex until marriage compared to emerging adults who never attended or did not consider religion as important. These findings suggest that the context in which sexual activity occurs within a romantic relationship may be related to religiousness and vice versa.

Although not as common as marriage, cohabitation has grown increasingly prevalent among emerging adults (Eggebeen & Dew, 2009). Cohabitation may be related to religiousness and religious service attendance. For instance, cohabitation is particularly common in Sweden, a nation with low levels of religiousness and religious participation (e.g., Wiik, Bernhardt, & Noack, 2009). Similarly, Uecker and colleagues (2007, 2008) found that in the United States, cohabitation was associated with less religious service attendance. Moreover, adolescents who are high in religious fervor and attendance, and who identify as Conservative Protestant, mainline Protestant, or Catholic are less likely than are their less religiously affiliated peers to cohabit as emerging adults (Eggebeen & Dew, 2009). The authors also note that religiousness may be related to both the timing of when emerging adults choose to establish marital or cohabiting unions, and the quality of these unions. National data from the Add Health study indicate that about one-third of religious individuals cohabit, and when they do, their cohabiting unions are more likely to end in marriage relative to nonreligious individuals (Eggebeen & Dew, 2009; Uecker, Regnerus, & Vaaler, 2007). Compared to couples who did not cohabitate prior to marriage, those who engage in premarital cohabitation, however, are more likely to report lower levels of marital quality and a greater chance of divorce (see Stanley, Rhoades, & Fincham, 2011), which may be due in part to lower levels of religiousness among cohabiting men (but not women; Stanley, Whitton, & Markman, 2004).

## ▲ Negotiating Integration and Conflicts Between Religious and Sexual Domains

How do emerging adults negotiate and make meaning of intersections and potential conflicts between the religious dimensions of their lives and sexual experiences? In this section, we attend to this question with a particular focus on religiousness and religious identity given their often institutional and publically mediated natures. Although spirituality may overlap with these areas, for many individuals, spiritual domains may be construed as more private and personalized (Zinnbauer & Pargament, 2006), and therefore may not involve the same integration challenges that may arise with religious domains.

For emerging adults who participate in organized religious settings, religious experiences may constitute a powerful source of social control (see Chapter 8). Depending upon the relevance and salience of religious institutions, experiences in such contexts may serve as guidance or be used to formulate young people's own views and practices (Oser, Scarlett, & Bucher, 2006; Regnerus, 2007). By providing common ideologies and offering specific codes for morality, religious institutions may socialize members to adhere to particular norms associated with sexuality, while discouraging adoption of beliefs or behaviors that are considered aberrant.

The elements of behavior and belief emphasized by particular religious contexts may differ markedly from one another, however (Barry & Nelson, 2005). In some religious contexts, regular religious engagement and adherence may be emphasized, whereas in others, individuals may perceive greater openness either from the institution or its members to be selective about which aspects of belief and practice they choose to adhere. Additionally, religious contexts may vary in terms of the specific teachings on issues of sexuality and relationships that they communicate to their members. For instance, Mormon young people attend regular classes where explicit sexual socialization occurs by discussing sexual ethics, and they are restricted from religious rituals if they are sexually active (Uecker, 2008). Conversely, Black Protestant young adults rarely discuss sexual issues in church (Rubin, Billingsley, & Caldwell, 1994). Despite prohibitive messages about sexual activity in some conservative religious groups, some aspects of sexuality may be revered as sacred within particular religious contexts, such as honoring the body or connecting with the divine through appropriate sexual expression, thereby potentially encouraging individuals to engage in those behaviors or to adopt positive attitude or belief orientations toward them within the context of committed, loving marital relationships (Murray-Swank, Pargament, & Mahoney, 2005).

## Processes of Integration and Conflict

Consistent with developmental systems theory (Lerner et al., 2008), processes of identity and behavioral formation are both dynamic and contextually mediated. Building upon Erikson's (1968) conceptualization of identity as a "configuration" that may encompass multiple identifications arranged in various ways, Schachter (2004) points to the diversity of these processes by highlighting four forms of configuration processes with respect to religious and sexual identifications: assimilation and synthesis; choice and suppression; compartmentalization; and intentional dissonance.

In the process of assimilation and synthesis, aspects of identity and associated behaviors are integrated without conflict or introjected into frameworks in which potential conflicts are minimized (Schachter, 2004). This configuration may characterize the minority of emerging adults who, based upon their religious identities, report choosing to abstain from premarital sex and who remain faithful to conservative beliefs about sexuality or relationships espoused by their traditions (e.g., Freitas, 2008; Regnerus & Uecker, 2011). Nelson (2003) suggests that Mormon emerging adults tend to be particularly strong in their religious identifications and experience religious contexts that support adherence. Thus, many Mormon emerging adults report that compliance with the norms of their tradition is an important criterion for maturity and often tend not to engage in risky behaviors, including premarital sexual activity. Assimilation and synthesis of religious and sexual identities may often result in particular social and personal benefits, such as acceptance from others and feelings of coherence. For other individuals, however, such compliance (or periods of noncompliance) may not be without social and personal costs, such as relational difficulties or feelings of incongruence until integration is achieved.

Some emerging adults may instead construct configurations based upon processes of choice and suppression, elevating one aspect of identity and patterning other behaviors and beliefs on this chosen identification. For some individuals, this may involve complete rejection of conflicting domains of identity and behavior, whereas for others, selective rejection of specific opposing parts (Schachter, 2004). Certain emerging adults may choose to give up previously formed religious identities and practices because of conflicts they perceive with currently unfolding aspects of identity and behavior (Uecker, Regnerus, & Vaaler, 2007). For example, many sexual-minority young people, especially those in more sexually conservative traditions, report that due to perceived incongruence between their religious and sexual identities and ostracism they experience within their respective religious traditions, they opt to reject previous religious identifications (Yarhouse & Tan, 2005; see Chapter 12).

Other emerging adults may selectively choose to integrate certain elements of religious identities and behaviors with their sexual lives but permit other facets to remain in conflict (Schachter, 2004). Emerging adults who identify with more sexually conservative religious traditions may be more selectively permissive, whereas this may not be the case for others who identify with traditions that are already more liberal with respect to sexual issues. For example, Regnerus and Uecker (2011) found that Evangelical Protestant emerging adults may adhere to prohibitions about premarital intercourse but may still engage in an array of other sexual activities, such as oral sex or masturbation. Additionally, although young people who identify as Catholic may persist in other parts of identification with their faith, many report selective interpretation and adherence to official doctrines concerning issues of sexuality, such as using contraception and accepting same-sex sexuality and marriage despite adhering to the Church's teachings on abortion or other issues (Barry & Nelson, 2005; Dillon, 1996).

A third way that individuals negotiate conflicts between religious and sexual spheres of their lives during this time may involve identity processes based upon compartmentalization, wherein multiple aspects of identity and behavior are maintained but kept in separate spheres (Schachter, 2004). For example, some emerging adults who identify with sexually conservative traditions may maintain such identities but also may choose to embrace sexually permissive attitudes and behaviors, fully practicing and identifying with both identities but reconciling potential conflicts by keeping the two domains isolated in their lives (Regnerus & Uecker, 2011).

A fourth identity process that some emerging adults may utilize to negotiate such conflicts may be to construct intentionally dissonant identity configurations between their religious and sexual lives in order to experience a sense of excitement or challenge. For instance, Schachter (2004) described the experiences of modern orthodox Jewish emerging adults from Israel who formed intentionally permissive sexual identities, despite inconsistencies with their religious beliefs, because it made them feel distinct or unique.

### Consequences

Although for some individuals incongruence between religious and sexual identities and behaviors may not be distressing, for others, the cognitive, emotional, or behavioral dissonance that may be experienced can be associated with psychosocial difficulties or identity-related problems. Individuals also may experience significant social consequences, such as relational discord or estrangement from family members or faith communities.

For example, Freitas (2008) found that many Evangelical Protestant emerging adults who attended spiritual colleges (colleges that may be public or private wherein there may be spiritual resources, but a specific tradition is not embraced by the majority of students) reported heightened experiences of conflicts between aspects of their religious and spiritual identities and practices and their sexual desires and behaviors. Instead of being able to assimilate or synthesize these domains easily, these emerging adults indicated that they still felt pressure from others to comply with religious expectations on sexual issues, despite their actual behaviors, desires, or true personal beliefs. In such cases, individuals may experience anxiety, shame, or depression due to being unable to reconcile meaningful aspects of the self (e.g., Barry & Nelson, 2005; Freitas, 2008; Yarhouse & Tan, 2005). Nelson and colleagues (2010) found that Mormon emerging-adult men who reported using pornography experienced greater psychosocial difficulties associated with the incongruence of violating the prohibitions of their faith, lower levels of religious engagement, and lower levels of relationship-oriented identity development relative to Mormon emerging-adult men who did not use pornography or experience similar conflicts. Managing sexual desire in permissible ways may be difficult, then, in particular contexts.

Nonetheless, if one's religious or spiritual identity or the effect of other mediating contextual factors is only minimally salient or not relevant, then identity and behavioral incongruencies may be more personally and socially acceptable to the individual and may not necessarily entail psychological distress (Wimberly, 1989). For those who do experience distress, however, helping individuals to resolve conflicts between personally relevant aspects of their identities may be an important priority for promoting adaptive meaning-making and development during emerging adulthood.

## ▲ Limitations and Future Directions

In this section, we point to specific limitations in current research and suggest a number of areas for promising research directions. First, although several studies suggest that the effects of religiousness are stronger for women's sexuality than men's (e.g., Brelsford et al., 2011; Burris et al., 2009), many studies conduct analyses separately for men and women (Ahrold & Meston, 2010; Farmer et al., 2009). In this regard, we recommend that future research carefully consider intersections between gender and religiousness. Similarly, researchers should further consider the intersection between culture and religion and how it affects sexuality. For instance, Magana and Clark (1995) argue that Catholic religion may be especially integrated into Mexican culture, which may affect Mexican emerging adults' sexual attitudes and behaviors in unique ways. Additionally, we acknowledge that current research in this area may be affected by response biases and reporting errors as some groups, particularly individuals who identify with more conservative religions, may be more likely relative to other groups to underreport their sexual behaviors due to perceived stigma in admitting their actual sexual behaviors (see Freitas, 2008), whereas others, such as emerging-adult men, may overestimate their sexual activity because it may invite praise from others consistent with the sexual double standard (Crawford & Popp, 2003; Lefkowitz, Gillen, & Vasilenko,, 2011). Future research should seek to be especially attentive to these issues in order to ensure accurate portrayals of emerging adults' sexual lives.

## ▲ Conclusion

As highlighted in this chapter, religiousness and spirituality may shape emerging adults' sexual attitudes, beliefs, and behaviors in important ways. Integrating religious or spiritual domains with sexual identities and behaviors is important but sometimes a challenging task for emerging adults. To this end, we conclude by providing recommendations as to how this process may be facilitated. Many religious or spiritual contexts may be silent about issues of sexuality or send messages to young people that their sexuality (at least prior to marriage) cannot be reconciled with their religious faith, which may lead to identity conflicts, confusion, and risky behaviors (Freitas, 2008). Instead, we believe that it is important that religious or spiritual communities be intentional in seeking to support young people in navigating these issues. These communities should not simply emphasize problem-based perspectives but assist emerging adults to consider healthy, normative aspects of sexual and relational development. This assistance might include creating spaces for active discussions about issues of sexuality and sexual development, offering counseling, critiquing media messages about unhealthy sexuality, providing educational programs, or offering exposure to role models who have successfully negotiated the interface between religiousness, spirituality, relationships, and sexuality.

Religious institutions also should consider that emerging adults may negotiate intersections and conflicts between religiousness and sexuality in diverse ways. With time, careful thought, and appropriate support in navigating the intersections between religion, spirituality, and sexuality, emerging adults may be better able to reconcile these critical aspects of their lives.

## ▲ Acknowledgments

The authors would like to thank Carolyn Barry and Mona Abo-Zena, who provided helpful comments on earlier versions of this draft.

## ▲ References

Abell, J. W., Steenbergh, T. A., & Boivin, M. J. (2006). Cyberporn use in the context of religiosity. *Journal of Psychology and Theology, 34,* 165–171. doi: 10.1007/s10802-005-9011-x

Adamczyk, A. (2008). The effects of religious contextual norms, structural constraints, and personal religiosity on abortion decisions. *Social Science Research, 37,* 657–672. doi: 10.1016/j.ssresearch.2007.09.003

Adamczyk, A. (2009). Understanding the effects of personal and school religiosity on the decision to abort a premarital pregnancy. *Journal of Health and Social Behavior, 50,* 180–195. doi: 10.1177/002214650905000205

Adamczyk, A., & Felson, J. (2008). Fetal positions: Unraveling the influence of religion on premarital pregnancy resolution. *Social Science Quarterly, 89,* 17–38. doi: 10.1111/j.1540-6237.2008.00519.x

Ahrold, T. K., & Meston, C. M. (2010). Ethnic differences in sexual attitudes of U.S. college students: Gender, acculturation, and religiosity factors. *Archives of Sexual Behavior, 39,* 190–202. doi:10.1007/s10508-008-9406-1

Arnett, J. J. (2004). *Emerging adulthood: The winding road from the late teens through the twenties.* New York, NY: Oxford University Press.

Arnett, J. J., & Jensen, L. A. (2002). A congregation of one: Individualized religious beliefs among emerging adults. *Journal of Adolescent Research, 17,* 451–467. doi: 10.1177/0743558402175002

Baltazar, A., Helm, H. W., McBride, D., Hopkins, G., & Stevens, J. V. (2010). Internet pornography use in the context of external and internal religiosity. *Journal of Psychology and Theology, 38,* 32–40. Retrieved from http://journals.biola.edu/jpt

Barry, C. M., & Nelson, L. J. (2005). The role of religion in the transition to adulthood for young emerging adults. *Journal of Youth and Adolescence, 34,* 245–255. doi: 10.1007/s10964-005-4308-1

Brelsford, G. M., Luquis, R., & Murray-Swank, N. A. (2011). College students' permissive sexual attitudes: Links to religiousness and spirituality.

*International Journal for the Psychology of Religion, 21*, 127–136. doi: 10.1080/10508619.2011.557005

Brewster, K. L., Cooksey, E., Guilkey, D., & Rindfuss, R. (1998). The changing impact of religion on the sexual and contraceptive behavior of adolescent women in the United States. *Journal of Marriage and Family, 60*, 493–504. doi: 10.2307/353864

Brody, S., Rau, H., Fuhrer, N., Hillebrand, H., Rudiger, D., & Braun, M. (1996). Traditional ideology as an inhibitor of sexual behavior. *The Journal of Psychology, 130*, 615–626. doi: 10.1080/00223980.1996.9915035

Buhi, E. R., Marhefka, S. L., & Hoban, M. T. (2010). The State of the Union: Sexual health disparities in a national sample of U.S. college students. *Journal of American College Health, 58*, 337–346. doi: 10.1080/07448480903501780

Burris, J. L., Smith, G. T., & Carlson, C. R. (2009). Relations among religiousness, spirituality, and sexual practices. *Journal of Sex Research, 46*, 282–289. doi:10.1080/00224490802684582

Centers for Disease Control and Prevention (2010). *Sexually transmitted disease surveillance, 2010*. Hyattsville, MD: National Center for Health Statistics. Retrieved from http://www.cdc.gov

Chara, P. J., & Kuennen, L. M. (1994). Diverging gender attitudes regarding casual sex: A cross sectional study. *Psychological Reports, 74*, 57–58. doi:10.2466/pr0.1994.74.1.57

Coleman, L. M., & Testa, A. (2008). Sexual health knowledge, attitudes, and behaviours: Variations among a religiously diverse sample of young people in London, UK. *Ethnicity & Health, 13*, 55–72. doi:10.1080/13557850701803163

Crawford, M., & Popp, D. (2003). Sexual double standards: A review and methodological critique of two decades of research. *Journal of Sex Research, 40*, 13–26. doi: http://dx.doi.org/10.1080/00224490309552163

Dillon, M. (1996). The persistence of religious identity among college Catholics. *Journal for the Scientific Study of Religion, 35*, 165–170. doi:10.2307/1387083

Edwards, L. M., Haglund, K., Fehring, R. J., & Pruszynski, J. (2011). Religiosity and sexual risk behaviors among Latina adolescents: Trends from 1995 to 2008. *Journal of Women's Health, 20*, 871–877. doi:10.1089/jwh.2010.1949

Eggebeen, D., & Dew, J. (2009). The role of religion in adolescence for family formation in young adulthood. *Journal of Marriage and Family, 71*, 108–121. doi: 10.1111/j.1741-3737.2008.00583.x

Erikson, E. (1968). *Identity: Youth and crisis*. New York, NY: Norton.

Esposito, C. L., & Basow, S. A. (1995). College students' attitudes toward abortion: The role of knowledge and demographic variables. *Journal of Applied Social Psychology, 25*, 1996–2017. doi: 10.1111/j.1559-1816.1995.tb01828.x

Essizoglu, A., Yasan, A., Yildirim, E. A., Gurgen, F., & Ozkan, M. (2011). Double standard for traditional value of virginity and premarital sexuality in Turkey: A university student's case. *Women & Health, 51*, 136–150. doi: 10.1080/03630242.2011.553157

Farmer, M. A., Trapnell, P. D., & Meston, C. M. (2009). The relation between sexual behavior and religiosity subtypes: A test of the secularization hypothesis. *Archives of Sexual Behavior, 38*, 852–865. doi:10.1007/s10508-008-9407-0

Farrell, J. (2011). The young and the restless: The liberalization of young Evangelicals. *Journal for the Scientific Study of Religion, 50*, 517–532. doi: 10.1111/j.1468-5906.2011.01589.x

Fielder, R. L., & Carey, M. P. (2010). Prevalence and characteristics of sexual hookups among first-semester female college students. *Journal of Sex & Marital Therapy, 36*, 346–359. doi: 10.1080/0092623X.2010.488118

Freitas, D. (2008). *Sex and the soul: Juggling sexuality, spirituality, romance, and religion on America's college campuses.* New York, NY: Oxford University Press.

Grello, C. M., Welsh, D. P., & Harper, M. S. (2006). No strings attached: The nature of casual sex in college students. *Journal of Sex Research, 43*, 255–267. doi:10.1080/00224490609552324

Halpern, C. T., Waller, M. W., Spriggs, A., & Hallfors, D. D. (2006). Adolescent predictors of emerging adult sexual patterns. *Journal of Adolescent Health, 39*, 926.e1–926.e10. doi:10.1016/j.jadohealth.2006.08.005

Herbenick, D., Reece, M., Schick, V., Sanders, S. A., Dodge, B., & Fortenberry, J. D. (2010a). Sexual behaviors in the United States: Results from a national probability sample of men and women ages 14–94. *Journal of Sexual Medicine, 7*, 255–265. doi: 10.1111/j.1743-6109.2010.02012.x

Herbenick, D., Reece, M., Schick, V., Sanders, S. A., Dodge, B., & Fortenberry, J. D. (2010b). Sexual behaviors, relationships, and perceived health status among adult women in the United States: Results from a national probability sample. *Journal of Sexual Medicine, 7*, 277–290. doi: 10.1111/j.1743-6109.2010.02010.x

Hess, J. A., & Rueb, J. D. (2005). Attitudes toward abortion, religion, and party affiliation among college students. *Current Psychology: A Journal for Diverse Perspectives on Diverse Psychological Issues, 24*, 24–42. doi: 10.1007/s12144-005-1002-0

Kogan, S. M., Brody, G. H., Gibbons, F. X., Murry, V. M., Cutrona, C. E., Simons, R. L. et al. (2008). The influence of role status on risky sexual behavior among African Americans during the transition to adulthood. *Journal of Black Psychology, 34*, 399–420. doi: 10.1177/0095798408320716

Kridli, S. A., & Scott-Baer, D. (2004). Jordanian Muslim women's intention to use oral contraceptives. *Research and Theory for Nursing Practice: An International Journal, 18*, 345–356. doi: 10.1891/rtnp.18.4.345.64096

Lefkowitz, E. S. (2005). "Things have gotten better": Developmental changes among emerging adults after the transition to university. *Journal of Adolescent Research, 20*, 40–63. doi:10.1177/0743558404271236

Lefkowitz, E. S., Gillen, M. M., Shearer, C. L., & Boone, T. L. (2004). Religiosity, sexual behaviors, and sexual attitudes during emerging adulthood. *Journal of Sex Research, 41*, 150–159. doi:10.1080/00224490409552223

Lefkowitz, E. S., Gillen, M. M., & Vasilenko, S. (2011). Putting the romance back into sex: Sexuality in romantic relationships. In F. Fincham & M. Cui (Eds.), *Romantic relationships in emerging adulthood* (pp. 213–233). New York, NY: Cambridge University Press.

Lerner, R. M., Boyd, M. J., & Lynch, A. D. (2008). Developmental systems theory. In. D. Carr (Ed.), *Encyclopedia of the life course and human development* (Vol. 1, pp. 134–137). Farmington Hills, MI: Gale.

Lottes, I., Weinberg, M., & Weller, I. (1993). Reactions to pornography on a college campus: For or against? *Sex Roles, 29,* 69–89. doi: 10.1007/BF00289997

Magana, A., & Clark, N. M. (1995). Examining a paradox: Does religiosity contribute to positive birth outcomes in Mexican-American populations? *Health Education Quarterly, 22,* 96–109. doi: 10.1177/109019819502200109

Morgan, E. M. (2011). Associations between young adults' use of sexually explicit materials and their sexual preferences, behaviors, and satisfaction. *Journal of Sex Research, 48,* 520–530. doi: 10.1080/00224499.2010.543960

Murray-Swank, N. A., Pargament, K. I., & Mahoney, A. (2005). At the crossroads of sexuality and spirituality: The sanctification of sex by college students. *International Journal for the Psychology of Religion, 15,* 199–219. doi:10.1207/s15327582ijpr1503_2

Nelson, L. J. (2003). Rites of passage in emerging adulthood: Perspectives on young Mormons. *New Directions for Child and Adolescent Development, 100,* 33–49. doi:10.1002/cd.73

Nelson, L. J., Padilla-Walker, L. M., & Carroll, J. S. (2010). "I believe it is wrong but I still do it:" A comparison of religious young men who do versus do not use pornography. *Psychology of Religion and Spirituality, 2,* 136–147. doi:10.1037/a0019127

Oser, F., Scarlett, W. G., & Bucher, A. (2006). Religious and spiritual development throughout the life span. In W. Damon & R. Lerner (Eds.), *Handbook of child psychology* (6th ed.; pp. 942–998). New York, NY: Wiley.

Pluhar, E., Frongillo, E. A., Jr., Stycos, J. M., & Dempster-McClain, D. (1998). Understanding the relationship between religion and the sexual attitudes and behaviors of college students. *Journal of Sex Education & Therapy, 23,* 288–296. Retrieved from Ebscohost.

Reece, M., Herbenick, D., Schick, V., Sanders, S. A., Dodge, B., & Fortenberry, J. D. (2010). Sexual behaviors, relationships, and perceived health among adult men in the United States: Results from a national probability sample. *Journal of Sexual Medicine, 7,* 291–304. doi: 10.1111/j.1743-6109.2010.02009.x

Regnerus, M. D. (2007). *Forbidden fruit: Sex and religion in the lives of American teenagers.* New York, NY: Oxford University Press.

Regnerus, M., & Uecker, J. (2011). *Premarital sex in America: How young Americans meet, mate, and think about marrying.* New York, NY: Oxford University Press.

Rostosky, S. S., Regnerus, M. D., & Wright, M. L. C. (2003). Coital debut: The role of religiosity and sex attitudes in the Add Health Survey. *Journal of Sex Research, 40,* 358–367. doi:10.1080/00224490209552202

Rubin, R. H., Billingsley, A., & Caldwell, C. H. (1994). The black church and adolescent sexuality. *National Journal of Sociology, 8,* 131–148. Retrieved from Ebscohost.

Schachter, E. P. (2004). Identity configurations: A new perspective on identity formation in contemporary society. *Journal of Personality, 72,* 167–200. doi: 10.1111/j.0022-3506.2004.00260.x

Smith, C. (with Snell, P.). (2009). *Souls in transition: The religious and spiritual lives of emerging adults.* New York, NY: Oxford University Press.

Stanley, S. M., Rhoades, G. K., & Fincham, F. D. (2011). Understanding romantic relationships among emerging adults: The significant roles of cohabitation and ambiguity. In F. D. Fincham & M. Cui (Eds.), *Romantic relationships in emerging adulthood* (pp. 234–251). New York, NY: Cambridge University Press.

Stanley, S. M., Whitton, S. W., & Markman, H. J. (2004). Maybe I do: Interpersonal commitment and premarital or nonmarital cohabitation. *Journal of Family Issues, 25*, 496–519. doi: 10.1177/0192513X03257797

Stoppa, T. M. (2009). *The varieties of spiritual experiences revisited.* Unpublished dissertation. University Park, PA: The Pennsylvania State University.

Uecker, J. E. (2008). Religion, pledging, and premarital sexual behavior of married young adults. *Journal of Marriage & Family, 70*, 728–744. doi:10.1111/j.17413737.2008.00517

Uecker, J. E., Regnerus, M., & Vaaler, M. L. (2007). Losing my religion: The social sources of religious decline in early adulthood. *Social Forces, 85*, 1667–1692. doi:10.1353/sof.2007.0083

Wiik, K. A., Bernhardt, E., & Noack, T. (2009). A study of commitment and relationship quality in Sweden and Norway. *Journal of Marriage and Family, 71*, 465–477. doi: 10.1111/j.1741-3737.2009.00613.x

Wimberly, D. W. (1989). Religion and role identity: A structural symbolic interactionist conceptualization of religiosity. *Sociological Quarterly, 30*, 125–142. doi: 10.1111/j.1533-8525.1989.tb01515.x

Yarhouse, M. A., & Tan, E. S. N. (2005). Addressing religious conflicts in adolescents who experience sexual identity confusion. *Professional Psychology: Research and Practice, 36*, 530–536. doi:10.1037/0735-7028.36.5.530

Zinnbauer, B. J., & Pargament, K. I. (2006). Religiousness and spirituality. In R. F. Paloutzian & C. Park (Eds.), *Handbook of the psychology of religion and spirituality* (pp. 21–42). New York, NY: Guilford.

# 12 ◢

## Sexual Minorities

GEOFFREY L. REAM AND ERIC M. RODRIGUEZ

In 2005, 16-year-old Zach Stark told his parents that he was gay. Trying to do what was, within their religious frame of reference, the best thing for him, Zach's parents sent him to Refuge, a residential program. Refuge was part of Love in Action, a conservative Christian ministry focused on "treatment" of homosexuality (graduates of such "reorientation" or "reparative" therapy sometimes identify as "ex-gay"). Before leaving, Zach posted on MySpace, telling the story and expressing his apprehensions. The post "went viral," and sexual-minority community activists held demonstrations at Refuge during Zach's stay (Fox, 2011). Once Zach was "back on the grid," he acted to take control of his story, wiping out his post with its hundreds of accumulated comments and asking for privacy (britzkrieg, 2005). The story had, however, already become bigger than him. Despite Love in Action's arguments that government should have no control over a ministry, a government investigation determined that Refuge was operating as an unlicensed mental health facility (Fox, 2011). It closed in 2007. The following is from a speech by Brandon Tidwell, a former Refuge resident turned activist, upon the occasion:

> *God loves gay men and women and does not demand us to change our identity. As an ex-gay survivor and former client of Love in Action, I know how important this simple message is . . . Today, I stand here as a gay man of Christian faith, a man with hopes, dreams, and aspirations to live a life of authenticity and service to this world. Through Soulforce [a gay-affirming Christian activist organization] and other partner groups, I hope to be a voice among many who are calling for God's love and acceptance to prevail in this struggle.* (Airhart, 2007; Fox, 2011)

A documentary (Fox, 2011) that tells the story of Zach, Brandon, and other Refuge residents also answers the question of "where are they now?" as emerging adults. Zach, interviewed in his college dormitory room, said:

*Of course I wish it didn't happen, and it was really sad, coming out, and that happening...I haven't changed my mind because of anything that happened to me...my life right now, I just work a lot, so it's more, I guess, normal...with my parents, if we don't talk about the issue, then it's not an issue...they're leaving it up to me.* (Fox, 2011)

Zach's and Brandon's stories touch on several themes discussed in this chapter, which synthesizes scholarship from multiple disciplines into an ecological perspective on sexual-minority emerging adults' experiences with religion and spirituality. We begin on the macro level, describing the forces involved in society's current religious-ideological struggles as they affect emerging adults, including what the current cohort went through as adolescents. Then, we narrow our focus to individual-level developmental tasks set forth for sexual minorities within this context. These include coming out to self and others, becoming involved with a sexual-minority community, and (for those involved with nonaffirming religion) reconciling individual religious/spiritual and sexual-minority identity. Finally, we highlight unique opportunities for the development of self and religiousness/spirituality that membership in the current generation of emerging adults offers to sexual minorities, and close with suggestions for practice and research.

For the purposes of this chapter, "sexual minority" refers to those who are in a social out-group on the basis of same-sex attraction, dating, sexual behavior, or orientation identity, commonly labeled as gay, lesbian, or bisexual (Cohen & Savin-Williams, 2012). Intersex, transgender, and gender-atypical people are *gender* minorities, and it would not be possible to give proper attention to their unique experiences within the scope of this chapter. We distinguish between religiousness and spirituality in a way that is generally consistent with contemporary research on sexual minorities and other chapters in this volume, while acknowledging that many religious and spiritual people and institutions make this distinction differently or not at all. Spirituality refers to personally held faith and search for the sacred, including beliefs, morality, and ethics emerging from this process. Religiousness refers to participation in institutions organized around spirituality, including identification with an institution and adherence to institutions' doctrines and practices (Stark & Bainbridge, 1985).

Existing social scientific scholarship on sexual minorities' experiences with religion and spirituality is substantial, but it has its limitations: Much of it is about American Christianity or "religion" in general with only a few studies about experiences unique to other religions, and most describes lesbians and gays or "sexual minorities" in general with a few studies addressing unique experiences associated with bisexuality (Rodriguez, 2010). The few studies specifically about young people, many of which we review later, generally do not distinguish emerging adults from either adolescents or adults. Finally, not many studies are situated within established theories of psychosocial, spiritual, or sexual orientation identity development. This chapter, therefore, attempts to assemble a three-dimensional picture from two-dimensional images which do not have its subject in focus. Nevertheless, we believe some useful insights, or at least conjectures, can be drawn from the current literature and we discuss these possibilities in the sections that follow.

## ▲ Nonaffirming Organizations and Movements

We begin with a macro-level perspective because "developmental tasks" are informed by what is needed to adapt to a particular context (Erikson, 1968), and the experiences with religion that define the current cohort of sexual-minority emerging adults in the United States involve having grown through a particular context. Specifically, if it were not the case that "contemporary [sexual minorities] have a uniquely problematic relationship with religion and spirituality because same-sex desire, behavior, and identity have historically been understood from the religious frame not simply as wrong but...antithetical to fundamental, sacred truths" (Fontenot, 2013, p. 618), sexual-minority youths' experiences would not be systematically different from other youths', and this would be a very short chapter. One experience shared by the current cohort of emerging adults is of having been adolescents during a particular episode of the generations-long conflict between sexual minorities and conservative religion: the Christian Right's culture wars.

The Christian Right is a broad and powerful coalition of conservative political and religious (mostly Roman Catholic and Evangelical Christian) leaders that emerged in the late 1970s (Hudson, 2008). They are the main proponents of the ideas, long discredited in the mainstream scientific discourse, that homosexuality is pathological, can be changed through therapy, and is a dangerous and destructive "lifestyle" somehow connected with pedophilia (Herek, 1998; Just the Facts Coalition, 2008). They also advocate for protection of public expression of anti-gay views on grounds of freedom of religion and freedom of speech (Macgillivray, 2004). When challenged with the idea that these assertions themselves are hurtful and destructive, voices within the Christian Right tend to argue that they are just trying to address a social problem and contribute to public health, or that they should at least have the right within a postmodern discourse to contribute a minority opinion and maintain an alternative frame of reference more comfortable for their adherents (Yarhouse & Burkett, 2002). However, this does not address the criticism that their efforts erode the legitimacy of sexual-minority identity itself (Ganzevoort, van der Laan, & Olsman, 2011) and the community-level agency that comes with it (Fontenot, 2013). Their detractors within progressive Christian circles argue that the Christian Right's true motive is to combat a perceived threat to their political hegemony (White, 2006).

It is critically important to note, for our purposes, that the Christian Right's efforts were not limited to communicating its views through sermons and their various media outlets. The movement was politically engaged, as large institutionalized religions in general (Berger, 1967) and the Evangelical movement in particular (Noll, 1994) tend to be, and its efforts to change cultural values and social policies touched even the lives of non-adherents. It is unknown how many current emerging adults were affected by "school board battles" in which Christian Right activists manipulated local school boards, trying to control what is taught in health classes and which books were allowed in the library. Points of contention included not only homosexuality but issues like "abstinence only" that had direct relevance to heterosexual youths' health (Deckman, 2004). Christian Right activists also forestalled passage of Michigan's anti-bullying "Matt's Safe School Law" (named for Matt Epling, an eighth grader who died by suicide in 2002 after a "welcome to High School" hazing incident; see Matt Epling.Com, 2006) for years until it eventually passed the Senate with a caveat that "this section does not prohibit a statement of a sincerely held religious beliefs or moral conviction" (Michigan State Senate, 2011). This was ostensibly for the protection of religious students' First Amendment rights, but media sources (e.g., Sullivan, 2011) framed it as an exception for religion-based verbal harassment of sexual minorities. This unsympathetic analysis was not without support: Sexual-minority youth experience peer victimization at higher rates than do heterosexual youth (Friedman et al., 2011); almost all perpetrators in the random school shootings that occurred during modern emerging adults' childhood and early adolescence had been called "gay" at school (Kimmel & Mahler, 2003), and most people in the United States believe religion contributes to gay suicide (Greene, 2010).

## ▲ Progressive Organizations and Movements

There are progressive and affirming movements, organizations, and denominations within most major American religions that seek to be a space where religion and sexual orientation are not in conflict. Some, like "open and affirming" United Churches of Christ (Scheitle, Merino, & Moore, 2010), are mainstream movements that are inclusive of sexual minorities. Others, such as the Metropolitan Community Church, are explicitly sexual-minority movements. Typically, such religious organizations are distinguished by being labeled either "gay-friendly" or "gay-positive." Gay-friendly refers to a denomination that is openly supportive of sexual minorities and encourages their participation in the religious and spiritual life of the group, while gay-positive refers to a religious organization that ministers specifically to both the sexual and gender minority communities (Rodriguez & Ouellette, 2000).

Conceivably, just as sexual minorities in the "Bible Belt"—where institutional Christianity touches on all aspects of life—experience serious conflicts between sexuality and religion (Barton, 2010), sexual-minority emerging adults raised in and still adherent to a progressive/affirming/gay-friendly religious context would never have a conflict between their sexuality and their religiousness to reconcile. Progressive movements also serve as a source of affirming "religious human capital" (refers to knowledge of rituals and doctrines as well as friendships with co-religionists; see Iannaccone, 1990) for those experiencing such conflict and wishing to reconcile their religious and sexual-minority identities (Rodriguez & Ouellette, 2000). Common strategies for this identity reconciliation include exegetically challenging anti-gay interpretations of Scripture passages, challenging the moral authority of individual religious leaders or the religious institution as a whole, and affirming the inherent healthiness and worthiness before God of same-sex relationships (Pitt, 2010; Siraj, 2012; Yip, 1997).

A major difference between more religiously liberal and more religiously conservative denominations/movements within a major religion, which social science usually does not address directly, is accepted methods for interpreting sacred scripture. Most conservative denominations/movements tend toward a view of scripture as the literal, infallible word of God, while most liberal denominations/movements tend to apply a historical-critical method, which takes into account the culture within which Scripture passages emerged before applying them to modern life (Glesne, 2004). Conservative versus liberal theological orientation and their associated ways of interpreting scripture are connected with attitudes toward homosexuality (Hall, 2013). For instance, conservative Christianity and Judaism takes a verse like Leviticus 20:13 (NRSV: "If a man lies with a male as with a woman, both of them have committed an abomination; they shall be put to death; their blood is upon them") at face value to indicate that a condemning and intolerant attitude toward homosexuality is appropriate, if not the death penalty itself. More liberal traditions, in contrast, argue that the ancient texts could not refer to modern, consensual, egalitarian gay/lesbian relationships because these were generally unheard of at the time, but that they could apply to exploitative or nonconsensual relationships, or to rape (Glesne, 2004).

Affirming and progressive movements are also, like the Christian Right, not merely promulgating their views but engaging in activism for change within their denominations and in society at large. In Soulforce's Equality Ride, young adult sexual-minority activists take a national bicycle tour of higher education institutions that allow discrimination against sexual minorities (Soulforce, 2012). The Metropolitan Community Church is a global presence and is prominent within sexual-minority communities, with one of its pastors serving as grand marshal of the 2011 New York City Pride Parade (Ladzinski, 2011). While Reform Judaism has historically been welcoming and supportive of sexual minorities (Shokeid, 1995), progressive efforts within Conservative Judaism recently resulted in the creation of guidelines for gay marriage (Markoe, 2012). While an affirming movement of Muslims has resulted in the emergence of at least an online safe space for sexual minorities (Siraj, 2012), care must be taken when generalizing Western cultural notions of religion, spirituality, and sexual identity to Eastern Islamic contexts. Halstead and Lewika (1998), for example, have argued that the concept of having a gay, lesbian, or bisexual identity (as opposed to just engaging in same-sex sexual behavior) is a uniquely Western concept that does not translate to Muslim cultures.

Several organizations providing homeless sexual-minority youth with emergency housing, transitional living, case management, life-skills training, community building, and advocacy in New York City are based in progressive and affirming religious organizations (New Alternatives, 2010; Shelter of Peace, 2011; Trinity Place Shelter, 2007). Although their efforts could be cynically framed as meager reparations for the damage caused by conservative religion, the data actually create a picture of a genuine attempt to reach out to young people who have fallen through (or been pushed through) the cracks of several potentially supportive systems and institutions: Although sexual minorities are greatly overrepresented among the general population of homeless youth (Center for American Progress, 2010), only 14%–39% were even explicitly turned out for being sexual minorities—most become homeless because of the "usual" reasons of family poverty, conflict in the home, and family substance use (Berberet, 2006; Cochran, Stewart, Ginzler, & Cauce, 2002; Mallon, 1998). Parents' individually-held religious beliefs are not found to be a major factor in youth homelessness (Hyde, 2005). About two-thirds of sexual-minority homeless youth, however, were involved in the child welfare system (Berberet, 2006), within which experiences of homophobic harassment are nearly universal and from which about half leave for the *relative safety* of the streets at some point (Mallon, 1998). By reaching out to these youth, sometimes incurring greater than normal risk to physical property and volunteers' safety, these organizations create an unconventional and arguably transgressive stand for people whom the system apparently believes should not be helped.

A caveat has to be added here that it is unclear how many sexual-minority emerging adults are actually reached by progressive religious organizations' efforts. The emerging-adult years have always been a time of somewhat lower average involvement with religion, as people are generally busy with work, family, and school (Smith, 2009). Religious attendance is especially low for this generation, however, especially among the mainline Protestant Christian churches that create the context for affirming and progressive movements (Smith, 2009), and research on sexual minorities in general finds particularly low rates of religious involvement among them (Halkitis et al., 2009). Among sexual minorities, not all who try to transition from their familiar religious involvement to a gay-friendly religious space have transformative or even good experiences, and they may prefer to stay in a context that is nonaffirming but appealing in other ways (Pitt, 2010). Although access to affirming and progressive religious ideas and participation are definitely available to emerging adults given their freedom, mobility, and facility with new communications technology, the work of finding out how much they are actually making contact and benefiting from it has yet to be done.

## ▲ Developing a Positive, Individual-Level Identity

Recent research shows that one of the key developmental issues facing sexual minorities is the process of coming out as a sexual minority, both to themselves and to others (Rodriguez, 2006; Savin-Williams, 2001b; Shallenberger, 1998). The coming-out process is an intensely personal one that can hold both positive (e.g., bringing one closer to family and friends, no longer having to hide gay identity, connecting to others in the sexual-minority community) and negative (alienation from family and friends, negative mental health outcomes such as loneliness, depression, and/or anxiety) connotations for any emerging adult. This holds true whether sexual-minority emerging adults had come out in adolescence and are presently enjoying/dealing with the results or they come out during emerging adulthood. Sexual-minority emerging adults who also happen to be people of faith may need to both (1) come out to their friends and family as sexual minorities, and (2) come out to their sexual-minority community as a person of faith.

With respect to coming out as a sexual minority to friends and family, Shallenberger (1998) noted several common themes in the social scientific research literature. These themes include difficult self-questioning, growing self-recognition and self-identification with one's sexual orientation, disclosure to loved ones that may be either slow or sudden, and eventual involvement with the gay, lesbian, and bisexual community. When coming out to one's sexual minority peers as a person of faith, however, Shallenberger (1998) noted additional themes in the coming-out process, including self-questioning regarding how sexual orientation fits in with religious and/or spiritual beliefs, reintegrating religious and sexual identities, and reclaiming both sexual orientation and their religious beliefs, typically by becoming part of a community of accommodating people. Both coming-out processes can involve conflict between emerging adults' sexual orientation and their religious and/or spiritual beliefs.

Rodriguez and Ouellette (2000) describe four pathways for dealing with identity conflict between sexual orientation and religious/spiritual beliefs: (1) remove the gay identity (e.g., via involvement in "ex-gay" or "reparative" therapy), (2) remove the religious identity (i.e., secularization or distancing oneself from established religion), (3) compartmentalization (i.e., keeping the two identities rigidly separate, as in the case of a gay man who goes to bathhouses all night and then attends worship services the next day as if nothing were different), and (4) identity integration, where the two identities are merged together into a new, positive whole. A recent analysis of data from diverse adults recruited from sexual-minority communities in the greater Sacramento area (Herek, Gillis, & Cogan, 1999), almost all of whom were raised in some religious background (81% Christian) and most of whom (80%) maintained some religious and/or spiritual beliefs, found that secularization and identity integration were connected with more positive mental health outcomes than removing the gay identity and compartmentalization (Rodriguez, 2006). A related secondary analysis of data from readers of an Internet magazine for sexual-minority youth (Kryzan, 2000) found, among sexual minorities from a Christian background ages 13–25, comparable mental health outcomes among those who had reconciled spiritual and sexual identity to those who reported no conflict (Ream & Savin-Williams, 2005). An important feature of both findings is that, although mental health outcomes were not significantly better for those who had integrated their identities than for those who were not (as far as could be discerned from our indicators) engaged with this process, neither were they significantly worse. This challenges the assumption that religion is generally psychologically unhealthy for sexual minorities (Greene, 2010).

Another important "take-home message" from this research is that the assumption that all religious sexual minorities experience identity conflict (the "conflict assumption") is invalid. Several of Rodriguez's (2006) respondents did not experience religious/sexual-minority identity conflict, for reasons including (1) never encountering anti-gay religious rhetoric, (2) encountering anti-gay rhetoric, but never internalizing it, (3) devaluing Church teachings, (4) coming out at a late age, (5) attending seminary, and (6) God's all-encompassing love (Rodriguez, 2006). For those who do experience conflict, the end result is not necessarily negative mental health consequences. Sexual minorities of faith may actually exemplify positive psychological concepts of stress-related growth and coming-out growth (Rodriguez & Vaughan, 2013): Even though hearing religious leaders proclaim that same-sex attraction is unnatural and an abomination can be troubling on several levels, it may occur to some as one of many challenges on their spiritual path, and growth through challenge is integral to identity (Arnett, 2005) and spiritual (Oser, Scarlett, & Bucher, 2006) development.

## ▲ Solidarity and Opportunity in Emerging Adulthood

After sexual minorities weather the relatively vulnerable stage of adolescence, the life stage of emerging adulthood holds much promise for them. One advantage is the potential for solidarity with the rest of their generation over experiences with religion. The current cohort of emerging adults as a whole is characterized as rigorously nonjudgmental (Regnerus, 2007), oriented toward friends (Smith, 2009), unwilling to take ideological positions that create barriers between people (Kinnaman & Hawkins, 2011), and marginally political or apolitical (Smith, Christoffersen, Davidson, & Herzog, 2011). It is also important to note again here that sexual minorities were not the only youth touched by the Christian Right's "school board battles," which encompassed evolution, prayer in schools, and several other signature "culture war" issues (Deckman, 2004). The Christian Right also tried to replace evidence-informed comprehensive sexuality education with ineffective and often scientifically inaccurate abstinence-only curricula, knowingly at the risk of increasing this generation's burden of teenage pregnancy and sexually transmitted infections (Fortenberry, 2005; Waxman Report, 2004). All of this perhaps contributed to emerging adults' impression of mainstream American conservative religion's boundaries around sexuality as inconsistent, unworkably strict, self-contradictory, at variance with normative practices of their adherents and the health interests of society, exploding the boundary of who is not living up to their expectations to include almost everyone (Regnerus, 2007), and arguably giving the entire generation of emerging adults the experience of being an "out-group" on the basis of their sexuality. Even though the average attitude found among modern emerging adults toward homosexuality is actually neutral to negative (Regnerus, 2007), their actual response to the issue will likely be in terms of solidarity with friends. Evangelical Christian author Rachel Held Evans, not much older than the current generation at age 31, warned in a frequently-cited blog post that the Christian Right might "win a culture war and lose a generation" over opposition to gay marriage (Evans, 2012).

Sexual-minority emerging adults, for their part, have access to this life stage's free field of options to pursue their own paths. The epilogue to the documentary we described earlier (Fox, 2011) reports college-age Zach Stark studying computer science and math, with no plans to become an activist for sexual-minority rights, and Brandon Tidwell pursuing an MBA and an eventual career in sustainability management. Although both emerging adults were building on features of their adolescent experiences (Zach with computers, Brandon with activism), neither was defined by his past. By getting their lives back on track after these negative religious experiences, they demonstrated an underemphasized characteristic of sexual-minority youth, which is resiliency (Savin-Williams, 2001a). Their lives also demonstrate the unique opportunity that emerging adulthood represents for sexual minorities, in that they are apparently unencumbered by religious social control. While emerging adulthood is a time of particularly low support and control from social structures (Arnett, 2011), sexual-minority youth are arguably used to low support. The correspondingly low control, along with their peers' solidarity, frees them to author their own lives.

## ▲ Final Thoughts: Implications for Both Practice and Research

In conclusion, we offer three key suggestions that could impact both future practice and future research in this area:

1. *Religion/spirituality is not just the province of the sexual majority.* Rodriguez (2010) has argued that we are in the midst of a major cultural shift in which sexual minorities are no longer simply compared and contrasted against religious "others" but are instead viewed as religious and spiritual beings in their own right. We repeat that call here and hope that practitioners and researchers find ways to incorporate this zeitgeist change into their work.

2. *There are worship opportunities for sexual minority emerging adults.* For those individuals who are attempting (and even struggling) to integrate their sexual orientation with their religious/ spiritual beliefs, there are worship opportunities out there. In Reform Judaism, liberal denominations of Christianity (i.e., the Evangelical Lutheran Church of America [ELCA], the Metropolitan Community Churches [MCC], and the United Church of Christ [UCC]) and even in many of the non-Western religious traditions (i.e., Buddhism, Daoism, Hinduism, Wicca),

sexual minority status is perceived by many as a welcome dimension of diversity. Such congregations are, however, not available in all geographical areas.

3. *More diversity in research (thus leading to more diversity in practice) is needed.* In the social scientific study of gay, lesbian, and bisexual people of faith, there has been a call for research to reflect a wider range of diversity, including issues of race/ethnicity and gender minorities, along with both non-Western religious practices and Eastern spiritual beliefs. In this chapter, we have described the experiences of emerging adults as a distinct population from both adolescents and adults, and we believe this and other developmental considerations should be taken up in future work.

## ▲ References

Airhart, M. (2007, July 18). Former ex-gays tell of harm at Exodus "Love in Action" program. *Ex-Gay Watch.* Retrieved July 6, 2012, from http://www.exgay-watch.com/wp/2007/07/ former-ex-gays-tell-of-harm-at-exodus-love-in-action-program/

Arnett, J. J. (2005). The developmental context of substance use in emerging adulthood. *Journal of Drug Issues, 35*(2), 235–254. doi: 10.1177/002204260503500202

Arnett, J. J. (2011). Emerging adulthood(s): The cultural psychology of a new life stage. In L. A. Jensen (Ed.), *Bridging cultural and developmental approaches to psychology: New syntheses in theory, research, and policy* (pp. 255–275). New York, NY: Oxford University Press.

Barton, B. (2010). "Abomination"—Life as a Bible Belt gay. *Journal of Homosexuality, 57*(4), 465–484. doi: 10.1080/00918361003608558

Berberet, H. M. (2006). Putting the pieces together for queer youth: A model of integrated assessment of need and program planning. *Child Welfare, 85*(2), 361–384.

Berger, P. L. (1967). *The sacred canopy: Elements of a sociological theory of religion.* Garden City, NY: Doubleday.

britzkrieg. (2005, August 1). Update on teen at center of gay therapy controversy. *Dark Christianity.* Retrieved November 15, 2012, from http://asylums.insanejournal.com/ dark_christian/216822.html

Center for American Progress. (2010, June 21). Gay and transgender youth homelessness by the numbers. Retrieved July 21, 2012, from http://www.americanprogress.org/issues/ 2010/06/homelessness_numbers.html/

Cochran, B. N., Stewart, A. J., Ginzler, J. A., & Cauce, A. M. (2002). Challenges faced by homeless sexual minorities: Comparison of gay, lesbian, bisexual, and transgender homeless adolescents with their heterosexual counterparts. *American Journal of Public Health, 92*(5), 773–777.

Cohen, K. M., & Savin-Williams, R. C. (2012). Coming out to self and others: Developmental milestones. In P. Levounis, J. Drescher, & M. E. Barber

(Eds.), *The LGBT casebook* (pp. 17–33). Arlington, VA: American Psychiatric Publishing.

Congregation Beit Simchat Torah. (2011). Shelter of Peace. Retrieved August 27, 2012, from http://shelterofpeace.org/

Deckman, M. M. (2004). *School board battles: The Christian right in local politics.* Washington, DC: Georgetown University Press.

Erikson, E. H. (1968). *Identity, youth, and crisis.* New York, NY: Norton.

Evans, R. H. (May 9, 2012). How to win a culture war and lose a generation. Retrieved July 24, 2012, from http://rachelheldevans.com/win-culture-war-lose-generation-amendment-one-north-carolina

Fontenot, E. (2013). Unlikely congregation: Gay and lesbian persons of faith in contemporary U.S. culture. In K. I. Pargament, J. J. Exline, & J. W. Jones (Eds.), *APA handbook of psychology, religion, and spirituality (Vol 1): Context, theory, and research* (pp. 617–633). Washington, DC: American Psychological Association.

Fortenberry, J. D. (2005). The limits of abstinence-only in preventing sexually transmitted infections. *Journal of Adolescent Health, 36*(4), 269–270. doi: 10.1016/j.jadohealth. 2005.02.001

Fox, M. J. (Writer), & Fox, M. J. (Director). (2011). *This is what Love in Action looks like.* United States: Sawed-off Collaboratory Productions.

Friedman, M. S., Marshal, M. P., Guadamuz, T. E., Wei, C., Wong, C. F., Saewyc, E., & Stall, R. (2011). A meta-analysis of disparities in childhood sexual abuse, parental physical abuse, and peer victimization among sexual minority and sexual nonminority individuals. *American Journal of Public Health, 101*(8), 1481–1494. doi: 10.2105/AJPH.2009.190009

Ganzevoort, R. R., van der Laan, M., & Olsman, E. (2011). Growing up gay and religious. Conflict, dialogue, and religious identity strategies. *Mental Health, Religion & Culture, 14*(3), 209–222. doi: 10.1080/13674670903452132

Glesne, D. N. (2004). *Understanding homosexuality: Perspectives for the local church.* Minneapolis, MN: Kirk House Publishers.

Greene, R. A. (2010, October 21). Churches contribute to gay suicides, most Americans believe. *CNN Belief Blog.* Retrieved July 23, 2012, from http://religion.blogs.cnn.com/2010/ 10/21/churches-contribute-to-gay-suicides-most-americans-believe/

Halkitis, P. N., Mattis, J. S., Sahadath, J. K., Massie, D., Ladyzhenskaya, L., Pitrelli, K.,…Cowie, S. A. E. (2009). The meanings and manifestations of religion and spirituality among lesbian, gay, bisexual, and transgender adults. *Journal of Adult Development, 16*(4), 250–262. doi: 10.1007/s10804-009-9071-1

Hall, C. J. A. (2013). *A thorn in the flesh: How gay sexuality is changing the Episcopal Church.* New York, NY: Rowman & Littlefield.

Halstead, J. M., & Lewicka, K. (1998). Should homosexuality be taught as an acceptable alternative lifestyle? A Muslim perspective. *Cambridge Journal of Education, 28*(1), 49–64. doi: 10.1080/0305764980280105

Herek, G. M. (1998). Bad science in the service of stigma: A critique of the Cameron group's survey studies. In G. M. Herek (Ed.), *Stigma and sexual orientation: Understanding prejudice against lesbians, gay men, and bisexuals* (pp. 223–255). Thousand Oaks, CA: Sage.

Herek, G. M., Gillis, J. R., & Cogan, J. C. (1999). Psychological sequelae of hate-crime victimization among lesbian, gay, and bisexual adults. *Journal of Consulting and Clinical Psychology, 67*(6), 945–951. doi: 10.1037/0022-006X.67.6.945

Hudson, D. W. (2008). *Onward Christian soldiers: The growing political power of Catholics and Evangelicals in the United States* (1st Threshold Editions hardcover ed.). New York, NY: Threshold Editions.

Hyde, J. (2005). From home to street: Understanding young people's transitions into homelessness. *Journal of Adolescence, 28*(2), 171–183. doi: 10.1016/j.adolescence.2005.02.001

Iannaccone, L. R. (1990). Religious practice: A human capital approach. *Journal for the Scientific Study of Religion, 29*(3), 297–314.

Just the Facts Coalition. (2008). Just the facts about sexual orientation and youth: A primer for principals, educators, and school personnel. Retrieved August 27, 2012, from http://www.apa.org/pi/lgbt/resources/just-the-facts.pdf

Kimmel, M. S., & Mahler, M. (2003). Adolescent masculinity, homophobia, and violence: Random school shootings, 1982-2001. *American Behavioral Scientist, 46*(10), 1439–1458. doi: 10.1177/0002764203046010010

Kinnaman, D., & Hawkins, A. (2011). *You lost me: Why young Christians are leaving church—and rethinking faith.* Grand Rapids, MI: BakerBooks.

Kryzan, C. (2000, November). Outproud/Oasis internet survey of queer and questioning youth. Retrieved March 14, 2013, from http://www.cyberspaces.com/qys2000/pdf/ qys2000_overview.pdf

Ladzinski, E. (2011, April 21). Hell's Kitchen reverend to serve as Pride March Grand Marshal. *DNAinfo.com New York.* Retrieved August 27, 2012, from http://www.dnainfo.com/new-york/20110420/chelsea-hells-kitchen/hells-kitchen-reverend-serve-as-pride-march-grand-marshal

Macgillivray, I. K. (2004). Gay rights and school policy: A case study in community factors that facilitate or impede educational change. *International Journal of Qualitative Studies in Education, 17*(3), 347–370. doi: 10.1080/0951 839042000204652

Mallon, G. P. (1998). *We don't exactly get the Welcome Wagon: The experiences of gay and lesbian adolescents in child welfare systems.* New York, NY: Columbia University Press.

Markoe, L. (June 5, 2012). Conservative Jews' gay wedding rules mostly met with a shrug. *The Washington Post: On Faith.* Retrieved August 27, 2012, from http://www.washington post.com/national/on-faith/conservative-jews-gay-wedding-rules-mostly-met-with-a-shrug/2012/06/05/gJQABeheGV_story.html.

Matt Epling.Com. (2006). About Matt. Retrieved March 13, 2013, from http://mattepling. webs.com/aboutmatt.htm

Michigan State Senate. (2011, November 2). Matt's Safe School Law. Retrieved November 15, 2012, from http://www.legislature.mi.gov/documents/2011-2012/billengrossed/Senate/ htm/2011-SEBS-0137.htm

New Alternatives. (2010). New alternatives for homeless LGBT youth. Retrieved August 27, 2012, from http://www.newalternativesnyc.org/

Noll, M. A. (1994). *The scandal of the Evangelical mind*. Grand Rapids, MI: William B. Eerdmans Publishing.

Oser, F. K., Scarlett, W. G., & Bucher, A. (2006). Religious and spiritual development throughout the life span. In R. M. L. W. Damon (Ed.), *Handbook of child psychology. Vol. 1: Theoretical models of human development* (6th ed., pp. 942–998). Hoboken, NJ: Wiley.

Pitt, R. N. (2010). "Killing the messenger": Religious Black gay men's neutralization of anti-gay religious messages. *Journal for the Scientific Study of Religion, 49*(1), 56–72. doi: 10.1111/j.1468-5906.2009.01492.x

Ream, G. L., & Savin-Williams, R. C. (2005). Reconciling Christianity and positive non-heterosexual identity in adolescence, with implications for psychological well-being. *Journal of Gay and Lesbian Issues in Education, 2*(3), 19–36. doi: 10.1300/ J367v02n03_03

Regnerus, M. (2007). *Forbidden fruit: Sex & religion in the lives of American teenagers*. New York, NY: Oxford University Press.

Rodriguez, E. M. (2006). At the intersection of church and gay: Religion, spirituality, conflict, and integration in gay, lesbian, and bisexual people of faith. *Dissertation Abstracts International: Section B. The Sciences and Engineering, 67*(3-B), 1742.

Rodriguez, E. M. (2010). At the intersection of church and gay: A review of the psychological research on gay and lesbian Christians. *Journal of Homosexuality, 57*(1), 5–38. doi: 10.1080/00918360903445806

Rodriguez, E. M., & Ouellette, S. C. (2000). Gay and lesbian Christians: Homosexual and religious identity integration in the members and participants of a gay-positive church. *Journal for the Scientific Study of Religion, 39*(3), 333–347. doi: 10.1111/0021-8294.00028

Rodriguez, E. M., & Vaughan, M. D. (2013). Stress-related growth in the lives of lesbian and gay people of faith. In J. D. Sinnott (Ed.), *Positive psychology: Advances in understanding adult motivation* (pp. 291–307). New York, NY: Springer.

Savin-Williams, R. C. (2001a). A critique of research on sexual-minority youths. *Journal of Adolescence, 24*(1), 5–13.

Savin-Williams, R. C. (2001b). *Mom, dad. I'm gay. How families negotiate coming out*. Washington, DC: American Psychological Association.

Scheitle, C. P., Merino, S. M., & Moore, A. (2010). On the varying meaning of "open and affirming." *Journal of Homosexuality, 57*(10), 1223–1236. doi: 10.1080/00918369. 2010.517064

Shallenberger, D. (1998). *Reclaiming the spirit: Gay men and lesbians come to terms with religion*. New Brunswick, NJ: Rutgers University Press.

Shokeid, M. (1995). *A gay synagogue in New York*. New York, NY: Columbia University Press.

Siraj, A. (2012). "I don't want to taint the name of Islam": The influence of religion on the lives of Muslim lesbians. *Journal of Lesbian Studies, 16*(4), 449–467. doi: 10.1080/ 10894160.2012.681268

Smith, C. (with Denton, M. L.). (2009). *Souls in transition: The religious and spiritual lives of emerging adults*. New York, NY: Oxford University Press.

Smith, C., Christoffersen, K. M., Davidson, H., & Herzog, P. S. (2011). *Lost in transition: The dark side of emerging adulthood.* New York, NY: Oxford University Press.

Soulforce. (2012). 2012 Equality Ride. Retrieved August 27, 2012, from http:// www.soulforce. org/programs/er2012/

Stark, R., & Bainbridge, W. S. (1985). *The future of religion.* Berkeley, CA: University of California Press.

Sullivan, A. (2011, November 4). Why does Michigan's anti-bullying bill protect religious tormenters? *Time Swampland.* Retrieved July 20, 2012, from http://swampland. time.com/2011/11/04/why-does-michigans-anti-bullying-bill-protect-religious-tormenters/

Trinity Place Shelter. (2007). Trinity Place: A shelter for homeless LGBTQ youth. Retrieved August 27, 2012, from http://www.trinityplaceshelter.org/

Waxman Report. (2004). The content of federally funded abstinence-only education programs. Retrieved July 3, 2012, from http://www.apha.org/apha/PDFs/HIV/The_Waxman_ Report.pdf

White, M. (2006). *Religion gone bad: The hidden dangers of the Christian Right.* New York, NY: J.P. Tarcher/Penguin.

Yarhouse, M. A., & Burkett, L. A. (2002). An inclusive response to LGB and conservative religious persons: The case of same-sex attraction and behavior. *Professional Psychology: Research and Practice, 33*(3), 235–241. doi: 10.1037/0735-7028.33.3.235

Yip, A. K. T. (1997). Attacking the attacker: Gay Christians talk back. *British Journal of Sociology, 48*(1), 113–127.

# 13 ▲

# Religion, Spirituality, and Emerging Adults: Processing Meaning Through Culture, Context, and Social Position

MONA M. ABO-ZENA AND SAMEERA AHMED

*The late Friday afternoon sun is barely visible. Shira is committed to the environment and inviting other undergraduates to Shabbat dinner. Michael alternates between attending the Bible study group at a burrito bar and mass at the campus chapel. Ahmed and Yusuf are most likely to lead the prayer for the Muslim Students Association, but Yasmin and Karen are most likely to lead its executive committee meetings. Rashi volunteers in the largest campus food drive organized by the Hindu student group, but spends most of her free time with other* desis[1] *in the South Asian Cultural Club. While Selina is generally at the Buddhist Society, she is a regular in all faith circles. These emerging adults have carved a space and a place for their religious and spiritual explorations in their university Interfaith Center. They have learned that vegetarian fare is the easiest way to accommodate most of the dietary restrictions. While their focus is largely with their co-religious/spiritual peers, together they have discussed shared and different aspects of their faith. Most tensions are readily diffused by recalling their common position: the campus faith center is in the basement of a building on the edge of campus.*

Although religion is a central component of human development, and inextricably linked with culture (Holden & Vittrup, 2009), it remains an understudied area within cross-cultural psychology (Tarakeshwar,

1. A term that has come to refer to the people, culture, or products from the Indian subcontinent (India, Pakistan, Bangladesh, and Sri Lanka).

220

Stanton, & Pargament, 2003). Culture, religion, spirituality, and other aspects of one's identity (e.g., race, ethnicity, gender, socioeconomic status) are dimensions consisting of complex personal and social contexts within which individuals interact and develop over time. While the nexus of these relations is important to study throughout the lifespan, the late teens and twenties provide a particularly important window. This period includes numerous changes such as physiological ones, reduced family interaction and influence, increased peer and diverse social influences, and changes in societal expectations that vary according to specific familial and cultural norms (Arnett, 2004). While the juggernaut of societal messages condones living for the moment and instructs us to "just do it," individuals and families from diverse cultural groups may struggle with conflicting messages, while they attempt to resolve issues related to identity, professional direction, and relationships. Some emerging adults resolve these issues within frameworks directly or indirectly influenced by religion and spirituality. Religion and culture may play a central role, sometimes clarifying and other times complicating developmental directions and processes.

The overlap of cultural influences on religiousness and spirituality is the central focus of this chapter. We begin with an empirical and theoretical overview primarily among emerging adults in the United States. Then, we provide a conceptualization of the interaction of religion, spirituality, culture, and context, while highlighting the sources of variation and why such variations may not currently be reflected in research. Finally, we present implications for research and clinical interventions.

## ▲ Religion Among Emerging Adults

Understanding the role of religion and spirituality in the meaning-making process for emerging adults is critical in order to account for the complexities in young people's development. In a nationally representative sample of religion and youth culture, Smith (2009) studied the religious lives of 18–23 year olds and found that moralistic therapeutic deism (MTD) that was prevalent during the adolescent years (Smith, 2005) had continued, but in a more diffuse form among emerging adults. Many emerging adults reported believing that religions were generally good, that world religions shared common principles, and that religious particularities are peripheral. A less typical theme was that their specific religion is right and that faith is really important.

Despite Smith's (2009) pioneering efforts, the study is limited by its minimal representation of racial and religious minority as well as immigrant-origin youth. Increasingly, developmental science is explicitly attending to the role of culture and religious variation (Holden & Vittrup, 2009) due to findings suggesting that some theoretical perspectives and empirical findings may not be generalizable to other religious and/or cultural groups (Barry & Nelson, 2005). For example, religion and religious communities may serve different roles in the positive development of immigrant-origin and racially diverse youth compared to nonimmigrant European American youth (Suárez-Orozco, Singh, Abo-Zena, Du, & Roeser, 2011). Given previously limited attention to the role of culture in the study of emerging adults' religion, coupled with changing US demographics (Eck, 2002), this chapter aims to integrate the role of culture in the study of religion and spirituality in order to unpack the pervasive role of culture in human development.

## Defining Culture and Human Development

Our present understanding in the field of the psychology of religion and spirituality is dominated by a largely Protestant Christian orientation within a European American cultural context (Hill & Pargament, 2003). In addition, Spencer (2006) points out several conceptual flaws that limited earlier human development scholarship such as considering the experiences of White youth as "normative," ignoring the role of context, lacking a developmental perspective that incorporates minority youth and viewing them from a deficit perspective, and failing to acknowledge the role of racism in shaping minority youth's developmental outcomes.

As a result, current research on religion and spirituality is limited in its religious and cultural context and may not adequately be applicable to the diversity represented in world faith traditions. The need to incorporate culture and context into human developmental theories is moving the field slowly away from universal theories and toward contextualized approaches that reflect diverse populations and experiences (Mistry & Saraswathi, 2003), including religiously and spiritually diverse ones. Instead of assuming culture to be a broad characteristic of racially nondominant or minority youth (i.e., non-White), this conceptualization describes culture as informing the values, practices, and the developmental outcomes of all individuals.

In considering the role of culture in religious and spiritual development, scholars have warned against equating culture with race-based proxies in order to explore thinking about how ethnicity, culture, race, and religiousness are linked (Mattis, Ahluwalia, Cowie, & Kirkland-Harris, 2006). Cultural values and practices exist at multiple contextual levels (e.g., family, neighborhood, socioeconomic, religious affiliation, and geographic) and range in the manner in which they may fit or conflict with one another given their complex relation with other personal and social factors (e.g., religiousness, race, ethnicity, immigrant status, gender, and sexual orientation). Consider three emerging adults who self-identify as Black but have distinct cultural, religious, and regional contexts that may lead to different developmental experiences: Deborah is Catholic and Haitian who grew up in Boston with her aunt; Amanda is biracial and grew up Baptist attending a racially diverse church in an affluent Atlanta suburb; and Jamal grew up in a Muslim household in Los Angeles. Given the role of context, studies of culture should be anchored within social stratification theory incorporating the role of racism, discrimination, oppression, and segregation on the developmental competencies of minority children and families (García Coll et al., 1996).

In addition, it is important to take into account culture-bound assumptions that infuse current Western social science scholarship on religiousness. Examples of such culture-bound assumptions may include the presumed division between sacred and secular domains of life or an assumption of an independent self (i.e., the spirit is distinct from one's body as the primary unit of analysis and the individual can be separated from others). Similarly, constructing notions of youth and youth development that privilege chronological time over "social" time and assume a link between them (Mattis et al., 2006, p. 284) are among culture-bound assumptions. Finally, macro-level forces also should be considered such as interethnic, intercultural, and interracial contexts that affect individuals' journeys in implicit and explicit ways. The developmental experiences of emerging adults may vary based on the cultural context, personal beliefs, and personal practices, as well as the degree of integration and acceptance in broader social contexts.

### Religion, Culture, Context, and Human Development

According to classic identity theory, identity development occurs along three clusters, society-inward, person-outward, and an interaction between individual and society, which includes the domains of gender, vocation, religion, and ethnicity (Erikson, 1968). These domains are not merely descriptive categories but also reflect the attribution of value-laden meaning to each domain, leading to different identity processes for privileged versus stigmatized groups (Breakwell, 1983; McIntosh, 1988). To illustrate, Schlosser (2003) argues the existence of Christian privileges that favor the dominant religious group in the United States over adherents of other faith groups or nonreligious people. Hierarchies of privilege may exist within religious communities (e.g., status of Seventh-Day Adventists relative to other Christian denominations) as well as within cultural groups with some racial or ethnic subgroups afforded greater privilege than members of other subgroups (e.g., status of Cuban Americans relative to other Latino Americans). These hierarchies illustrate the need to study within-group and between-group variations, and they include person-centered perspectives that attend to contextual variations.

## ▲ Person-Centered and Contextually Grounded Developmental Conceptualization

Challenges to studying and measuring culture in the development of religiousness and spirituality include difficulties to operationalize a multidimensional phenomenon. A conceptualization must be person-centered and fluid to allow varied fit at multiple ecological levels within a broader pluralistic society.

### Person Centered

Individual characteristics may influence people's religious and spiritual values, beliefs, practices, and overall religious and spiritual trajectory. Since individuals vary considerably, understanding meaning-making needs to include how individuals navigate particular religious and spiritual content within interrelated levels of context. For example, Feldman (2008) described his struggle as a Jewish emerging adult with undiagnosed hypoglycemia. His battle with frequent fasts, required by his faith, contributed to his abandoning a conservative practice of Judaism in favor of incorporating the broader culture of his faith. The relative fit between a context (and variations in the support, challenge, or trauma associated with it) and individuals' internal resources may affect their developmental processes and trajectory (Lerner, 2002).

Studies of religion have considered the degree to which individuals are intrinsic versus extrinsic in their religious orientation, or prefer literal and structural interpretations, as opposed to ones that are broader or metaphoric (Park, 2005). These individual characteristics, including personality traits, interact with a social context that incorporates a range of influences, many cultural. For example, religious music and dance may inspire some believers, while leaving others empty, depending on the individual and how the religious context portrays or limits such expressions. What young people are searching for in a religious experience (i.e., spiritual connection, intellectual contentment, lifestyle, fellowship or mentorship) also may be related to their religious expectations, experiences, and meaning-making processes. The relations between an individual and his or her context also may be bidirectional, as in the case of religiously inspired social justice work (e.g., King & Furrow, 2004).

### Fluid

Emerging adults' responses to religious identity tasks vary based on individual characteristics, social influences, and contextual situations, which may change over time. Developmental studies of religiousness generally have focused on accounting for significant changes in religious practice (King & Roeser, 2009), but they have yet to explore the reasons and circumstances associated with such changes or development (Marks & Dollahite, 2011). Thus, developmental studies have not fully described the nature and meaning of the practice (or its lack) to individuals. Some emerging adults may adopt a cafeteria-like view of religion and spirituality (Smith, 2009) and may infuse a wide range of spiritual beliefs and practices that cut across traditions (e.g., a Bu-Jew, someone who combines tenets of Buddhism and Judaism). Longitudinal analyses of religious beliefs and practices also may fail to identify the contours of questions of faith that occur across the religious calendar (e.g., Advent, Passover, or Ramadan) or even throughout a particular day (e.g., sunrise or sunset), or in response to experiences and life events (e.g., divorce, religious retreat). Although fluctuations in faith and spirit were central to early psychology of religion scholarship (James, 1902/1985), such matters are currently considered more within the purview of chaplains and clergy.

*Developmentally Integrated*

Religious identity and religiousness are closely linked to other aspects of development, particularly ethnic and gender identity development. For example, immersion in a co-ethnic or co-racial congregation may contribute to an overlap, or perhaps conflation, of culture and religion. In a qualitative study of Indian American Hindu and Muslim emerging adults, participants described entry into college as an important beginning of self- and religious discovery (Levitt, Barnett, & Khalil, 2011). Prior to being in the diverse college setting, many participants had difficulty distinguishing religious practices from their ethnic cultural practices. However, exposure to other observant religious groups or nonreligious cultural groups allowed them to decouple religion and culture (see Chapter 9). Culture itself can serve as a de facto "religion," where cultural practices are codified, even though they may not be grounded in the religion (e.g., henna parties as part of South Asian Muslim marriage traditions). Some emerging adults who had observed the influence of culture on religion in ways that were not theologically grounded have sought to purge cultural innovations from religion in order to return to a purer, fundamental form of religious practice (Levitt et al., 2011). Others negotiate their ethnic, religious, and linguistic identities based on the barriers and demands of a particular context (Jaspal & Coyle, 2010).

Religious teachings and practices may influence individuals' developmental outcomes through direct and indirect messages, including ones about gender and age. Despite the espoused gender equality in US society, men and women may perceive differing levels of empowerment within religious settings, thereby creating a gendered developmental context that affords different opportunities and responsibilities to each gender. Gendered messages may facilitate involvement and entitlement, while in other cases they may give rise to feelings of not belonging or self-doubt. Although social commentaries on religion and religious institutions generally suggest that they are patriarchal and afford limited opportunities for women, practices should be interpreted from a framework that attempts to construe the behavior within its values and context as opposed to the dominant framework (see Chapter 10).

Similarly, in religious contexts, age and coming of age may be operationalized differently than in "mainstream" US culture. The age of maturity may range in religious contexts between the ages of 10 and 15 years, depending on religious beliefs. Maturation may be a private or a public transition that involves a combination of physical maturation and belief acquisition, understanding, or acceptance, which may not align with mainstream society, where "adult" responsibility is often delayed. Emerging adults may need to reconcile conflicting social and religious responsibilities and expectations.

## Contextually Grounded

Individuals develop within multiple overlapping contexts (e.g., home, neighborhood), so emerging adults must be considered within their respective social and structural contexts. Changes in physical location and social circumstances, such as moving from living with parents to living on a college campus, can alter the context, and thus the development of emerging adults (see Chapters 5 and 9). Social contexts may overlap, as illustrated, in a study seeking to identify the role of neighborhood context in the identity formation of Jewish Canadian adolescents (Markstrom, Berman, & Brusch, 1998). The authors could not attribute differences in identity scores solely to neighborhood context because many parents in the Jewish dominant neighborhood also chose to enroll their high school children in Jewish schools. This finding underscores the need for scholars to consider parental socialization practices, particularly related to religion (see Chapter 4) and the complex role of socializing agencies (e.g., religious schools), as they relate to school and neighborhood choice, socioeconomic status, and differences within religious and ethnic subgroups. While being a religious minority may touch on common elements across the United States, there may be differences related to the geographic context and the concentration of a religious minority group within a particular sociocultural context (e.g., being Jewish in New York versus North Dakota; see Chapter 8).

For youth living in pluralistic contexts, the exposure to multiple religious beliefs, appreciation for diversity in the United States, and youth culture that promotes "finding one's self" may result in exploration of religious systems different from their birth religion in order to clarify personal values and beliefs. Just as social, religious, and cultural contexts may reinforce each other, it is also important to consider how emerging adults navigate through mainstream social contexts that may conflict with religious expectations (e.g., premarital sex). Failure to acknowledge how religion interacts with key ecological factors, such as culture, social class, and ethnicity, and how it unfolds in individuals may result in missing key developmental tasks and their individual variations.

*Layers of Culture Embedded in Context*

Developmental contextualism portrays culture as influencing development primarily through engagement in culturally meaningful practices
(Rogoff, 2003). Culture is embedded, enacted, and recreated through
involvement in multiple layers of contexts that range from proximal
levels (e.g., individual, family, and peers) to the more complex (e.g.,
religious institutions and society).

### Developmental Niche

While considering culture at a macro-contextual level, equally important is
exploring the micro-level contextual ecology of one's developmental niche
(Super & Harkness, 1986). Although designed to understand child development, this theoretical model specifies the meaning of variation by focusing on the physical context, the values of socializing agents (e.g., parents,
mentors), and the particular practices in which they engage. Describing
the variation of these contexts is beyond the scope of a single chapter, but
it includes parental practices. Homes may feature indifference, outward
rejection of religion, or even multiple religions given intermarriage or conversion (Lambert & Dollahite, 2010). Beyond the home, emerging adults
are exposed to diverse references to religion, as in yard displays, marketing to religious groups (e.g., diverse holiday postal stamps), and religious
attire (e.g., hijab, yammaka, dastar). The media may constitute the most
pervasive influence, with televised Christmas specials, news accounts
about religion, and other features that may heighten feelings of curiosity
or fear as well as inclusion or marginalization based on the individual and
the relative fit with the religious context (see Chapter 6).

### Religious Contexts

Religious contexts are multifaceted and include variations across and
within groups. These contexts not only include religious and spiritual
teachings but also the congregational connections within which emerging adults develop. These contexts may provide social support and
sanctions at individual and institutional levels, fellowship, socialization
opportunities, and mentors (Roehlkepartain & Patel, 2006).

### Religious Content

The study of religion must attend, at some level, to the specific content
embodied in particular religious and spiritual teachings. Variations in

religious content may lead to particularly different cultural and developmental expectations and experiences. Religious content may promote values and behavioral expectations that may differ from those promoted by mainstream society, which may affect whether an individual seeks and adheres to religious guidelines. Especially for more socially conservative religious groups, these challenges may surface in navigating everyday encounters, such as decisions about religious attire. Perhaps the most tenuous negotiations include those associated with addressing intimate and romantic relationships, given religious and/or cultural guidelines that forbid premarital sex (see Chapters 5 and 11). Although coupling and dating are common, emerging adults who are religious or come from religious families may face additional challenges in how to navigate both the desires and pressures to engage in sexual relationships prior to marriage (Regnerus & Uecker 2011). Similarly, pursuing marital options with individuals outside the cultural or religious group or same-sex marriages may be challenging. While such behaviors and exploration may be of minimal concern for some emerging adults, for others the stakes may be dramatically higher.

### Mentors and Peers

Throughout childhood and adolescence, some emerging adults may have developed co-religious peer associations that promote both interdependence and social embeddedness, thereby promoting positive development (King & Furrow, 2004). In addition, emerging adults may have developed connections with religious group mentors and nonparental influences, which have generally been found to be related significantly to a variety of decreased risk factors, such as reducing dropout rates for at-risk adolescents (Schwartz, Bukowski, & Aoki, 2006). For some emerging adults, religious leaders and youth ministries are important for their religious and spiritual development (Nelson, 2003). These relationships may range from formal perfunctory associations to personal ones where individuals attempt to clarify religious feelings, make life decisions, and examine their identity and purpose in life (e.g., birth rite trip to Israel). For others, the lack of youth-affirming congregations, mentors, relevant discourse, or hypocritical behaviors of religious role models can contribute to confusion, negative experiences, and greater distancing from the religious community.

### Congregational Culture

Religious contexts influence socialization by providing clear guidance, promoting specific values and priorities, establishing behavioral expectations, providing social support, and serving as sources for individual and group identity development. Religious congregations are socializing agents and often become multifaceted centers of community life, but little explicit attention has focused on their role in the developmental context of children and adolescents (Roehlkepartain & Patel, 2006). Congregations have their own internal cultures and may promote particular values or priorities. For example, an ethnographic case study considered the particularly high civic participation levels in a Catholic church and found that parish culture, beyond denominational culture, affects individuals' civic participation (DiSalvo, 2008). Religious congregations and communities may seek to establish and communicate particular values, such as youth-friendly, racially diverse, or LGB-affirming cultures. For ethnic or racial minority and immigrant-origin youth, worship in mostly co-ethnic religious communities may serve multiple functions of religious, racial, ethnic, or cultural socialization. Given the overlap between religion and culture and the cultural interactions that arise organically (Levitt, 2007), studies on emerging adults need to explore the role of congregations, method of influence, and functions in the meaning-making process of emerging adults and how they may fluctuate throughout development.

Differences in congregational culture can highlight varied religious approaches, promote ideological alternatives and exploration, and encourage cultural expression. The surge in social media can augment in-person fellowship and socialization with virtual congregations and numerous online mechanisms to facilitate religious and spiritual exchanges (e.g., online convert support groups). In addition to deepening their own faith connections, Millennials may directly explore other faith traditions through "friending" others or researching diverse faith traditions online (see Chapters 5 and 6). The degree to which religious exploration is promoted within the congregational community may vary across religious groups. While some traditions may tolerate certain types of exploration within the religion, they may condemn explorations beyond that particular religious system. Consequently, the extent to which emerging adults explore their own or another faith tradition in person or virtually may result in varied responses from their faith community, which in turn may create cognitive dissonance.

## Embedded Congregations

Congregations and religious communities are embedded within a larger social context. It is important to consider the degree of similarity of the religious group to the dominant framework as well as the familiarity, acceptance, or discrimination from society. For religious and or ethnic minorities, group categorization by others can have both positive and negative aspects, depending on the status of the religion and the relative merit attributed to the religion in a given context (Sirin & Fine, 2007). In addition, external dimensions of religious life (e.g., congregational prayer, religious organization attendance) may increase individuals' belonging to a collective group. Thus, individuals may experience benefits from a sense of belonging, which may include a sense of fellowship, social support, and other material support (Portes & Raumbaut, 2006). However, perceived low religious group status within society (e.g., Scientologists) also may result in emerging adults distancing themselves from their religious group. The relative fit between the status of religious affiliation with those considered normative in broader society may affect individuals' meaning-making process and sense of belonging.

## Implications

The ability to conceptualize and operationalize the varying developmental factors impacting the meaning-making process of emerging adults is critical to an understanding of religion and spirituality in the lives of emerging adults. The implication of this conceptualization can be applied directly to research and applied settings.

### Research

Studies of religion may not adequately capture the salient experiences related to religious experiences of emerging adults, due both to the content of the studies and sampling limitations. Many of the large-scale studies have limited samples of religious minorities because of a lack of prevalence within a representative sample (Smith, 2009). Such underrepresentation of religious minorities and their experiences in large-scale, empirical work inadvertently may perpetuate the representation that "normative" religious and spiritual development largely overlap with experiences by mostly Christian, White, individuals from middle to higher socio-economic backgrounds without the necessary caveats to represent how experiences may diverge. In the future, scholars should sample the range of religious and spiritual affiliations (or the unaffiliated) including religious minorities, take into account the beliefs and practices of nontheistic traditions, and validate measures that account for the particularities of religious and spiritual dimensions of the developmental context (Tarakeshwar, Pargament, & Mahoney, 2003).

In addition, most studies do not account for the personal reasons, processes, and contextual factors that explain the meanings surrounding the "correlational landscape" (Marks & Dollahite, 2011, p. 182). It is important that researchers expand their understanding of the role of culture, religion, and spirituality in the lives of emerging adults by exploring factors that affect both their integration and attempts to decouple them. Mixed-method developmental studies should examine the personal and social nature of religious and spiritual socialization, variations in how religion and spirituality are experienced in context, and the fluid nature of person-context fit. To account for the complexities in the religious and spiritual life of emerging adults better, while maintaining a firm grounding in the theology and culture of religion and spirituality, researchers must broaden their sample, constructs being studied, methods, and disciplinary perspectives.

### Applied and Clinical Implications

A more culturally inclusive developmental conceptualization of the role that culture has on the religious and spiritual lives of emerging adults can assist professionals from various applied settings. For example, in higher education, it may guide recruitment and retention efforts as well as curricular and extracurricular offerings and how they relate to personal and professional negotiations (e.g., handshaking in interviews, intersection between religion and finance). In the areas of public health, a culturally inclusive developmental conceptualization can help to guide policy efforts on government programs and funding, as well as youth development and empowerment efforts, by highlighting the complex interaction that occurs between culture and religion. In addition, awareness of specific risk factors within particular religious and cultural subgroups may help to define culturally and religiously sensitive interventions.

For health practitioners (e.g., clinicians, physicians), understanding the developmental context can help to direct assessment and treatment interventions for emerging adults. Religiously based beliefs may influence how an individual views the explanatory models of health and wellness. In addition, religious beliefs combine with a host of social and cultural factors and affect whether an individual perceives out-group health professionals as able to understand the cultural dimension of his or her situation (Cinnirella & Loewenthal, 1999). A nuanced approach to assessment that explores how the presenting problem is impacted by individuals' personal characteristics, the linked and fluid nature of development, and multiple overlapping contexts will enable clinicians to contextualize the presenting problem within individuals' lives. For example, a clinician working with a Muslim emerging adult coming to terms with his alcohol usage may not fully appreciate the depth and level of the struggle related to religious prohibition, associated cultural stigma, and the implications such behaviors may have on marriage prospects and group membership. As such, it is recommended that practitioners expand their assessment of religion by including questions about the different components of faith (e.g., beliefs, doubts, practices, personal interpretation), coupling or decoupling of religion and culture for the individual, religious context, the manner of interaction and influence on the presenting problem, and available support systems. A thorough assessment enables clinicians to develop a stronger therapeutic alliance and identify religiously and culturally sensitive treatment interventions, such as helping to navigate and clarify their personal values and beliefs, as well as utilizing nontraditional sources of support (i.e., congregational community, ethnic community) for therapeutic intervention.

## ▲ Conclusion

As noted, the interaction between religion, spirituality, and culture in the lives of emerging adults is complex and results in varying developmental trajectories. Researchers and individuals working within applied settings are encouraged to adopt a more culturally inclusive developmental conceptualization that integrates the numerous and often overlapping personal and social contexts in which an individual interacts and develops over time. Adopting such a conceptualization will no doubt increase our depth and understanding of the meaning-making process of emerging adults residing in culturally and religiously diverse communities.

## ▲ Acknowledgments

The authors would like to thank Catherine Loewenthal and Carolyn Barry for helpful comments on earlier versions of this chapter.

# ▲ References

Arnett, J. J. (2004). *Emerging adulthood: The winding road from the late teens through the twenties.* New York, NY: Oxford University Press.

Barry, C. M., & Nelson, L. J. (2005). The role of religion in the transition to adulthood for young emerging adults. *Journal of Youth and Adolescence, 34,* 245– 255. doi: 10.1007/s10964-005-4308-1

Breakwell, G. M. (Ed.). (1983). *Threatened identities.* New York, NY: Wiley.

Cinnirella, M., & Loewenthal, K. M. (1999). Religious and ethnic group influences on beliefs about mental illness: A qualitative interview study. *British Journal of Medical Psychology, 72,* 505–524. doi 10.1348/000711299160202

DiSalvo, K. (2008). Understanding an outlier: How parish culture matters in a highly participatory Catholic Church. *Review of Religious Research, 49*(4), 438–455.

Eck, D. L. (2002). *A new religious America: How a "Christian country" has become the world's most religiously diverse nation.* San Francisco, CA: Harper.

Erikson, E. H. (1968). *Identity: Youth and crisis.* New York, NY: Norton.

Feldman, D. H. (2008). The role of developmental change in spiritual development. In R. M. Lerner, R. Roeser, & E. Phelps (Eds.), *Positive youth development and spirituality: From theory to research* (pp. 167–196). West Conshohocken, PA: Templeton Foundation Press.

García Coll, C., Lamberty, G., Jenkins, R., McAdoo, H. P., Crnic, K., Wasik, B. H., & Vazquez, G. H. (1996). An integrative model for the study of developmental competencies in minority children. *Child Development, 67*(5), 1891– 1914. doi: 10.1111/j.1467-8624.1996.tb01834.x

Hill, P. C., & Pargament, K. (2003). Advances in the conceptualization and measurement of religion and spirituality. *American Psychologist, 58,* 64–74. doi: 10.1037/0003066X.58.1.64

Holden, G. W., & Vittrup, B. (2009). Religion. In M. H. Bornstein (Ed.), *Handbook of cultural developmental science* (pp. 279–295). New York, NY: Routledge.

James, W. (1902/1985). *The varieties of religious experience.* Cambridge, MA: Harvard University Press.

Jaspal, R., & Coyle, A. (2010). "Arabic is the language of the Muslims—that's how it was supposed to be:" Exploring language and religious identity through reflective accounts from young British-born South Asians. *Mental Health, Religion and Culture, 13*(1), 17–36. doi: 10.1080/13674670903127205

King, P. E., & Furrow, J. L. (2004). Religion as a resource for positive youth development: Religion, social capital, and moral outcomes. *Developmental Psychology, 40*(5), 703–713. doi 10.1037/1941-1022.S.1.34

King, P. E., & Roeser, R.W. (2009). Religion and spirituality in adolescent development. In R. M. Lerner & L. Steinberg (Eds.), *Handbook of adolescent psychology* (3rd ed.; pp. 435–478). Hoboken, NJ: Wiley.

Lambert, N. M. & Dollahite, D. C. (2010). Development of the faith activities in the home scale (FAITHS). *Journal of Family Issues, 31*(11), 1442–1464. doi: 10.1177/0192513X10363798

Lerner, R. M. (2002). *Concepts and theories of human development* (3rd ed.). Mahwah, NJ: Lawrence Erlbaum.

Levitt, P. (2007). *God needs no passport: Immigrants and the changing American religious landscape*. New York, NY: New Press.

Levitt, P., Barnett, M., & Khalil, N. A. (2011). Learning to pray: Religious socialization across generations and borders. In K. F. Olwig & M. Rytter (Eds.), *Mobile bodies, mobile souls* (pp. 139–159). Aarhus, Denmark: Aarhus University Press.

Marks, L. D., & Dollahite, D. C. (2011). Mining the meaning and pulling out the processes from psychology of religion's correlation mountain. *Psychology of Religion and Spirituality, 3*(3), 181–193. doi: 10.1037/a0022206

Markstrom, C.A., Berman, R.C., & Brusch, G. (1998). An exploratory investigation of identity formation among Jewish adolescents according to context. *Journal of Adolescent Research, 13*, 202–222. doi: 10.1177/0743554898132006

Mattis, J. S., Ahluwalia, M. K., Cowie, S. E., & Kirkland-Harris, A. M. (2006). Ethnicity, culture, and spiritual development. In E. C. Roehlkepartain, P. E. King, L. Wagener, & P. L. Benson (Eds.), *The handbook of spiritual development in childhood and adolescence* (pp. 283–296). Thousand Oaks, CA: Sage.

McIntosh, P. (1988). *White privilege and male privilege: A personal account of coming to see correspondences through work in women's studies*. Working Papers Committee of the Wellesley College Center for Research on Women.

Mistry, J., & Saraswathi, T. S. (2003). The cultural context of child development. In R. M. Lerner, M. A. Easterbrooks, & J. Mistry (Vol. Eds.). (2003). *Developmental psychology. Vol. 6: Handbook of psychology* (pp. 267–291). New York, NY: Wiley.

Nelson, L. J. (2003). Rites of passage in emerging adulthood: Perspectives of young Mormons. *New Directions for Child and Adolescent Development. Special issue: Exploring Cultural Conceptions of the Transition to Adulthood, 100*, 33–50, doi: 10.1002/cd.73

Park, C. L. (2005). Religion and meaning. In R. F. Paloutzian & C. L. Park (Eds.), *Handbook of the psychology of religion and spirituality* (pp. 295–314). New York, NY: Guilford Press.

Portes, A., & Rumbaut, R.G. (2006). *Immigrant America: A portrait*. Berkeley, CA: University of California Press.

Regnerus, M., & Uecker, J. (2011). *Premarital sex in America: How young Americans meet, mate, and think about marrying*. New York, NY: Oxford University Press.

Roehlkepartain, E. C., & Patel, E. (2006). Congregations: Unexamined crucibles for spiritual development. In E. C. Roehlkepartain, P. E. King, L. Wagener, & P. L. Benson (Eds.), *The handbook of spiritual development in childhood and adolescence* (pp. 324–336). Thousand Oaks, CA: Sage.

Rogoff, B. (2003). *The cultural nature of human development*. New York, NY: Oxford University Press.

Schlosser, L. W. (2003). Christian privilege: Breaking a sacred taboo. *Journal of Multicultural Counseling and Development, 31*, 44–51. doi: 10.1002/j.2161-1912.2003.tb00530.x

Schwartz, K. D., Bukowski, W. M., & Aoki, W. T. (2006). Mentors, friends, and gurus: Peer and nonparent influences on spiritual development. In E. C. Roehlkepartain, P. E. King, L. Wagener, & P. L. Benson (Eds.), *The handbook of spiritual development in childhood and adolescence* (pp. 310–323). Thousand Oaks, CA: Sage.

Sirin, S. R., & Fine, M. (2007). Hyphenated selves: Muslim American youth negotiating identities on the fault lines of global conflict. *Applied Developmental Science, 11*(3), 151–163.

Smith, C. (with Denton, M. L). (2005). *Soul searching: The religious and spiritual lives of American teenagers*. New York, NY: Oxford University Press.

Smith, C. (with Snell, P.). (2009). *Souls in transition: The religious and spiritual lives of emerging adults*. New York, NY: Oxford University Press.

Spencer, M. B. (2006). Phenomenology and ecological systems theory: Development of diverse groups. In W. Damon & R. M. Lerner (Eds.). *Handbook of child psychology: An advanced textbook* (829–893). Hoboken, NJ: Wiley.

Suárez-Orozco, C., Singh, S., Abo-Zena, M.M., Du, D., & Roeser, R.W. (2011). The role of religion and religious organizations in the positive youth development of immigrant youth. In A. E. A. Warren, R. M. Lerner, & E. Phelps, (Eds.), *Thriving and spirituality among youth: Research perspectives and future possibilities* (pp. 255–288). Hoboken, NJ: Wiley.

Super, C. M., & Harkness, S. (1986). The developmental niche: A conceptualization at the interface of child and culture. *International Journal of Behavioral Development, 9*(4), 545–569. doi: 10.1177/016502548600900409

Tarakeshwar, N., Pargament, K., & Mahoney, A. (2003). Measures of Hindu pathways: Developmental and preliminary evidence of reliability and validity. *Cultural Diversity and Ethnic Minority Psychology, 9*(4), 316–332. doi: 10.1037/1099-9809.9.4.316

Tarakeshwar, N., Stanton, J., & Pargament, K. I. (2003). Religion: An overlooked dimension in cross-cultural psychology. *Journal of Cross-Cultural Psychology, 34*(4), 377–394. doi: 10.1177/0022022103253184.

# 14 ◭

# Nonreligious and Atheist Emerging Adults

LUKE W. GALEN

Who are the "Nones" and why are there so many of them? Media attention and scholarly inquiry have increasingly been focused on these questions for the following reasons. First, there are roughly 43 million adults in the United States (20%) who are religiously unaffiliated (or "Nones"), and this group has the fastest rate of growth of the major religious groups (Kosmin, Keysar, Cragun, & Navarro-Rivera, 2009). The Nones include those who identify as atheist, agnostic, or secular; however, most are religious yet unaffiliated. Other designations that are considered nonreligious are the "spiritual but not religious" and those responding to religious inquiries with "don't know" or "don't care." Thus, the Nones are a diverse group. Second, this group is growing. The 18- to 29-year-old age range (the "Millennials") cohort is less religious than older Americans with fully one in three religiously unaffiliated (Pew Research Center, 2012). Historically, cohorts have shown a drop in religiousness in adolescence followed by an increase during the family formation stage (Roozen, 1980); however, the current cohort of young adults is also less likely to be affiliated or attend religious services than earlier generations were at the same age (Pew Research Center, 2012). Therefore, this chapter focuses on the substantial number of emerging adults who identify as either completely nonreligious, unaffiliated, or who develop substantial religious doubts. The chapter first describes the basic demographic and cognitive aspects of the nonreligious, followed by the educational, personality, familial, and social influences that contribute to their self-identification.

## ◭ Definitions, Demographics, Cognition, and Education

For both theoretical and practical reasons, most previous studies have typically focused on the effect of religion itself or on a comparison of different denominations or levels of religious behavior (e.g., church attendance), rather than being focused on nonreligiousness per se. As a result, and because of small numbers, studies often utilize the unaffiliated as a general catchall category that includes subgroups that differ in significant ways. Those with no religious belief or behavior and who self-label as atheists and agnostics constitute roughly one-third of the unaffiliated emerging adults (or 6% of all US adults; Pew Research Center, 2012). These nonreligious individuals are disproportionately men (e.g., two-thirds to three-quarters), overrepresented within ethnic groups of European Americans and Asian Americans, and with higher numbers residing in the west and northeast regions of the United States. They tend to come from families with high levels of education and socio-economic status. For example, although the percentage of the highly educated (i.e., graduate degree) among the unaffiliated as a whole (13%) resembles the general population (11%), it is higher among the nonreligious (20%). Thus, subsequent comparisons may reflect demographic rather than religious effects.

Nonreligious youth are characterized by a preference for intellectualism (Hunsberger & Brown, 1984), a lesser emphasis on emotion than the religious (Burris & Petrican, 2011), and the ability to generate multiple perspectives on existential issues ("integrative complexity;" Hunsberger et al., 1996). This cognitive style is linked to transitioning away from childhood religion. Young adults who process material with greater complexity also have more religious doubts that increase with age (Hunsberger, Pratt, & Pancer, 2002) and more often cite cognitive influences on their religious views than do those who increase in religiosity (Altemeyer & Hunsberger, 1997). Such individuals engage in "divergent cognition" or seeking information from belief-inconsistent (e.g., nonreligious) sources as opposed to convergent sources that support previous beliefs. These youth are characterized by high levels of "Quest" religious orientation, open-ended beliefs linked to complex cognition and greater doubts over time (Burris et al., 1996). These processes suggest that religiousness becomes polarized, such that adolescents with greater initial doubts continue to decrease in religiousness over time (Ozorak, 1989).

There has been much interest in the relatively few individuals raised in highly religious households who as adults have low levels of religiousness, often referred to as "apostates" or "disaffiliates." In studies that contrasted these college-aged individuals with those who increased their religiousness, the former group was identified as having good academic records and who engaged in a process of intellectual struggle that resulted in giving up their childhood beliefs (Altemeyer & Hunsberger, 1997). Many weakly religious youth (who tend to have been raised in marginally or nominally religious households) do not possess a coherent knowledge of basic religious tenets (Smith, 2009). In contrast, the completely nonreligious have more religious knowledge than youth from most religious groupings (Pew Research Center, 2010), consistent with a process of deliberation and rejection of family beliefs. Although those who disaffiliate from religion provide a range of reasons for leaving, these do not differ substantially by previous faith (e.g., Catholic vs. Protestant). However, the most common explanation is a rejection of the teachings of their faith (Public Religion Research Institute, 2012). It is possible that those with differing "trajectories" of nonreligiousness may differ in substantive ways. For example, one typology by Zuckerman (2011) distinguishes "mild" apostasy (in the weakly religious, and thus associated with little disruption) from transformative apostasy (in the strongly devout, and therefore associated with more psychological reorientation). However, the literature has yielded little empirical information to date regarding how developmental trajectories of nonbelief correspond to psychological profiles.

This preference for intellectualism and complexity may extend to actual cognitive ability. Lower levels of religiousness are associated with higher performance on elementary cognitive tasks and overall intelligence (Bertsch & Pesta, 2009; Kanazawa, 2010; Lewis, Ritchie, & Bates, 2011; Nyborg, 2009). Recent experimental research indicates that analytical (as opposed to intuitive) thought is linked to lower levels of religious and spiritual beliefs (Gervais & Norenzayan, 2012; Shenhav, Rand, & Green 2011). There is also evidence that a strong tendency to mentalize (i.e., the capacity to represent and reason about agents' thoughts) or use "theory of mind" is necessary for many types of spiritual or religious beliefs, such that those who have lower mentalizing ability (e.g., Asperger's disorder) also tend to have lower levels of belief in God. Lower mentalizing abilities in men may even account for the overrepresentation of men among the nonreligious (Norenzayan, Gervais, & Trzesniewski, 2012). Therefore, these findings suggest that analytical cognitive tendencies are related to young adults' nonreligiousness.

The disproportionately high levels of education associated with irreligion has led some to suggest that higher education itself "secularizes" or is corrosive of religious belief. However, recent longitudinal studies indicate that although college students report lower levels of religiousness relative to when they were adolescents, this is even more the case for those who do not attend (Mayrl & Uecker, 2011). Rather, college attendance may decrease aspects of specific beliefs that are exclusivist, literalistic, and sectarian (Hill, 2011), possibly due to an exposure to different worldviews or critical scientific thinking. These findings suggest that, as with most individuals, the nonreligious may "self-select" or expose themselves to educational and social influences based on relatively early-developing factors. In addition to cognitive style, such influences also may include basic personality and temperamental factors.

## ▲ Personality

The stable patterns in which individuals can interact with and view the world have been conceptualized as several basic personality dimensions upon which individuals can vary. Research using the Big Five model of personality has indicated that, relative to the religious, the nonreligious tend to be higher on the trait of Openness to Experience and lower on traits associated with prosociality such as Conscientiousness and Agreeableness (Saroglou, 2002). However, there are problems in generalizing results of the "low religious" to the completely nonreligious or concluding that personality differences are due primarily to religiousness itself. Because most religious young adults are also members of religious communities (e.g., churches, temples, mosques), personality measures may reflect active social group participation rather than metaphysical belief. There are many putative benefits of religious groups (e.g., social support, structuring norms; Graham & Haidt, 2010) corresponding with prosocial traits, but unrelated to religious beliefs themselves. Group membership involves having strong convictions and diligence regarding duties and attendance, traits that are related to having conscientious personalities. Nonreligious individuals who are members of organized groups (e.g., the Center for Inquiry, Secular Student Alliance, or other secular humanist groups) display few differences in comparison with religious individuals on these traits (Galen & Kloet, 2011), and those with strong convictions, whether religious or secular, are more conscientious than indifferent or nonparticipatory individuals. Within the nonreligious, those who self-identify as spiritual are more agreeable than are atheists and agnostics (Galen, 2009), suggesting that personality differences as a function of belief also may be attributable to stylistic and expressive effects rather than metaphysical beliefs. Alternatively, nonbelievers may genuinely lack agreeable social traits, rendering them unsuited to organized groups (McCullough et al., 2005). It is also likely that the nonreligious are lower in Agreeableness because they are members of a stigmatized minority by definition, "going against the flow" socially. For example, communal traits are correlated with religiousness only when the culture is predominantly religious, such as in the United States as opposed to Europe (Gebauer, Paulhus, & Neberich 2013; Saroglou, 2010).

The nonreligious tend to be undogmatic, open-minded, and low on authoritarian characteristics (obedience, social conformity, and out-group aggression; Altemeyer & Hunsberger, 1997; Hunsberger & Altemeyer, 2006). This constellation of cognitive and personality features suggests that secular young adults share common traits extending beyond a mere rejection of religious views. For example, Openness is connected to nonreligiousness because of characteristics common to both personality and metaphysical worldviews (e.g., divergent cognition). Youth with such traits are likely to become less religious over time, whereas those with high Conscientiousness in adolescence increase in religiousness in young adulthood (McCullough, Tsang, & Brion, 2005). Taken as a whole, nonreligious youth appear to differ from their religious counterparts in terms of basic personality, and these tendencies are also reflected in their broader worldviews.

## ▲ Social Views, Values, and Morality

On one level the typical nonreligious young adult's sociopolitical views are not terribly surprising. For example, the nonreligious are more likely to be socially liberal and to vote Democratic or Independent rather than Republican (Kosmin & Keysar, 2008). The nonreligious are also more supportive of gay marriage and accepting of homosexuality than are the religious (Gallup, 2010). Although religiousness or the lack thereof may influence some social attitudes, others are more shaped by race, class, socioeconomic status, and political orientation. In fact, other than "culture war" issues such as abortion, gay marriage, premarital sex, and marijuana legalization, highly religious emerging adults do not greatly differ from the least religious on a variety of social issues such as gun control, capital punishment, or affirmative action. For example, in one study of college students, approval for the death penalty differed 6% between students with high and low religiousness, whereas approval of abortion differed by 54% (Higher Education Research Institute, 2003). Similarly, White Catholics are more supportive than Hispanic Catholics of both the death penalty (47% vs. 30%) and legal abortion (56% vs. 43%; PRRI, 2012). Likewise, Black Protestants and White Evangelicals are religiously similar, but dissimilar on issues such as support for the death penalty and abortion. It appears that on most issues, relative liberalism or conservatism across religions is more relevant than differences between religions. Consequently, the social views of the nonreligious resemble those of religious liberals. On fundamental moral issues such as lying, cheating, stealing, or bullying among college students there is virtually no relation to church attendance (Weeden, Cohen, & Kenrick, 2008). Why does religiousness or the lack thereof relate to some moral views rather than others?

It may be useful to examine further how nonreligious young adults differ on broader values beyond specific sociopolitical issues. Nonreligiousness is associated with greater valuation of achievement, hedonism, stimulation, and self-direction, whereas religiousness is associated with valuing traditionalism and conformity (Schwartz & Huismans, 1995). In the area of social values, nonreligious people tend to rank universalism (the protection of the welfare of all people) more highly than the religious, whereas religious individuals tend to rank benevolence (enhancing the welfare of familiar people) more highly (Saroglou, Delpierre, & Dernelle, 2004). In other words, the nonreligious make less of a distinction between in- and out-group members. Thus, there is a close relation between specific moral judgments and broader values of the nonreligious.

Jonathan Haidt has demonstrated that individuals often differ regarding the ways in which they evaluate moral concepts. For example, liberals and the nonreligious emphasize caring and fairness, whereas conservatives and the more religious are concerned with obedience to authority, in-group loyalty, and purity (Graham & Haidt, 2010). The disproportionate emphasis on care and fairness ("individualizing" concerns) exemplifies the "ethics of autonomy"—people should be allowed to live as they choose as long as others are not affected negatively. Secular ethics tends to emphasize individuality over embeddedness within the collective (Farias & Lalljee, 2008). The "group binding" concerns of sanctity/purity, in-group, and authority (stressed by religious individuals) prioritize conformity to tradition and community standards. Therefore, nonreligious youth may hold different views on social issues such as gay marriage because they base their views on fairness rather than on authority or sanctity concerns. Moral disagreements with teachings may occasionally precipitate breaking with previous religious traditions. For example, 4% of individuals who disaffiliate cite a specific social or sexual issue conflict with their religion (Public Religion Research Institute, 2012). Other research has suggested that nonreligious college students place a relatively greater emphasis on moral consequentialism relative to religious individuals, who emphasize rule-based or deontological morality (Piazza, 2012). These findings may explain why religiousness appears to play a smaller role in social issues of helping, charity, or forgiveness than it does with purity or group-related morality (Weeden et al., 2008). Another possibility is that moral views develop less through social learning and inculcation than by more general familial and class-based worldviews.

## ▲ Family

The nonreligious tend to show distinct family demographic patterns, such as being overrepresented among the single, never married, and cohabiting (Pew Research Center, 2012). This may be because, compared to more religiously conservative individuals, secular emerging adults have an older age of marriage and a broader spacing of sexual activity, marriage, and childbearing. This more drawn-out "social clock" (Neugarten, 1979) relative to the religious appears to come from several social, group, and familial factors. In contrast to specific religious sanctions against cohabitation and sex outside of marriage (with increased normative pressure to marry soon after sexual initiation), the nonreligious appear to regard the achievement of higher education as the indicator of maturity rather than childbearing (Cahn & Carbone, 2010). As a result, in contrast to the stereotype that the likelihood of divorce is a function of moral sanctions of religious groups, the completely nonreligious have a relatively lower divorce rate, due in part to older age at marriage and higher education (Denton, 2012; Pew Research Center, 2012). Nonreligious families in the United States tend to have fewer children than the religious, even after controlling for parents' education (Mosher, Williams, & Johnson, 1992). As such, the normative pattern of increased religious behavior in conjunction with marriage and childbearing is absent or attenuated (McCullough et al., 2005). Therefore, secular emerging adults' marriage patterns are likely a result of worldviews reflected in demographic and social trends.

The family milieu in which youth are raised likely plays a role in the values, personality, and worldviews mentioned earlier. Compared to the religious, seculars value autonomy more in children relative to obedience, and the use of reason rather than corporal punishment in regard to discipline (Ellison & Sherkat, 1993). The general low authoritarian philosophy of secular parents (e.g., viewing individuals as fundamentally benevolent; Starks & Robinson, 2007) may account for the nonreligiousness of the developing youth as much as any specific nonreligious instruction. Although socialization by parents exerts a strong influence on developing young adults' religiousness, core characteristics such as personality develop largely prior to religiousness (Saroglou, 2010), indicating the possibility that genetically based temperamental factors that underlie personality also contribute to nonreligiousness (McCullough, Tsang, & Brion, 2005). This would imply that emerging adults who are raised religiously may disaffiliate or drop out over time due to dispositional factors.

## ▲ Mental Health, Well-Being, and Prosociality

Large-scale studies and reviews have shown a modest but significant association between greater religiousness and a lower incidence of mental health and behavioral problems in emerging adults (Smith, 2009; Yonker, Schnabelrauch, & DeHaan, 2012). Youth with higher religious engagement have been found to have better family relationships, more prosocial behavior (e.g., civic engagement), and lower substance abuse and delinquency (Dew et al., 2008). Based on an inference of the causal role of the putative benefits of religiousness (e.g., optimism, moral guidance, coherent worldview; Regnerus & Smith, 2005), it is commonly posited that the nonreligious must, therefore, be at a comparative disadvantage. However, other work also has found that there are few differences as a function of religiousness in regard to mental well-being (Hunsberger, Pratt, & Pancer, 2001). In one study, youth with either stable belief ("abiders") or stable disbelief ("atheists") were equivalent in many outcomes such as health and well-being (Pearce & Denton, 2011). How can these conclusions be reconciled? The vast majority of research on emerging adults has focused on a religiously normative population, limiting the extension of findings to the low end of the religiousness continuum. Common religious measures are problematic when used inversely as measures of nonreligiousness. That is, disaffiliation, infrequent church attendance, or views of religion as unimportant do not differentiate atheists from the indifferently religious. For example, only a fifth of the "nonreligious" category in Smith (2009) did not believe in God, indicating that the "religiously disengaged" are not equivalent to the completely nonreligious. Almost all studies have confounded religious belief with social engagement or strong convictions and are better characterized as answering the question "Do more religiously engaged youth have better outcomes than less religiously engaged youth?" rather than "Is religiousness associated with better outcomes than nonreligiousness?"

The use of church attendance to ascertain whether the religiously uninvolved are at a disadvantage confounds religious belief with factors such as social support and capital, institutional guidance, or exposure to community programs (Ellison & George, 1994). This is problematic not only because it is typically the religious dimension most associated with mental and social well-being (Beyerlein & Hipp, 2006) but also because subsequent findings are often not qualified as representing a confounding of belief with group effects. The advantages in religiously engaged youth (e.g., service projects, donation of money or time) may be artifacts of service components in religious programs (Donahue & Benson, 1995). Despite unique elements in church participation (e.g., rituals), participation in both religious *and* nonreligious social clubs is associated with positive psychosocial adjustment (Good, Willoughby, & Fritjers, 2009). Therefore, the nonreligious may be at a disadvantage in regard to positive outcomes not because they do not believe in God, but rather because they are not embedded in a normative social group (Regnerus, 2003), which is an effect illustrated in cross-national comparisons (see later).

Interestingly, when studies include the full continuum of religious beliefs, those with the highest levels of mental distress are typically the weakly religious, whereas highly religious as well as nonreligious youth tend to be the least distressed (Eliassen, Taylor, & Lloyd, 2005); a curvilinear effect suggesting that mental well-being is associated with strong convictions either way (Donelson, 1999). Another measurement factor that has led to spurious results is that indices designed to tap "spirituality" make little sense when used with nonreligious youth because they are contaminated by predicted criteria. For example, scales assessing perceived meaningfulness or existential well-being are not surprisingly associated with general well-being (Dew et al., 2008) because items often assess positivity in general rather than spiritual beliefs (e.g., "There is a larger meaning to life"). In sum, the literature appears to indicate that the actively religious have better mental health and prosociality than the uncommitted or indifferent, but there is scant evidence that the confidently nonreligious differ from the confidently religious when social and group effects are considered (Galen, 2012).

Those who were raised in highly religious familial environments who later reject that identity have garnered attention regarding personal adjustment and etiological contributing factors. Some scholars have suggested that college students who are so-called apostates are marked by poorer mental health and parental relationships than are those who retain childhood religious beliefs (Brinkerhoff & Mackie, 1993; Hunsberger & Brown, 1984), though this may depend on the degree or depth of change from the previous level of religiousness (Zuckerman, 2011). On one hand, any guilt, anxiety, and familial conflict may be a result of breaking away from a religious milieu (Altemeyer & Hunsberger, 1997). Alternatively, parental conflict, death, or abandonment may precede a weakening or relinquishment of religious beliefs (Burris et al., 1996; Wilson & Sherkat, 1994). However, other studies have failed to uncover definitive patterns of maladjustment or family conflict (Hunsberger, 1980). Further, parental loss in childhood is related to religious change in either direction and may reflect general instability rather than irreligion specifically (Pasquale, 2010). Thus, studies focusing on "apostasy" may reflect stressors related to a contrast with the family or loss of social support rather than a lack of religiousness or may depend on the family religiousness from which the individual is departing.

## ▲ Societal Forces

Nonreligious emerging adults experience the stigma of being a distrusted and immoral societal "other," having rejected sacred normative beliefs (Edgell, Gerteis, & Hartmann, 2006), although few nonreligious report wanting to "convert" others (Altemeyer & Hunsberger, 1997; Brinkerhoff & Mackie, 1993). Many of the associations with personality or prosociality discussed earlier are related to conflicts with contextual normativity rather than factors inherent in irreligion. For example, although having two nonreligious parents is not problematic, the presence of parents with two different religions is associated with familial conflict (Cragun, Kosmin, Keysar, Hammer, & Nielsen, 2012). Similarly, the positive association between religiousness and psychological well-being exists only in religious countries

(Gebauer, Sedikides, & Neberich, 2012). Thus, any putative liability to mental health that irreligion poses may reflect nonnormative social status and a lack of group belonging rather than the absence of religious content.

## ▲ Caveats and Future Directions

As we have seen, information regarding the nonreligious is largely based on extensions of research focused on religious emerging adults (e.g., including terminology reflecting a deficit or deviance approach; Cragun & Hammer, 2011) or has lumped low religious ("unaffiliated," "none," or "disengaged"; Smith, 2009) together with the completely nonreligious (Lim, MacGregor, & Putnam, 2010). Future research is likely to be beneficial to the extent that it does not treat nonreligious youth as a homogeneous group. Contextual factors will become increasingly relevant as the increase in the nonreligious alters their minority status. Greater numbers of children being raised with at least one nonreligious parent may increase secularization because of increasing availability of nonreligious spouses (Merino, 2012). They may experience "coming out" as a social movement much as gay youth did in the past decade, which itself is likely to reduce prejudice (Gervais, 2011). The growth in organized nonreligious groups (Galef, 2010) also will result in normalizing as secular youth find peer support (Baker & Smith, 2009) and the concomitant benefits of cohesive social groups.

## ▲ References

Altemeyer, B., & Hunsberger, B. (1997). *Amazing conversions: Why some turn to faith and other abandon religion.* Amherst, NY: Prometheus Books.

Baker, J. O. B., & Smith, B. (2009). The nones: Social characteristics of the religiously unaffiliated. *Social Forces, 87,* 1251–1263. doi: 10.1353/sof.0.0181

Bertsch, S., & Pesta, B. J. (2009). The Wonderlic Personnel Test and elementary cognitive tasks as predictors of religious sectarianism, scriptural acceptance and religious questioning. *Intelligence, 37,* 231–237. doi: 10.1016/j.intell.2008.10.003

Beyerlein, K., & Hipp, J. R. (2006). From pews to participation: The effect of congregation activity and context on bridging civic engagement. *Social Problems, 53,* 97–117. doi:10.1525/sp.2006.53.1.97

Brinkerhoff, M. B., & Mackie, M. M. (1993). Casting off the bonds of organized religion: A religious-careers approach to the study of apostasy. *Review of Religious Research, 34,* 235–258.

Burris, C. T., Jackson, L. M., Tarpley, W. R., & Smith, G. J. (1996). Religion as quest: The self-directed pursuit of meaning. *Personality and Social Psychology Bulletin, 22*, 1068–1076. doi: /10.1177/01461672962210010

Burris, C. T., & Petrican, T. (2011). Hearts strangely warmed (and cooled): Emotional experience in religious and atheistic individuals. *International Journal for the Psychology of Religion, 21*, 183–197. doi:10.1080/10508619.2011.581575

Cahn, N., & Carbone, J. (2010). *Red families v. blue families: Legal polarization and the creation of culture*. New York, NY: Oxford University Press.

Cragun, R. T., & Hammer, J. H. (2011). "One person's apostate is another person's convert:" What terminology tells us about pro-religious hegemony in the sociology of religion. *Humanity & Society, 35*, 149–175. doi: 10.1177/016059761103500107

Cragun, R. T., Kosmin, B. A., Keysar, A., Hammer, J. J., & Nielsen, M. E. (2012). On the receiving end: Discrimination toward the non-religious. *Journal of Contemporary Religion, 27*, 105–127. doi:10.1080/13537903.2012.642741

Denton, M. L. (2012). Family structure, family disruption, and profiles of adolescent religiosity. *Journal for the Scientific Study of Religion, 51*, 42–64. doi: 10.1111/j.1468-5906.2011.01619.x

Dew, R. E., Daniel, S. S., Armstrong, T. D., Goldston, D. B., Triplett, M. F., & Koenig, H. G. (2008). Religion/ spirituality and adolescent psychiatric symptoms: A review. *Child Psychiatry and Human Development, 39*, 381–398. doi: 10.1007/s10578-007-0093-2

Donahue, M. J., & Benson, P. L. (1995). Religion and the well-being of adolescents. *Journal of Social Issues, 51*, 145–160. doi: 10.1111/j.1540-4560.1995.tb01328.x

Donelson, E. (1999). Psychology of religion and adolescents in the United States: Past to present. *Journal of Adolescence, 22*, 187–204. http://dx.doi.org/10.1006/jado.1999.0212

Edgell, P., Gerteis, J., & Hartmann, D. (2006). Atheists as "other": Moral boundaries and cultural membership in American society. *American Sociological Review, 71*, 211–234. doi:10.1177/000312240607100203.

Eliassen, A. H., Taylor, J., & Lloyd, D. A. (2005). Subjective religiosity and depression in the transition to adulthood. *Journal for the Scientific Study of Religion, 44*, 187–199. doi:10.1111/j.1468-5906.2005.00275.x

Ellison, C. G., & George, L. K. (1994). Religious involvement, social ties, and social support in a southeastern community. *Journal for the Scientific Study of Religion, 33*, 46–61. doi:10.2307/1386636

Ellison, C. G., & Sherkat, D. E. (1993). Obedience and autonomy: Religion and parental values reconsidered. *Journal for the Scientific Study of Religion, 32*, 313–329. doi: 10.2307/1387172

Farias, M., & Lalljee, M. (2008). Holistic individualism in the age of Aquarius: Measuring individualism/collectivism in New Age, Catholic, and atheist/agnostic groups. *Journal for the Scientific Study of Religion, 47*, 277–289. doi: 10.1111/j.1468-5906.2008.00407.x

Galef, J. (2010, September 6. Fall Brings Record Numbers of Atheist, Agnostic Student Organizations on Campus. http://www.secularstudents.org/recordnumbergroups2010

Galen, L. W. (2009). Profiles of the Godless: Results from a survey of the nonreligious. *Free Inquiry, 29*, 41–45.

Galen, L. W. (2012). Does religious belief promote prosociality? A critical examination. *Psychological Bulletin, 138*, 876–906. doi: 10.1037/a0028251

Galen, L. W., & Kloet, J. (2011). Personality and social integration factors distinguishing nonreligious from religious groups: The importance of controlling for attendance and demographics. *Archive for the Psychology of Religion, 33*, 205–228.

Gallup (2010). Americans' acceptance of gay relations crosses 50% threshold. http://www.gallup.com/poll/135764/americans-acceptance-gay-relations-crosses-threshold.aspx

Gebauer, J. E., Paulhus, D. L., & Neberich, W. (2013). Big two personality and religiosity across cultures: Communals as religious conformists and agentics as religious contrarians. *Social Psychological and Personality Science, 4*, 21–30. doi: 10.1177/1948550612442553

Gebauer, J. E., Sedikides, C., & Neberich, W. (2012). Religiosity, social self-esteem, and psychological adjustment: On the cross-cultural specificity of the psychological benefits of religiosity. *Psychological Science, 23*, 158–160. doi:10.1177/0956797611427045.

Gervais, W. M. (2011). Finding the faithless: Perceived atheist prevalence reduces anti-atheist prejudice. *Personality and Social Psychology Bulletin, 37*, 543–556. doi:10.1177/0146167211399583.

Gervais, W. M., & Norenzayan, A. (2012). Analytic thinking promotes disbelief. *Science, 336*, 493. doi: 10.1126/science.1215647

Good, M., Willoughby, T., & Fritjers, J. (2009). Just another club? The distinctiveness of the relation between religious service attendance and adolescent psychosocial adjustment. *Journal of Youth and Adolescence, 38*, 1153–1171. doi: 10.1007/s10964-008-9320-9

Graham, J., & Haidt, J. (2010). Beyond beliefs: Religions bind individuals into moral communities. *Personality and Social Psychology Review, 14*, 140–150. doi:10.1177/1088868309353415.

Higher Education Research Institute (2003). The spiritual life of college students. http://spirituality.ucla.edu/docs/reports/Spiritual_Life_College_Students_Full_Report.pdf

Hill, J. P. (2011). Faith and understanding: Specifying the impact of higher education on religious belief. *Journal for the Scientific Study of Religion, 50*, 533–551. doi:10.1111/j.1468-5906.2011.01587.x

Hunsberger, B. (1980). A reexamination of the antecedents of apostasy. *Review of Religious Research, 21*, 158–170. http://www.jstor.org/stable/3509881

Hunsberger, B., Alisat, S., Pancer, S. M., & Pratt, M. (1996). Religious fundamentalism and religious doubts: Content connections, and complexity of thinking. *International Journal for the Psychology of Religion, 6*, 201–220. doi:10.1207/s15327582ijpr0603_7

Hunsberger, B. E., & Altemeyer, R. A. (2006). *Atheists: A groundbreaking study of America's nonbelievers*. Amherst, NY: Prometheus Books.

Hunsberger, B., & Brown, L. B. (1984). Religious socialization, apostasy, and the impact of family background. *Journal for the Scientific Study of Religion, 23*, 239–251.

Hunsberger, B., Pratt, M., & Pancer, S. M. (2001). Religious versus nonreligious socialization: Does religious background have implications for adjustment? *International Journal for the Psychology of Religion, 11*, 105–128. doi:10.1207/S15327582IJPR1102_03.

Hunsberger, B., Pratt, M., & Pancer. S. M. (2002). A longitudinal study of religious doubts in high school and beyond: relationships, stability, and searching for answers. *Journal for the Scientific Study of Religion, 41*, 255–266. doi:10.1111/1468-5906.00115

Kanazawa, S. (2010). Why liberals and atheists are more intelligent. *Social Psychology Quarterly, 73*, 33–57. doi: 10.1177/0190272510361602

Kosmin, B. A., & Keysar, A. (2008). American nones: A profile of the no religion population. http://commons.trincoll.edu/aris/files/2011/08/NONES_08.pdf

Kosmin, B. A., Keysar, A., Cragun, R. T., & Navarro-Rivera, J. (2009). *American nones: The profile of the no religion population.* Hartford, CT: Institute for the Study of Secularism in Society and Culture.

Lewis, G., Ritchie, S., & Bates, T. (2011). The relationship between intelligence and multiple domains of religious belief: Evidence from a large adult US sample. *Intelligence, 39*, 468–472. doi:10.1016/j.intell.2011.08.002

Lim, C., MacGregor, C. A., & Putnam, R. D. (2010). Secular and liminal: Discovering heterogeneity among religious nones. *Journal for the Scientific Study of Religion, 49*, 596–618. doi:10.1111/j.1468-5906.2010.01533.x

Mayrl, D., & Uecker, J. E. (2011). Higher education and religious liberalization among young adults. *Social Forces, 90*, 181–208. doi: 10.1093/sf/90.1.181

McCullough, M. E., Enders, C. K., Brion, S. L., & Jain, A. R. (2005). The varieties of religious development in adulthood: A longitudinal investigation of religion and rational choice. *Journal of Personality and Social Psychology, 89*, 78–89. doi:10.1037/0022-3514.89.1.78.

McCullough, M. E., Tsang, J. A., & Brion, S. (2005). Personality traits in adolescence as predictors of religiousness in early adulthood: Findings from the Terman longitudinal study. *Personality and Social Psychology Bulletin, 29*, 908–991. doi: 10.1177/0146167203253210

Merino, S. M. (2012). Irreligious socialization? The adult religious preferences of individuals raised with no religion. *Secularism and Nonreligion, 1*, 1–16.

Mosher, W. D., Williams, L. B., & Johnson, D. P. (1992). Religion and fertility in the United States: New patterns. *Demography, 29*, 199–214. doi: 10.2307/2061727

Neugarten, B. L. (1979). Time, age, and the life cycle. *The American Journal of Psychiatry, 136*, 887–894.

Norenzayan, A., Gervais, W. M., & Trzesniewski, K. (2012). Mentalizing deficits constrain belief in a personal God. *PLoS ONE, 7*, e36880. doi:10.1371/journal.pone.0036880

Nyborg, H. (2009). The intelligence–religiosity nexus: A representative study of white adolescent Americans. *Intelligence, 37*, 81–93. doi: 10.1016/j.intell.2008.08.003

Ozorak, E. W. (1989). Social and cognitive influences on the development of religious beliefs and commitment in adolescence. *Journal for the Scientific Study of Religion, 28*, 448–463. doi:10.2307/1386576

Pasquale, F. L. (2010). An assessment of the role of early parental loss in the adoption of atheism or irreligion. *Archive for the Psychology of Religion, 32,* 375–396.

Pearce, P. L., & Denton, M. L. (2011). *A faith of their own: Stability and change in the religiosity of American adolescents.* New York, NY: Oxford University Press.

Pew Research Center (2012). "Nones" on the rise: One-in-five adults have no religious affiliation. http://www.pewforum.org/uploadedFiles/Topics/Religious_Affiliation/ Unaffiliated/NonesOnTheRise-full.pdf

Pew Research Center. (2010). U.S. Religious Knowledge Survey. http://www.pewforum.org/U-S-Religious-Knowledge-Survey-Who-Knows-What-About-Religion.aspx.

Piazza, J. (2012). "If you love me keep my commandments": Religiosity increases preference for rule-based moral arguments. *International Journal for the Psychology of Religion, 22,* 285–302. doi:10.1080/10508619.2011.638598

Public Religion Research Institute (2012). The 2012 American Values Survey. http://publicreligion.org/site/wp-content/uploads/2012/10/AVS-2012-Pre-election-Report-for-Web.pdf

Regnerus, M. D., & Smith, C. (2005). Selection effects in studies of religious influence. *Review of Religious Research, 47,* 23–50. http://www.jstor.org/stable/4148279

Regnerus, M. D. (2003). Religion and positive adolescent outcomes: A review of research and theory. *Review of Religious Research, 44,* 394–413. http://www.jstor.org/stable/3512217

Roozen, D. A. (1980). Church dropouts, changing patterns of disengagement and re-entry. *Review of Religious Research, 21,* 427–450.

Saroglou, V. (2002). Religion and the five factors of personality: A meta-analytic review. *Personality and Individual Differences, 32,* 15–25. doi:10.1016/S0191-8869(00)00233-6

Saroglou, V. (2010). Religiousness as a cultural adaptation of basic traits: A five-factor model perspective. *Personality and Social Psychology Review, 14,* 108–125. doi:10.1177/1088868309352322.

Saroglou, V., Delpierre, V., & Dernelle, R. (2004). Values and religiosity: A meta-analysis of studies using Schwartz's model. *Personality and Individual Differences, 37,* 721–734. doi:10.1016/j.paid.2003.10.005.

Schwartz, S. H., & Huismans, S. (1995). Value priorities and religiosity in four western religions. *Social Psychology Quarterly, 58,* 88–107.

Shenhav, A., Rand, D. G., & Greene, J. D. (2011). Divine intuition: Cognitive style influences belief in God. *Journal of Experimental Psychology: General, 141,* 423–428. doi: 10.1037/a0025391

Smith, C. (with Snell, P.). (2009). *Souls in transition: The religious and spiritual lives of emerging adults.* New York, NY: Oxford University Press.

Starks, B., & Robinson, R.V. (2007). Moral cosmology, religion, and adult values for children. *Journal for the Scientific Study of Religion, 46,* 17–35. doi: 10.1111/j.1468-5906.2007.00338.x

Weeden, J., Cohen, A. B., & Kenrick, D. T. (2008). Religious attendance as reproductive support. *Evolution and Human Behavior, 29,* 327–334. doi:10.1016/j.evolhumbehav. 2008.03.004

Wilson, J., & Sherkat, D. E. (1994). Returning to the fold. *Journal for the Scientific Study of Religion, 33,* 148–161.

Yonker, J. I., Schnabelrauch, C. A., & DeHaan, L. G. (2012). The relationship between spirituality and religiosity on psychological outcomes in adolescents and emerging adults: A meta-analytic review. *Journal of Adolescence, 35,* 299–314. doi:10.1016/j.adolescence.2011.08.010

Zuckerman, P. (2011). *Faith no more: Why people reject religion.* New York, NY: Oxford University Press.

# Part V ▲
## CONCLUSION

# 15 ▲

# Reflections on the Long and Winding Road of Meaning-Making

MONA M. ABO-ZENA AND CAROLYN MCNAMARA BARRY

> *The unexamined life is not worth living.*
> —Socrates

In describing the role of religion and spirituality in the lives of emerging adults, Arnett (2004) claims that few people enter this period of life with clear ideas, and few people emerge without having clarified their position. The goal of this volume is to understand emerging adults' religiousness and spirituality more fully by bringing together diverse focal points on religious and spiritual content and a range of personal, social, and societal contexts. This developmental lens that assumes bidirectionality and considers multiple levels of person-context fit highlights the variations and patterns in how, why, and toward what ends emerging adults consider and engage in religiousness and spirituality. Moreover, we sought to situate emerging adults' religiousness and spirituality and their unique life situation as emerging adults within the entire lifespan.

Although each chapter in this volume focused on specific aspects of religious and spiritual development, our conclusion begins by highlighting the broad themes across the volume in emerging adults' search for meaning. Thereafter, we point to future scholarly directions; specifically, we discuss *when, how, at whom*, and *where* scholars look, as well as *for what* they look in order to advance the literature on emerging adults' religiousness and spirituality. Finally, we reflect upon the implications of the findings for secular and religious practitioners, as well as for emerging adults and their families.

## ▲ Broad Themes

This volume provides a broad framework that includes foundational issues, multiple socialization contexts, and how religiousness and spirituality vary by gender, sexual orientation, culture, and for a range of commitments from the nonreligious to the highly devoted. In keeping with Gestalt psychology (Schirillo, 2010), the *whole* body of research presented in this volume is greater than the *sum* of its parts. Despite each chapter's focus on a particular aspect of emerging adults' religiousness and spirituality, interconnections exist that were referenced throughout the chapters. Moreover, the volume highlighted four broad themes that emerged from the literature reviewed across the chapters.

### *Salience of Religiousness and Spirituality*

First, for many emerging adults in the United States, religiousness and spirituality are salient dimensions of their development within individual, family, and community contexts, as well as at a broader sociocultural context (see Chapters 4, 5, 8, 9, and 13). In fact, such dimensions are even salient to emerging adults who are currently distancing themselves from a particular religion or are nonreligious (see Chapter 14). The centrality of explicit and implicit aspects of religion and spirituality in individual, family, and human history affects behaviors, attitudes, and interactions across religious affiliations and among the unaffiliated (e.g., understanding concepts such as karma, engaging in religiously inspired social-justice work, and filling in crossword puzzles where some answers reference religion). Failure to understand the role of religiousness and spirituality in human development better would yield an incomplete and inaccurate portrayal of human development. The process of meaning-making may lead to adaptive and positive trajectories that yield to flourishing or others that are less optimal and may result in floundering during the transition to adulthood. Scholarship and applications related to religious and spiritual development may help to promote a range of outcomes and interventions for emerging adults to support their flourishing during this time period.

### *One of Many Paths*

Second, religiousness and spirituality represent pathways through which meaning-making can occur. Although these pathways (which may or may not be overlapping) have been associated with benefits concerning adjustment for many emerging adults in the United States (see Chapter 3), they are clearly not the only paths, as evidenced by positive adjustment outcomes among the nonreligious (see Chapter 14). Indeed, emerging adults may find meaning-making opportunities through a university spring break outreach trip rebuilding homes in El Salvador or through a close friendship that includes high levels of emotional intimacy and authenticity of self or through particular courses (e.g., physics class on the cosmos or ethics class on the existence of evil in the world), or even in a neighborhood young adult football league. These alternate pathways to meaning-making may remain separate, or emerging adults may incorporate them into their religious and/or spiritual worldviews.

### Person-Context Fit

Third, religiousness and spirituality can provide clear benefits to individuals, but they also may be detrimental to some emerging adults (see Chapter 3). Only by examining the person-context fit between an emerging adult's religious or spiritual tradition and his or her current beliefs and behaviors can scholars better identify the situations under which religion and religiousness may cause harm to an emerging adult or subgroup. For instance, sexual-minority emerging adults who strive to remain faithful to religious traditions that prohibit their sexual orientation often experience tremendous cognitive dissonance (see Chapter 12). Similarly, heterosexual emerging adults who adopt age norms of sexual liberation, while remaining affiliated with religious traditions that prohibit premarital sex, experience dissonance as well (see Chapter 11).

### Contextualism

Fourth, developmental contextualism is required to understand fully emerging adults' religious and spiritual lives. Like all people, emerging adults live amid multiple layers of contexts, all of which interact with each other to shape their daily lives (Bronfenbrenner, 1979; Rogoff, 2003). Drawing on one example of this sociocultural lens, we note that Bronfenbrenner's bioecological model (1979) is well represented throughout our volume, and it illustrates how religiousness and spirituality can be embedded at every level of emerging adults' lives. Specifically at the individual level, advances in all developmental domains contribute to emerging adults' own religious and spiritual development during the third decade (see Chapter 2). Relatedly, identities unique to each individual (see Chapters 10, 12, 13, and 14) in turn shape emerging adults' interactions at all subsequent levels. Key socializing agents (see Chapter 4, 5, and 6) as well as assorted types of secular and religious communities (see Chapters 8 and 9) serve as proximal influences. These agents can afford opportunities for finding others who may range from being like-minded to those with highly disparate views as well as experiences that may promote or challenge emerging adults' religiousness and spirituality.

The structure and policies inherent in religious communities and universities in general (see Chapters 8 and 9), let alone the particular religious affiliation (if applicable) and university and other contexts in which emerging adults participate, invariably shape their opportunities for religious and spiritual exploration. At more distal levels, emerging adults in the United States have a unique opportunity to engage in religious and spiritual development in a nation founded on religious liberty, yet whose laws have ebbed and flowed on the extent to which separation of "church" and state is embraced (see Chapter 7). Further, the societal norms concerning sexuality, gender, and culture (ranging from the United States generally to particular subcultures within it) contribute to all levels of influence as well (see Chapters 10–13). Lastly, the historical changes that have delayed the onset of adulthood have resulted in unique developmental tasks for these emerging adults in the United States (see Chapter 1) that shape the opportunities and extent to which emerging adults engage in meaning-making. Only by considering the multiple layers of influence on emerging adults can research on religiousness and spirituality truly advance.

In sum, four broad themes emerged: (a) religiousness and spirituality are salient to many emerging adults in the United States, (b) religiousness and spirituality are one among many possible pathways that promote positive adjustment in emerging adults, (c) religion and religiousness can be detrimental to some emerging adults given poor person-context fit, and (d) an ecological model should undergird our study of emerging adults' religious and spiritual lives. With these themes in mind, we discuss next steps for scholars of emerging adults' religiousness and spirituality.

## ▲ Future Research Directions

### When Do We Look?

The third decade is a particularly salient time to understand religiousness and spirituality, even though they are important facets of human development throughout the lifespan (Holden & Vittrup, 2009). Largely because theories on religious and spiritual development traditionally have assumed a requisite adult level of cognitive maturity, the preponderance of the scholarship to date has focused on adults. More recently, scholars (Boyatzis, 2013; King, Ramos, & Clardy, 2013) have investigated children's and adolescents' religiousness and spirituality to contribute to describing how this maturity develops. However, this burgeoning research generally groups individuals between 18 and 30 years either with adolescents or adults. This generalized grouping does not account adequately for emerging adults' unique developmental needs and tasks that are embedded within the sociocultural context of the United States. In order to understand better the developmental processes that shape emerging adults, as scholars and practitioners we need to consider their development at different points of time during these focal years, as well as their antecedents (i.e., through retrospective studies) and the adult years that follow.

### How Do We Look?

We scholars need to look in a manner that we see all that is there: the robust nature of religiousness and spirituality and the diverse range of ways that emerging adults navigate its multiple layers in different facets of their lives. Given that the preponderance of measures primarily were created for European-American Christians (Hill & Pargament, 2003), we need to create and use valid and reliable measures for religiously and spiritually diverse populations. Empirical and theoretical work needs to be built on the sound construction of nuanced measures and study designs; in so doing, we could then assess better how the diverse population of emerging adults are navigating this meaning-making process and to what extent they are immersed in religious and spiritual contexts.

Scholars in the fields of the psychology of religion and developmental psychology (with a focus on religious and spiritual development) utilize mostly quantitative methods that provide a distal depiction of trends. In addition, we scholars need to use dynamic and contextually oriented theoretical approaches to guide multimethod research studies, including some that focus on proximal levels of influence and variation (e.g., peers and family; Marks & Dollahite, 2011). Together, these approaches would provide both convergent and divergent data to illuminate the complexity of developmental change. Moreover, they would elucidate trajectories by documenting the prevalence and unpacking meanings of behaviors that may be difficult to measure (Yoshikawa, Weisner, Kalil, & Way, 2008). For example, a study that focuses on individual or collective prayer should incorporate both quantitative measures (to document the frequency of prayer done individually or in congregation as well as the types of prayer) and qualitative methods (to map the terrain of sincerity in prayer that is often considered a private matter and to address issues of attention, transcendence, or sincerity during prayer in part because of the difficulty in numerically measuring such experiences). Moreover, both quantitative and qualitative approaches should reflect in-group and out-group perspectives on the particular aspect of religiousness being studied, and account for personal, social, and societal factors (e.g., religious doubt or questioning, social desirability, and public regard of faith or faith-related practices).

The use of multimethod data and data analysis from a range of sources should inform a developmental model that accounts for the (sometimes conflicting) interaction between multiple individual and contextual layers immersed in particular religious and spiritual beliefs and practices (or lack thereof). *How* we scholars look must be aligned closely with *what* we look for as well as *when* we look. These methods and research designs may include a range of quantitative and qualitative methods of inquiry (e.g., logs of practices, diaries or reflections on practices, and retrospective, concurrent, longitudinal, and sequential designs). We also need to analyze the sociocultural context of emerging adults as extant data and to inform and contextualize research. For instance, scholars could analyze the art and music produced and consumed by emerging adults for religious and spiritual content. With the proliferation of virtual media, we can build on how emerging adults represent their religiousness and spirituality in their online profiles and other virtual representations (Bobkowski & Pearce, 2011).

We scholars need to develop interdisciplinary approaches and research teams that can highlight the many ways that religiousness and spirituality may shape the whole development of individuals from early childhood through their emerging-adult years and beyond. In addition to researchers from human development and psychology, other social scientists (e.g., sociologists, anthropologists, economists) should be included in order to provide their valuable research perspectives. While utilizing a developmental and lifespan lens, the contributors of this volume have moved the field a bit further because they represent a wide range of disciplines beyond psychology that include criminal justice, mass communication, religion, and higher education. Yet scholars in other related disciplines (e.g., theology, gender studies, and education) may inform research questions and methods as well as religious leaders, faculty mentors, clinicians, and service providers such as campus ministers and mental health counselors. Finally, we need to involve emerging adults more directly in helping to identify the terrain of their lives and the ways that religion and spirituality could serve as a resource or an impediment to their development. In so doing, the ecological validity of the study is likely to increase as well as emerging adults' opportunities for their own discernment.

## At Whom Do We Look?

We scholars need to look beyond the usual candidates who are surveyed in studies of religion and spirituality (i.e., European-American Christians). The goal of broadening this representation would be to represent meaningful variations across and between groups better. This broader sampling would include religious minorities (see Chapter 13) and other religious groups (e.g., Jehovah's Witnesses) currently underrepresented in the research, yet often who are more religious than are those who are currently studied (Smith, 2009). It also would highlight important developmental and contextual variations better that may inform developmental processes, such as the differentiated role of religion in historically oppressed or marginalized groups (e.g., African American, First Nation, immigrant), and how religion may serve as a factor to promote these young people's resilience.

Further, religious group membership alone may not document the within-group variations adequately. According to Scarlett (2006), all one knows about the religious self-identification is the label; you do not know what a label means to the individual. In fact, there may be more in common between individuals of different religious affiliations who share a certain level of religious commitment than do individuals of the same affiliation, but markedly different levels of commitment. For example, Smith (2005) outlined levels of religiousness topped by the smallest group of "Devoted" where many aspects of the nature of practice and belief may be similar across traditions (e.g., Evangelical Christian, Orthodox Jewish, Roman Catholic; p. 220). In addition, research about religiousness and spirituality needs to reflect the distribution of individuals and groups adequately across theistic and nontheistic traditions, and lived in formal and more individual contexts at varying levels of religious commitment and practice.

Finally, although contextualizing the study of emerging adults is important, a study of individuals in the United States also should be informed by cross-cultural research. While adults in the United States report higher rates of religious beliefs and practices than do those in Western European countries, they report lower rates than do those in the Middle-Eastern or African countries (Inglehart, Basanez, Diez-Medrano, Halman, & Luijkx, 2004). We scholars should conduct research that explores patterns and trajectories of religiousness and spirituality internationally in order to situate better how and to what extent religiousness and spirituality among emerging adults in the United States are significant compared to those in other sociocultural contexts.

## *Where Do We Look?*

Although colleges and universities are the most typical recruitment ground for participants in our studies, we scholars need to look in different contexts in order to understand elements of person-context fit and the social aspects of meaning-making better. Such contexts might include the military, community colleges (and other more transitory environments), retail stores where emerging adults may hold jobs, work-study and service programs like Peace Corp and Americorp, Headstart programs where we are likely to find parenting classes for young parents, and jails where there are high numbers of low-income emerging-adult men.

Our looking needs to explore the common locations, in both traditional and unconventional manners, where religious and spiritual exploration are very likely as well as less likely to occur. Additionally, we need to look at formal religious organizations and the many layers within them that may help us to understand better why emerging adults do or do not attend them, including affiliations that are more religiously liberal and inclusive of atheists and sexual minorities such as Unitarian Universalists (see Chapters 12 and 14) as well as less common religions such as Santería (see Chapter 7) and Wicca (see Chapter 6). Within religious organizations and communities this looking would include both opportunities for individual or collective worship. It also would pay attention to informal contexts of religious organizations and communities, such as a community viewing of the Super Bowl in the mosque, church, or temple social hall (see Chapter 8).

Finally, as scholars, we need to be immersed more fully in the everyday contexts of emerging adults in order to document more accurately how issues of religion and spirituality are related to their everyday practices. For example, consider how emerging adults with personal-religious narratives that include religious socialization about fiscal obligations and charity (e.g., tithing among Seventh-Day Adventists and Mormons, Muslims and almsgiving and prohibitions against interest) may navigate their increasing financial independence in manners different from individuals who have had less opportunity to engage in budgeting tasks in religious or other contexts. Lastly, we should document more comprehensively the intricate ways in which religion and spirituality (whether physically or virtually, in everyday interactions or in determining major life directions such as whether, who, and in what context to get married) may inform emerging adults' behavior and attitudes.

## *For What Do We Look?*

Building upon the greater variety of *where* we look, we scholars need to look in order to assess the best person-context fit from the level of the individual, family, peers, mentors, neighborhood, religion, religious community, and the broader society. The influence of such contexts may not all be aligned. How do individuals navigate these personal relationships with potentially conflicting messages and priorities? Do they integrate these messages, including the implicit and explicit socialization and reinforcement that they receive from their parents, peers, media, the law, religious communities, universities, and culture (see Chapters 4–9 and 13)? Do they compartmentalize the messages? Or do they selectively alternate between both? Consider emerging adults who may participate in activities that deviate from what is accepted within their religious context, such as those who view pornography and are attempting to balance personal desires and stay generally within religious community expectations (Nelson, Padilla-Walker, & Carroll, 2010; see Chapters 6, 11, and 12). Given their rationalizations, though, emerging adults may acknowledge inconsistency in their behaviors across contexts and compartmentalize, or may feel guilty about their behavior due to their inability to incorporate the sometimes different social expectations. We need to look for both the outcomes and practices that we might expect given what we know about human development and the importance of context, as well as to be open to identifying behaviors, attitudes, and trajectories that may somehow be outside the expectations of religious and spiritual communities.

## ▲ Implications

### Practitioners

Although this edited volume was designed primarily to inform scholars of emerging adults' religiousness and spirituality, there are important implications for secular and religious practitioners who work with emerging adults. First, although there are more religious communities, particularly informal ones, than we had originally thought (see Chapter 8). However, there is still a dearth of youth-affirming religious communities, especially for those marginalized by culture, economic position, or sexual orientation (see Chapters 12 and 13). Although informal young adult groups and other programming exists in mainline Protestant and Roman Catholic communities, it appears as though their approaches to programming are less effective than are those in other communities (e.g., Mormons, Black Protestants) in retaining emerging adults in their religious communities (Smith, 2009).

Similarly, there is a dearth of secular organizations (that are not affiliated with a university context) that are tailored to the interests and needs of emerging adults. Although several years ago the MacArthur Network on Transitions to Adulthood documented the challenges of these "forgotten half" of emerging adults (i.e., those not enrolled in higher education; Osgood, Foster, Flanagan, & Ruth, 2005; Settersten, Furstenberg, & Rumbaut, 2005), practitioners need to pay greater attention to providing meaning-making opportunities for these emerging adults. In fact, many community organizations have programming for adults, but not specifically for emerging adults. Consequently, these emerging adults have less structural support in place than do their peers attending universities to promote their central developmental task of identity achievement, which includes their values, beliefs, and worldviews. As s a result, they are more likely to flounder during their emerging-adult years compared to their peers at universities. In sum, we encourage practitioners affiliated with secular and religious communities to consider ways of expanding their programming in order to reach a wider range of emerging adults, as well as to consider how they provide meaning-making opportunities, which will be discussed next.

Second, some youth-affirming communities (both religious and secular) may not have provided relevant messaging for emerging adults given the nature of their current developmental needs and thirst for self-exploration during this decade. Just like infants who are effectively able to use their caregiver as a secure base to explore the toys around them (Bowlby, 1969), emerging adults need a secure base, often through religious or secular communities, to explore their religiousness and spirituality. Emerging adults in the United States are quite busy asking why (and *why not*) to their elders during this decade, and they are likely to be persuaded by complex and, if applicable to the community, theologically rich answers rather than a simple "because I (or the institution) said so." In other words, practitioners and community leaders need to respond in earnest to questioning and to religious and spiritual doubts of emerging adults in manners that facilitate emerging adults' meaning-making rather than devalue it. Even leaders and members of faith traditions that sanction relatively lower levels of questioning need to consider the cost of dismissing questions by emerging adults and risk marginalizing them; alternately, these leaders may consider how to socialize believers of all ages to incorporate their queries in a manner that is in keeping with the values of the tradition and help to address them. Third, practitioners need to "walk the walk" as such role modeling and mentoring does not go unnoticed by emerging adults, which includes limiting hypocritical behaviors. Indeed, both high-level scandals and their concealment (e.g., sexual abuse, embezzlement) as well as personal indiscretions (e.g., extramarital affairs, gossiping) are scrutinized by the media and by actual and prospective congregants. They may be particularly influential for emerging adults during this formative period as they individuate from their parents and seek to create their own religious and spiritual identities (Arnett, 2004). Moreover, emerging adults who witness unethical behaviors may be tempted to pursue the *"why not"* option as they engage in decision making about moral and ethical issues.

### Emerging Adults and Their Families

In addition to the implications for secular and religious practitioners, this volume has important implications for emerging adults and their families. First, given the dearth of youth-affirming communities, it behooves emerging adults to be intentional in seeking out communities that support them. Certainly parents, older siblings, and extended family members may be particularly helpful in making suggestions about where support may be found (e.g., InterVarsity Christian Fellowship or Theology on Tap). Ultimately, emerging adults need to take ownership of this process in order to find the right fit for them. Emerging adults who are passive and awaiting a community to find them are likely to flounder. Instead, emerging adults need to utilize their social networks (that often include their families) to find salient communities in order to forge close relationships with others that involve emotional intimacy, and not just companionship. In so doing, one by one, emerging adults may create a constellation of others who genuinely care for and support them. Thus, emerging adults must be willing to take social risks in attending community-sponsored events (e.g., a spinning class, a rock climbing wall, a job training program, scripture study), where they are likely to meet others who are willing to share their authentic selves. They are encouraged to grab a sibling, cousin, or trusted friend to accompany them on such occasions to increase the likelihood of going and returning on future occasions.

Second, if at first emerging adults do not succeed in finding youth-affirming communities, then, as the adage goes, "they should try, try again." Some of the communities that emerging adults encounter may not provide that secure base for exploration, which then will require emerging adults to discern to what extent they agree or disagree with the messages given by that community. As they recenter their relationships with their parents (Tanner & Arnett, 2011) and develop ideally a cadre of trusted others to whom they can turn, such advisors (e.g., coach, roommate, sibling, parent, job supervisor, religious mentor) can be quite useful in facilitating discernment. Although it is hoped that the family of origin (let alone their future spouses) will serve as a secure base for emerging adults, this ideal is not realized for all emerging adults in the United States. Certainly, families (particularly parents) can heed the suggestions noted for secular and religious communities in the previous section about providing opportunities for meaning-making. Further, parents should not assume that emerging adults' questioning or doubting is an indication of their competence as parents. Rather this searching process is developmentally normative, especially within the US mainstream culture (Arnett, 2004). Parents who are present both physically (or virtually) and emotionally to dialogue with their emerging adults as they search and quest are likely to forge more mature and honest relationships with their children during this tumultuous time and thereafter when their emerging-adult children become adults.

Third, although adults, particularly those involved in communities that promote meaning-making, should be pillars of support and model optimal behavior, emerging adults need to recognize that they are also people who, unfortunately, sometimes make mistakes. Indeed, this is a hard lesson to learn as we as humans often consider our elders as infallible. However, sometimes these revered adults (including parents) will stumble just as do emerging adults. In such cases, the adults should acknowledge their mistakes, too, and (if applicable) seek forgiveness from the emerging adults. Thereafter, the adults should keep the dialogue open with the emerging adults in order to promote healing of the relationship. In so doing, emerging adults' meaning-making can continue.

These suggestions for secular and religious practitioners as well as emerging adults and their families are not intended explicitly to promote religion, which can have both positive and negative impact on emerging adults. Instead, these suggestions are designed to promote positive outcomes (ranging from health benefits to well-being; see Chapter 3) for emerging adults through a range of meaning-making opportunities that may include religiousness and spirituality, in order to promote emerging adults' flourishing rather than floundering in the third decade of life.

## ▲ Conclusion

With the demographic shifts that delay the onset of adulthood to about age 30, many emerging adults in the United States today are faced with a decade free from major responsibilities to others (Arnett, 2004), which allows opportunities both for flourishing or floundering. The goal of this volume was to explore the ways in which emerging adults make sense of their complex lives during this third decade. Indeed, religiousness and spirituality have the potential to make both positive and negative contributions to emerging adults' lives. To us, the real value of religiousness and spirituality is that they often afford opportunities for emerging adults to engage with those bigger questions of life's purpose. As Smith (2011) notes, too many emerging adults in the United States do not engage adaptively in this transcendental quest, which in turn can result in a life filled with numerous accomplishments (i.e., an impressive resume) but may not bear the same fruit as would an "examined life." It is our sincere hope that this volume encourages more sophisticated scholarship on this meaning-making process, which then should inform practice and policies that promote emerging adults' positive development. To us, it is only from living this "examined life," in any variety of contexts from which emerging adults find meaning (e.g., religious community, young adult soccer league, Habitat for Humanity) that the greatest joys in life can be found. In so doing, these opportunities that arise on this long and winding road of development can invariably support their flourishing in the third decade so they are optimally equipped for the developmental responsibilities as adults.

## ▲ References

Arnett, J. J. (2004). *Emerging adulthood: The winding road from the late teens through the twenties.* New York, NY: Oxford University Press.

Bobkowski, P. S., & Pearce, L. D. (2011). Baring their souls in online profiles or not: Religious self-disclosure in social media. *Journal for the Scientific Study of Religion, 50,* 744–762. doi: 10.1111/j.1468-5906.2011.01597.x

Bowlby, J. (1969). *Attachment and loss: Vol. 1. Attachment.* New York, NY: Basic Books.

Boyatzis, C. J. (2013). The nature and functions of religion and spirituality in children. In K. I. Pargament (Ed.), *APA handbook of psychology, religion, and spirituality: Vol. 1. Context, theory, and research* (pp. 497–512). doi: 10.1037/14045-001.

Bronfenbrenner, U. (1979). *The ecology of human development: Experiments by nature and design.* Cambridge, MA: Harvard University Press.

Hill, P. C., & Pargament, K. (2003). Advances in the conceptualization and measurement of religion and spirituality. *American Psychologist, 58,* 64–74.

Holden, G. W., & Vittrup, B. (2009). Religion. In M. H. Bornstein (Ed.), *Handbook of cultural developmental science* (pp. 279–294). New York, NY: Routledge.

Inglehart, R. F., Basanez, M., Diez-Medrano, J., Halman, L., & Luijkx, R. (2004). *Human beliefs and values: A cross-cultural sourcebook based on the 1999-2002 value surveys.* Mexico City, Mexico: Siglo XXI.

King, P. E., Ramos, J. S., & Clardy, C. E. (2013). Searching for the sacred: Religion, spirituality, and adolescent development. In K. I. Pargament (Ed.), *APA handbook of psychology, religion, and spirituality: Vol. 1. Context, theory, and research* (pp. 513–528). Washington, DC: American Psychological Association. doi: 10.1037/14045-001

Marks, L. M., & Dollahite, D. C. (2011). Mining the meanings and pulling out the processes from psychology of religion's correlation mountain. *Psychology of Religion and Spirituality, 3,* 181–193. doi: 10.1037/a0022206

Nelson, L. J., Padilla-Walker, L. M., Carroll, J. S. (2010). "I believe it is wrong but I still do it:" A comparison of religious young men who do versus do not use pornography. *Psychology of Religion & Spirituality, 2,* 136–147. doi: 10.1037/a0019127

Osgood, D. W., Foster, E. M., Flanagan, C., & Ruth, G. R. (Eds.). (2005). *On your own without a net: The transition to adulthood for vulnerable populations.* Chicago, IL: University of Chicago Press.

Rogoff, B. (2003). *The cultural nature of human development.* New York, NY: Oxford University Press.

Scarlett, G. (2006). Toward a developmental analysis of religious and spiritual development. In E. C. Roehlkepartain, P. E. King, L. Wagener, & P. L. Benson (Eds.), *The handbook of spiritual development in childhood and adolescence* (pp. 21–33). Thousand Oaks, CA: Sage.

Schirillo, J. A. (2010). Gestalt approach. In E. B. Goldstein (Ed.), *Encyclopedia of perception* (pp. 469–471). Thousand Oaks, CA: Sage. doi: 10.4135/9781412972000

Settersten, R. A., Furstenberg, F. F., & Rumbaut, R. (Eds.). (2005). *On the frontier of adulthood: Theory, research, and public policy.* Chicago, IL: University of Chicago Press.

Smith, C. (with Denton, M. L). (2005). *Soul searching: The religious and spiritual lives of American teenagers.* New York, NY: Oxford University Press.

Smith, C. (with Snell, P.). (2009). *Souls in transition: The religious and spiritual lives of emerging adults.* New York, NY: Oxford University Press.

Smith, C. (with Christofferson, K., Davidson, H., & Herzog, P. S.). (2011). *Lost in transition: The dark side of emerging adulthood.* New York, NY: Oxford University Press.

Tanner, J. L., & Arnett, J. J. (2011). Presenting "emerging adulthood": What makes it developmentally distinctive? In J. J. Arnett, M. Kloep, L. B. Hendry, & J. L. Tanner (Eds.), *Debating emerging adulthood: Stage or process?* (pp. 13–30). New York, NY: Oxford University Press.

Yoshikawa, H., Weisner, T. S., Kalil, A., & Way, N. (2008). Mixing qualitative and quantitative research in developmental science: Uses and methodological choices. *Developmental Psychology, 44,* 344–354. doi: 10.1037/0012-1649.44.2.344

# Index ▲

meaning-making and religion (*Cont.*)
  congregations and communities in,
    142–48
  context of, 7
  culture, context, and social position,
    13–14
  developmental process of, 5, 6–7
  in emerging adults, 4–5
  foundational perspectives, 8–9
  gender and, 12, 181–82
  heterosexual sexuality and, 12–13
  ideological context of, 143–44
  media and, 10
  nonreligious and atheist emerging
    adults, 14
  overview, 3–5, 255
  parents and, 9, 23
  peers and, 10, 23–24
  religious affiliation and, 231
  religious communities and, 11
  religious freedom and, 10–11
  scholarship on, 268
  sexual minorities and, 13
  social context of, 144–45
  socialization, 9–12, 23
  summary, 7–8
  transcendent context of, 146–48
  universities and, 11–12
  variations in, 12–14
media
  engaging media, 98–100
  meaning-making and, 10
  Media Practice Model, 10, 94–95,
    98, 104–5
  religious media, 95–98, 103–4
  selection of, 95–98
  social media, 24, 76–77, 100, 103–4,
    182, 230
Media Practice Model, 10, 94–95, 98,
    104–5
mental health, 43–45, 211–12,
    244–47, 261
mentors/mentoring. *see also* role
    models
  access to, 48, 62, 64
  assessment of, 263
  from communities, 85, 140

faculty mentors, 261
  hypocritical behaviors, 265
  influence of, 49–50
  from nonparental adults, 33
  religious and spiritual
    perspectives, 24
  in religious context, 228, 229
  in social context, 144–45
Metropolitan Community Church,
    208, 209
Mexican culture, 198
Millennial generation, 25, 237
*Mitchell v. Helms* (2000), 124
moralistic therapeutic deism (MTD),
    25, 221
moral relativists, 25
morals/morality
  abortion and, 191
  in cocurricular life, 155
  codes of, 140, 194
  in congregations, 142
  decision making about, 265
  development of, 161
  formation of, 84
  identity of, 147
  ideological context, 143
  immorality, 4, 180, 246
  in nonreligious and atheist
    emerging adults, 241–43
  of religious leaders, 208
  religiously based, 99
  search for the sacred and, 205
  sexual behavior, 24
  sociomoral concerns, 178
  standards of, 95, 157
  worldviews, 42, 44–46, 51
Mormon emerging adults, 25–26, 86,
    98, 129, 194–95. *see also* Church of
    Jesus Christ of Latter-day Saints
Morrill Anti-Bigamy Act, 116
Muslim Americans
  community engagement among, 175
  higher education, influence on, 152
  hijab wearing, 174, 182
  Internet use by, 96
  Islam, 100, 146, 176, 182, 209
  orthodoxy of, 177

Protestants (*Cont.*)
  sexual relations, 24
  young adult groups, 264
psychospiritual transformation, 49–50

Quaker communities, 86, 153, 163

racism, 222–23
Refuge program, 204–5
religion and spirituality. *see also*
    gender-religion link; higher
    education and religious
    influence; meaning-making and
    religion
  contextualism, 257–58
  culture, defined, 222–23
  decline of, 3–4, 22, 25, 51, 135–38
  defining scope of, 5–6
  during emerging adulthood, 8
  family demographic patterns,
    243–44, 265–67
  influence on homosexual emerging
    adults, 188–89
  pathways of, 256–57
  person-context fit, 257
  piety, 12, 180, 182
  practitioners of, 264–65
  prayer/praying, 61, 63, 146, 260
  religion among, 221–24
  salience of, 256
  traditions in, 30–31
religion and spirituality, benefits and
    detriments, 8–9
  coming-of-age process, 48–51
  creation of worldview, 41–42
  influence on outcomes, 47–48
  in-groups *vs.* out-groups, 45–47
  potential benefits, 42–44
  potential detriments, 44–47
  religious doubt, 50–51, 163
  risk behaviors, reduction, 40, 42–43
  rites of passage, 48–50
religion and spirituality,
    development. *see also*
    parental roles
  beliefs, 24–25, 174
  developmental domains and, 29–34

non-stage models in, 27–28
practices, 25–26
prevalence of, 24–26
stage models in, 26–27
theories of, 26–29
underpinnings, 22–24
religion clauses of US Constitution
  Establishment Clause, 113–14,
    120–24
  foundation message of, 113–15
  Free Exercise Clause, 113–14, 116–20
  law emerging from, 116–24
  lessons for study of emerging
    adulthood, 127–29
  lessons learned from, 124–27
  overview, 109–13
  reshaping of efforts, 130
religious and spiritual identity,
    196–97, 212, 223, 225–27
religious authenticity, 180
religious congregations and
    communities
  as centers of meaning-making,
    142–48
  congregational culture, 229–30
  defined, 11, 134
  defining religious involvement in,
    134–35
  embedded congregations, 230–31
  Episcopal congregants, 175
  future directions, 148–49
  identity formation in ecological
    system, 140–42
  informal religious communities,
    138–40
  overview, 133–34
  participation trends, 135–36
  regular participants, 136–38
religious content and developmental
    conceptualization, 228–29
religious doubt, 14, 48, 50–51, 163,
    237–38
religious freedom, 110–11, 130
Religious Freedom Restoration Act
    (RFRA), 119–20
religious fundamentalism, 46–47, 158,
    177, 189

spirituality, defined, 134–35
spiritual role models, 48–50
stage models in religion and
    spirituality, 26–27
Stark, Zach, 204–5, 214
structural theory of faith
    development, 26–27
substance abuse
    alcohol use, 42–43, 188, 233
    binge drinking, 42–43, 82, 137
    marijuana use, 42, 98, 241
    underage alcohol consumption, 43
syncretistic spiritual practices, 25–26

teenage pregnancy, 213
"Theology on Tap," 138–39
Tidwell, Brandon, 204–5, 214
trait approach, 27
transcendent context of
    meaning-making, 146–48

Unitarian Universalists, 262
United Churches of Christ, 208
universities, and religion and
    spirituality, 11–12

US Bill of Rights, 111
US Constitution. *see* religion clauses
    of US Constitution

Vanderbilt University, 157
video game violence, 101
volunteering, 33, 137,
    145–46, 210

*Walz v. Tax Commission* (1970), 122
well-being measures, 142,
    244–46
White Evangelicals, 242
Wicca, 100, 262
*Wisconsin v. Yoder* (1972),
    117–18

Young Men's Christian Association
    (YMCA), 155–56
Young Women's Christian
    Association (YWCA), 155–56

*Zelman v. Simmons-Harris* (2002),
    123, 130
Zen Buddhism, 42

CPSIA information can be obtained
at www.ICGtesting.com
Printed in the USA
BVHW072147260319
543789BV00002B/115/P